A Handbook of Soil-Plant-Water-Fertilizer and Manure Analysis

nipa books for everyone PAPERBACKS

NIPA® GENX ELECTRONIC RESOURCES & SOLUTIONS P. LTD.

New Delhi-110 034

A Handbook of Soil-Plant-Water-Fertilizer and Manure Analysis

M.V. Durai

Presently
Institute of Forest Genetics & Tree Breeding
Indian Council of Forestry Research & Education (ICFRE)
Ministry of Environment & Forests (GoI)
R.S.Puram - 641 0002, Coimbatore (Tamil Nadu), India

Formerly
Forest Research Centre
Institute of Forest Productivity
Indian Council of Forestry Research & Education (ICFRE)
Mandar 835 214, Ranchi, Jharkhand

nipa books for everyone
® PAPERBACKS

NIPA® GENX ELECTRONIC RESOURCES & SOLUTIONS P. LTD.
New Delhi-110 034

nipa books for everyone
PAPERBACKS

NIPA® GENX ELECTRONIC RESOURCES & SOLUTIONS P. LTD.

101,103, Vikas Surya Plaza, CU Block
L.S.C. Market, Pitam Pura, New Delhi-110 034
Ph : +91 11 27341616, 27341717, 27341718
E-mail: newindiapublishingagency@gmail.com
www: www.nipabooks.com

For customer assistance, please contact
Phone: + 91-11-27 34 17 17
Fax: + 91-11- 27 34 16 16
E-Mail: feedbacks@nipabooks.com

ISBN 978-81-960462-3-1

Composed & Designed by NIPA

Preface

Soil, plants, water, fertilizers and manures are materials of common interest in the field of agriculture and forestry. Methods applicable to the analysis of chemistry soils, plant, water, fertilizers and manures are as numerous and varied as the field of chemistry itself. The extraction of a chemical constituents from the interested materials is purely a soil chemistry procedure, while determination of the extracted constituents is an analytical process, a few methods of analysis are accurate and precise. No doubt, a few good books are available for analysis of soil, plant, water and fertilizers but they are not comprehensive and not covered all relevant procedures and principles for soil, plant, water and fertilizers in single book.

In this book, I have complied together almost tested, proven and routinely used methods for the determination of nutrients in soil, plant and fertilizers and analysis of quality parameters in water, effluents and other polluted water. All essential parameters, which are concern with plant growth and environment, are duly covered. Besides systematic presentation of chapters, relevant principles, concepts and critical interpretations are included in this book, which will help the readers to understand the subject with ease. This book would meet the needs of teaching, research, advisory services, soil and plant testing laboratories and those interested in monitoring the nutrient contents of effluents/ polluted soil and water. It should be of interest to all these laboratories, R & D centre, and academic institutions interested in soil science, plant analysis, environment management, fertilizer production and environmental engineering.

I have duly acknowledged the sources of diagrams and tables that have been reproduced from text books and other publications. The author is ready to accept ideas and suggestions to improve the quality of the book, if any. The ultimate of aim of the author is to provide single comprehensive hand book on soil, plant, water, fertilizers and manures to the readers.

M V Durai
Coimbatore

Contents

1

Introduction

The role of plant nutrients in crop production is well established. Estimation of nutrients contents and forms in materials, which are involved in nutrient supply and dynamics is a crucial step in scientific nutrient management and crop production. There are 16 essential plant nutrients. These are carbon (C), hydrogen (H), oxygen (O), nitrogen (N), phosphorus (P), potassium (K), calcium (Ca), magnesium (Mg), iron (Fe), sulphur (S), zinc (Zn), manganese (Mn), copper (Cu), boron (B), molybdenum (Mo) and chlorine (Cl). These nutrients have to be available to the crops in quantities as required for a yield target. Any limiting or deficient nutrient (s) will limit crop growth.

The required nutrients may come from various sources, such as the atmosphere, soil, irrigation water, mineral fertilizers, manures and bio-fertilizers. The combinations, quantities and integration of nutrients to be supplied from various sources depend on various factors including type of crop, soils, availability of various resources, and ultimately on economic considerations, such as the level of production and costs of inputs and outputs.

Integrated nutrient management (INM) is a well accepted approach for the sustainable management of soil productivity and increased crop production. To implement this approach successfully, well equipped testing laboratories, among other things, are needed in order to evaluate the nutrient supplying capacities of various sources.

Accurate and timely analysis helps in determining the requirements of plant nutrients so as to arrange their supply through various sources. The analytical facilities required for chemical analysis of soils, plants, water and fertilizers are broadly identical in nature with a few specific requirements in terms of facilities and chemicals for certain estimations. In view of this, it is possible to set up integrated facilities for soil, plant, water and fertilizer analysis. A common facility saves on supervision and other costs, such as common equipment and chemicals.

Depending on the need, different types of laboratories can be set up. A soil, plant and water testing laboratory with an annual analysing capacity of about 10,000 - 12,000 samples requires a building space of about 370m^2. For a fertilizer testing laboratory with an analysing capacity of 2,000 samples, the space requirement is about 185m^2. A composite laboratory may require about 480 m^2. Given the increasing need for analysis of larger numbers of soil, plant, water and fertilizer samples by the service laboratories to serve the farmers more rapidly and more effectively, various types of equipment/techniques capable of multi-nutrient analysis may be useful. For example, auto-analysers, atomic absorption spectrometer (AAS) and inductively coupled plasma - atomic emission spectroscopy (ICP-AES). However, for service laboratories in developing countries that are limited in terms of facilities, skilled personnel and financial resources, such equipment is not advocated in general.

2

Basics of An Analytical Laboratory

Introduction

In chemical laboratories, the use of acids, alkalis and some hazardous and explosive chemicals is unavoidable. In addition, some chemical reactions during the analysis process may release toxic gases and, if not handled well, may cause an explosion. Inflammable gases are also used as a fuel/heating source. Thus, work safety in a chemical laboratory calls for special care both in terms of the design and construction of the laboratory building, and in the handling and use of chemicals.

For chemical operations, it is also necessary to provide special chambers. The air temperature of the laboratory and work rooms should be maintained constant at 20–25°C. Humidity should be kept at about 50 percent. Temperature and humidity often affect soil and fertilizer samples. Temperature also affects some chemical operations. Hence, maintaining the temperature and humidity as specified is critical.

Proper air circulation is also important in order to prevent hazardous and toxic fumes and gases from remaining in the laboratory for long. The release of gases and fumes in some specific analytical operations are controlled through fume-hoods or trapped in acidic/alkaline solutions and washed through flowing water. The maintaining of a clean and hygienic environment in the laboratory is essential for the good health of the personnel.

Care is required in order to ensure that acids and hazardous chemicals are stored in separate and safe racks. An inventory of all the equipment, chemicals, glassware and miscellaneous items in a laboratory should be maintained. A safe laboratory building should have suitable separate rooms for different purposes and for performing different operations as described below:

- Room 1. Reception, sample receipt, and dispatch of reports.
- Room 2. Sample storage and preparation room (separate for soil/plant and fertilizers).
- Room 3. Nitrogen digestion/distillation room (with fume hood for digestion).
- Room 4. Instrument room to house the Atomic absorption spectrophotometer (AAS), Flame photometer, Spectrophotometer, pH meter, conductivity meter, Hot air ovens, Centrifuge, Balances, Water still etc.
- Room 5. Chemical analysis room (separate for soil/plant and fertilizers):
  - To prepare reagents and chemicals and to carry out their standardization
  - To carryout extraction of soil and fertilizer samples with appropriate chemicals/reagents
  - To carryout titration, colour development, precipitation, filtration, etc.
  - All other types of chemical work.
- Room 6. Storage room for chemicals and spare equipment.
- Room 7. Office room with computers for data processing and record keeping.

Laboratory Safety Measures

Special care is required while operating equipment, handling chemicals and in waste disposal.

Equipment

Electrical cables, plugs and tubing need proper checking in order to avoid accidents. Various types of gas cylinders needed in the laboratory, such as acetylene, nitrous oxide and liquefied petroleum gas must be kept under watch and properly sealed/capped, and they must be stored in ventilated cupboards.

Chemical Reagents

Hazardous chemicals should be stored in plastic bottles. While working with chemicals, such as perchloric acid, a fume-hood must be used. Chemicals must be labelled properly, indicating their hazardous nature. Bottles with inflammable substances need to be stored in stainless steel containers.

Waste Disposal

Each country has special rules and methods for the disposal of hazardous waste. Cyanides, chromates, arsenic (As), selenium (Se), cobalt (Co) and molybdateare commonly used but hazardous chemicals. They should never be disposed of in the laboratory sink but collected in a metal container for proper disposal at the specified places and in the manner described in national legislation for waste disposal.

General Rules and Requirements

General safety rules and requirements for personnel working in a laboratory are

- Learn safety rules and the use of first aid kits. Keep the first-aid kit handy in a conspicuous place in the laboratory.
- Personal safety aids such as laboratory coats, protective gloves, safety glasses, face shields and proper footwear should be used.
- Observe normal laboratory safety practice in connecting equipment to the power supply, in handling chemicals and in preparing solutions of reagents.
- All electrical work must be done by qualified personnel.
- Maintain an instrument manual and logbook for each item of equipment in order to avoid mishandling, accidents and damage to equipment.
- Keep work tables/spaces clean.
- Clean up spillage immediately.
- Wash hands after handling toxic/hazardous chemicals.

- Never suck the chemicals by mouth but use automatic pipetting devices.
- Use forceps/tongs to remove containers from hotplates/ovens/furnaces.
- Do not use laboratory glassware for eating/drinking.
- Never open a centrifuge cover until the machine has stopped.
- Add acid to water and not water to acid when diluting the acid.
- Always put labels on bottles, vessels and wash-bottles containing reagents, solutions, samples and water.
- Handle perchloric acid and hazardous chemicals in fumehoods.
- With the wet oxidation method of sample digestion, destroy organic matter (OM) first with nitric acid.
- Read the labels on the bottles before opening them.

Quality Control of Analytical Procedures

Independent Standards

The ultimate aim of the quality control measures is to ensure the production of analytical data with a minimum of error and consistency. Once an appropriate method has been selected, its execution has to be done with utmost care. To check and verify the accuracy of analysis, independent standards are used in the system. The extent of deviation of an analytical value on a standard sample indicates the accuracy of the analysis. Independent standards can be prepared in the laboratory from pure chemicals. When a new standard is prepared, the remainder of the old ones always has to be measured as a mutual check. If the results are not within acceptable levels of accuracy, the process of calibration, preparation of the standard curve and the preparation of reagents should be repeated until acceptable results are obtained on the standard sample. After ensuring this, analysis on an unknown sample can start. Apart from independent standards, certified reference samples can also be used as "standard". Such samples are obtained from other selected laboratories where the analysis on a prepared standard is carried out by more than one laboratory. Such samples along with the accompanying analytical values are used as a check to ensure the accuracy of analysis.

Use of Blank

A blank determination is an analysis without the analyte or attribute; in other words, it is an analysis without a sample, going through all steps of the procedure with the reagents only. The use of blank is accounts for any contamination in the chemicals used in actual analysis. The "estimate" of the blank is subtracted from the estimates of the samples. "Sequence control" samples are used in long batches in automated analysis. Generally, two samples, one with a low content and the other with a very high content of known analyte (but the contents falling within the working range of the method) are used as standards to monitor the accuracy of analysis.

Blind Sample

A blind sample is one with a known content of analyte. The head of the laboratory inserts this sample in batches and at times unknown to the analyst. Various types of sample material may serve as blind samples, such as control samples or sufficiently large left-overs of test samples (analysed several times). It is essential that the analyst be aware of the possible presence of a blind sample but not be able to recognize the material as such.

Validation of Analysis Procedures

Validation is the process of determining the performance/ characteristics of a method/procedure. It is a prerequisite for assessing the suitability of produced analytical data for the intended use. This implies that a method may be valid in one situation but not in another. If a method is very precise and accurate but expensive for adoption, it may be used only when data with that order of precision are needed. The data may be inadequate if the method is less accurate than required. Two types of validation are followed.

Validation of Own Procedure

In-house validation of methods or procedures by individual user laboratories is a common practice. Many laboratories use their own version of even well established methods for reasons of efficiency, cost and convenience. Changes in the liquid-solid ratio in extraction procedures for available soil nutrients, shaking time, etc., result in changed values, hence they need validating. Such changes are often introduced in order to take account of local conditions, the cost of analysis and the required accuracy and efficiency. Validation of such changes is a part of quality control in the laboratory. It is also a kind of research project. Hence not all types of the laboratories may be in a position to modify the standard method. They should follow the given method as accepted and practiced by most other laboratories.

Apart from validating methods, laboratories need to employ a system of internal quality control in order to ensure that they are capable of producing reliable analytical data with a minimum of error. This requires continuous monitoring of operations and systematic day-to-day checking of the data produced in order to decide whether these are reliable enough to be released. Internal quality control requires implementing the following steps:

- Use a blank and a control (standard) sample of known composition along with the samples under analysis.
- Round off the analytical values to the second decimal place. The value of the third decimal place should be omitted if it is lower than 5. If it is higher than 5, the value of the second decimal should be raised by 1.

As quality control systems rely heavily on control samples, the sample preparation must be done with great care in order to ensure that

- the sample is homogenous
- the sample material is stable
- the material has uniform and correct particle size as sieved through a standard sieve and
- relevant information, such as properties of the sample and the concentration of the analyte, is available.

The sample under analysis must also be processed/ prepared in such a way that it has a similar particle size and homogeneity to that of the standard (control) sample. As and when internal checks reveal an error in the analysis, corrective measures should be taken. The error could be one of calculation or typing. Where it is not, it requires thorough checks on sample identification, standards, chemicals, pipettes, dispensers, glassware, calibration procedure and equipment. The standard may be old or prepared incorrectly. A pipette may indicate the wrong volume. Glassware may not have been cleaned properly. The equipment may be defective, or the sample intake tube may be clogged in the case of a flame photometer or an AAS. The source of error must be detected and the samples analysed again.

Validation of the Standard Procedure

This refers to the validation of new or existing methods and procedures intended for use in many laboratories, including procedures accepted by national systems or the ISO. It involves an inter laboratory programme of testing the method by a number of selected renowned laboratories according to a protocol issued to all participants. Validation is relevant not only when non-standard procedures are used but also when validated standard procedures are used, and even more so when variants of standard procedures are introduced. The results of validation tests should be recorded in a validation report, from which the suitability of a method for a particular purpose can be deduced.

Preparation and Standardization of Reagent Solutions

Chemical reagents are manufactured and marketed in different grades of purity. In general, the purest reagents are marketed as "analytical reagent" or AR-grade. Other labels are "LR", meaning laboratory reagent, and "CP", meaning chemically pure. The strength of chemicals is expressed as normality or molarity. Therefore, it is useful to have some information about the strength of the acids and alkalis most commonly used in chemical laboratories (Table 2). Some important terms that are often used in a laboratory for chemical analysis are explained below:

Molarity

A one molar (M) solution contains one mole or one molecular weight in grams of a substance in each litre of the solution. The molar method of expressing concentration is useful because equal volumes of equimolar solutions contain equal number of molecules.

Normality

The normality of a solution is the number of gram equivalents of the solute per litre of the solution. It is usually designated by the letter N. Semi-normal, penti-normal, desi-normal, centi-normal and milli-normal solutions are often required; these are written as 0.5N, 0.2N, 0.1N, 0.01N and 0.001N, respectively. However, molar expression is preferred because "odd" normalities such as 0.121N are clumsily represented in fractional form. The definition of normal solution uses the term "equivalent weight". This quantity varies with the type of reaction. Hence, it is difficult to give a clear definition of equivalent weight that covers all reactions. It often happens that the same compound possesses different equivalent weights in different chemical reactions. A situation may arise where a solution has a normal concentration when employed for one purpose and a different normality when used in another chemical reaction. Hence, the system of molarity is preferred.

Table 2.1 : Strength of commonly used acids and alkalis (approx.)

Reagent/ chemical	Normality	Molarity	Formula weight	% by weight	Specific gravity	Millilitre required for 1N/ litre solution	Millilitre required for1M/ litre solution
Nitric acid	16.0	16.0	63.0	70	1.42	63.7	63.7
Sulphuric acid	35.0	17.5	98.0	98	1.84	28.0	56.0
Hydrochloric acid	11.6	11.6	36.5	37	1.19	82.6	82.6
Phosphoric acid	45.0	15.0	98.0	85	1.71	22.7	68.1
Perchloric acid	10.5	10.5	100.0	65	1.60	108.7	108.7

Equivalent Weight

The equivalent weight (Eq.W) of a substance is the weight in grams that in its reaction corresponds to a gram atom of hydrogen or of hydroxyl, or half a gram atom of oxygen, or a gram atom of univalent ion. When one equivalent weight of a substance is dissolved in one litre, it gives 1N solution. The Annexure 3 gives the equivalent and molecular weights of some important compounds.

Milli-equivalent Weight

Equivalent weight when expressed as milli-equivalent weight (mEq. W) means the equivalent weight in grams divided by 1,000. It is commonly expressed as "me". It is the most convenient value because it is the weight of a substance contained in or equivalent to 1 ml of 1N solution. Therefore, it is a unit that is common to both volumes and weights, making it possible to convert the volume of a solution to its equivalent weight, and the weight of a substance to its equivalent volume of solution: number of mEq = volume × normality.

Buffer Solutions

Solutions containing either a weak acid and its salt or a weak base and its salt (e.g.$CH_3COOH + CH_3COONa$ and $NH_4OH + NH_4Cl$) possess the characteristic property of resisting changes in pH when some acid or base is added to them. Such solutions are called buffer solutions. The important properties of a buffer solution are

- It has a definite pH value.
- Its pH value does not alter on keeping for a long time.
- Its pH value is only altered slightly when a strong base or strong acid is added.
- Because of the above property, readily prepared buffer solutions of known pH are used in order to check the accuracy of pH meters used in the laboratory.

Titrations

Titration is a process of determining the volume of a substance required to just complete the reaction with a known amount of other substance. The solution of known strength used in the titration is called the titrant. The substance to be determined in the solution is called the titrate. The completion of the reaction is assessed with the help of an appropriate indicator.

Indicators

A substance that indicates the end point on completion of the reaction is called an indicator. The most commonly used indicators in volumetric analysis are:

- Internal indicators,
- External indicators and
- Self-indicators.

Internal Indicators

Indicators such as methyl red, methyl orange, phenolphthalein and diphenylamine that are added to the solution where reaction occurs are called internal indicators. On completion of the reaction of titrant on titrate, a colour change takes place owing to the presence of the indicator, which also helps in knowing that the titration is complete. The internal indicators used in acid–alkali neutralization solutions are methyl orange, phenolphthalein and bromo-thymol blue. The indicator used in precipitation reactions such as titration of neutral solution of NaCl (or chlorine ion) with silver nitrate ($AgNO_3$) solution is K_2CrO^{-4}. On completion of the titration reaction of $AgNO_3$ with Cl, when no more Cl is available for reaction with silver ions to form $AgCl_2$, the chromium ions combine with Ag^{2+} ions to form sparingly soluble Ag_2CrO_4, which is brick red in colour. This indicates that Cl_2 has been titrated completely and that end point has occurred.

Redox indicators are also commonly used. These are substances that possess different colours in the oxidized and reduced forms. Diphenylamine has a blue violet colour in the oxidation state and is colourless in reduced condition. Ferrocin gives a blue colour in the oxidation state and a red colour in reduced condition.

External Indicators

Some indicators are used outside the titration mixture. Potassium ferricyanide is used as an external indicator in the titration of potassium dichromate and ferrous sulphate in acid medium. In this titration, a few drops of indicator are placed on a white porcelain tile. A glass rod dipped in the solution being titrated is taken out and brought into contact with the drops of indicator on the tile. First, a deep blue colour is noticed, which turns greenish on completion of titration.

Self-Indicators

After completion of the reaction, the titrant leaves its own colour owing to its slight excess in minute quantities. In $KMnO_4$ titration with ferrous sulphate, the addition of $KMnO_4$ starts reacting with $FeSO_4$, which is colourless. On completion of titration, the slight excess presence of $KMnO_4$ gives a pink colour to the solution, which acts as a self-indicator and points to the completion of the titration.

Standard Solutions

A solution of accurately known strength (or concentration) is called a standard solution. It contains a definite number of gram equivalent or gram mole per litre of solution. If it contains 1 g equivalent weight of a substance/compound, it is 1N solution. If it contains 2g equivalent weights of the compound, it is 2N. All titrimetric methods depend on standard solutions that contain known amounts of the reagents in unit volume of the solution. A solution is prepared, having about the desired concentration. This solution is then standardized by titriting it with another substance that can be obtained in highly purified form. Thus, potassium permanganate solution can be standardized against sodiumoxalate, which can be obtained in a high degree of purity as it is easily dried and is non-hygroscopic.

Primary Standards

Primary standard is such a substance, whose weight and purity is stable, is called a "primary standard". A primary standard must have the following characteristics:

- It must be obtainable in a pure form or in a state of known purity.
- It must react in one way only under the condition of titration and there must be no side reactions.
- It must be non-hygroscopic. Salt hydrates are generally not suitable as primary standards.
- Normally, it should have a large equivalent weight in order to reduce the error in weighing.
- An acid or a base should preferably be strong, that is, it should have a high dissociation constant for being used as standards.

A primary standard solution is one that can be prepared directly by weighing the material and with which other solutions of approximate strength can be titrated and standardized. Some primary standards are:

- Acids
  - Potassium hydrogen phthalate
  - Benjoic acid
- Bases
  - Sodium carbonate
  - Borax
- Oxidizing agents
  - Potassium dichromate
  - Potassium bromate
- Reducing agents
  - Sodium oxalate
  - Potassium ferrocyanide
- Others
  - Sodium chloride
  - Potassium chloride.

Secondary Standards

Secondary standard solutions are those that are prepared by dissolving a little more than the gram equivalent weight of the substance per litre of the solution and then their exact standardization is done with primary standard solution. Some secondary standards are :

- Acids
  - Sulphuric acid
  - Hydrochloric acid
- Base
  - Sodium hydroxide.

Standardization of Common Non-Primary Standard Substances

The standard solutions of all the reagents required in a laboratory must be prepared and kept ready before commencing any analysis. However, their strength should be checked periodically, or fresh reagents should be prepared before analysis. All titrations involving acidimetry and alkalimetry require standard solutions. These may be prepared either from standard substances by direct weighing, or by standardizing a solution of approximate normality of materials by titrating against a prepared standard. The methods for preparing standard solutions of some non-primary standard substances in common use are given below.

Hydrochloric Acid (HCl)

Concentrated hydrochloric acid (HCl) is about 11N. Therefore, to prepare a standard solution, say, decinormal (0.1N) of the acid, it is diluted about 100 times. Take 10 ml of acid and make about 1 litre by dilution with distilled water. Titrate this acid against 0.1N Na_2CO_3 (primary standard) using methyl orange as indicator. The colour changes from pink to yellow when the acid is neutralized. Suppose 10 ml of acid and 12 ml of Na_2CO_3 are consumed in the titration, then,

Acid	Alkali
V1 × N1	= V2 × N2
10 × N1	= 12 × 0.1
10 N1	= 1.2
N1	= 0.12

Thus, the normality of the acid is 0.12.

Sulphuric Acid (H_2SO_4)

Similar to above, the normality of sulphuric acid (H_2SO_4) can be determined. It needs to be diluted about 350 times in order to reach about 0.1N because it has a normality of about 35. Then, titrate against standard Na_2CO_3 to determine the exact normality of H_2SO_4.

Sodium Hydroxide (NaOH)

As per the above method, the normality of HCl/H_2SO_4 has been fixed. Therefore, to determine the normality of sodium hydroxide (NaOH), titration is carried out by using either of these standard acids. To determine the molarity, molar standard solutions are used. In the case of the standardization of NaOH or any other alkali, potassium hydrogen phthalate can also be used as a primary standard instead of titration with secondary standards.

Preparation of Soil Extracts for Available Nutrients

Plants draw their nutrients from air, water and soil. The bulk of mineral nutrients come from soil. Soil available form of nutrients is that fraction which is distributed indifferent discrete chemical forms, which often exist in a state of dynamic equilibrium and constitute the pool from which plant draw it. Soil available form of a nutrient is also that fraction whose variation in amount is responsible for significant changes in yield and responses. The nutrient available to biological organisms is termed as bio- available nutrient. Available nutrients in the soil are water soluble and exchangeable. The reagent used for the extraction f this pool simulates the plant roots and extracts the same amount of available nutrient as the plant is able to take in. The following are various extractants for the available fraction of nutrients.

a). Preparation of soil-water extract for water soluble nutrients

The water soluble nutrients, which consist NH_4^+ of cations and anions in different proportion are Ca^{2+}, Mg^{2+}, K^+, Na^+, NH_4^+, Fe^{2+}, Mn^{2+}, Cu^{2+}, Zn^{2+}, SO_4^{-2}, Cl^-, MoO_4^{-2} and BO_3^{-3}. These are nutrients that can be extracted using distilled water with soil water ratio of 1:5.

Procedure

- Weigh 100g of soil passed through 2mm sieve into 1L reagent bottle

- Add 500ml of distilled water and small quantity of charcoal (decoloring agent) and shake the contents by end over end for 30 min. to get a clear extract
- Filter the contents through Whatman No. 1 filter paper
- Store the extract in a clean bottle for the estimation of soluble nutrients in the soil
- Add 2-3 drops of TEA (Tri Ethanolamine) to this extract to prevent algal growth and place in a refrigerator.

b). Preparation of chemical extracts for water soluble + exchangeable nutrients

There are a variety of extractants used for extracting available nutrients from soils.

Available P: Available P content in the soil is extracted by using two extractants depending up on pH.

i). Olsen's reagent: 0.5M $NaHCO_3$ solution of pH 8.5 for slightly acidic, neutral, alkaline and calcareous soils.

ii). Bray's reagent: 0.03M NH_4F + 0.025N HCl solution for acidic soils

Available K: neutral normal ammonium acetate (CH_3COONH_4) used.

Available S: 0.15% $CaCl_2$ solution used.

Available Micro-nutrients

i). ***Cationic micro-nutrients:*** 0.005M DTPA (Diethylene Triamine Penta Acetic Acid) + 0.01M $CaCl_2$ + 0.1M TEA.

ii). ***Anionic micronutrients***

- Available B by hot water
- Available Mo by Ammonium oxalate solution (or) Tamm's reagent
- Available Cl^- by water.

3

Methods for Soil Analysis

Introduction

Soil is the main source of nutrients for the plants. Soil also provides support for plant growth in various ways. Knowledge about soil health and its maintenance is critical to sustaining crop productivity. The health of soils can be assessed by the quality and stand of the crops grown on them. However, this is a general assessment made by the farmers. A scientific assessment is possible through detailed physical, chemical and biological analysis of the soils. Essential plant nutrients such as N, P, K, Ca, Mg and S are called macronutrients, while Fe, Zn, Cu, Mo, Mn, B and Cl are called micronutrients. It is necessary to assess the capacity of a soil to supply nutrients in order to supply the remaining amounts of needed plant nutrients (total crop requirement - soil supply). Thus, soil testing laboratories are considered nerve centres for nutrient management in crop production systems and plantation forestry.

Soils may have large amounts of nutrient reserves in them. All or a part of these reserves may not be of any use to crops because they may not be in plant-available form. For the purpose of estimation or analysis of plant-available soil nutrients, such methods are to be used that have been tested/verified for the correlation of nutrients extracted and their plant availability. This book describes internationally accepted and widely used methods. Apart from nutrients, soil pH estimation is also critical in the assessment of soil health. Generally, plants prefer soils that are close to either side of neutrality. However, there are acid-loving plants and also plants that can withstand high soil alkalinity. Hence, good yields and economic returns from farming are possible in acid and alkali soils. With proper amendments, still higher yields can be obtained in acid and alkali soils. Soil pH also has a considerable influence on the activity of soil micro-flora and on the availability of soil nutrients to crops. It is also important to estimate physical properties such as soil texture, structure, bulk density, soil colour, water content and soil temperature.

Soil Sampling

"The analysis can be no better than the sample" (Jackson, 1962)

The sampling of soils is a challenging problem, worthy of detailed consideration. Sampling includes taking the soil material so as to take in to account the variability of soils, handling and processing the sample and final sub-sampling for the actual determination. Soil sampling must take into account variations of soil according to profile depth and landscape area.

The methods and procedures for obtaining soil samples vary according to the purpose of the sampling. Analysis of soil samples may be needed for engineering and agricultural purposes. This guide describes soil sampling for agricultural and plantation forestry purposes, i.e. for soil fertility evaluation and fertilizer recommendations for both food crops and forest trees.

The results of even very carefully conducted soil analyses can only be as good as the soil samples themselves. Thus, the efficiency of a soil testing service depends on the care and skill with which soil samples are collected. Non-representative samples constitute the largest single source of error in a soil fertility programme. The most important phase of soil analysis takes place not in the laboratory but in the field where the soil is sampled.

Soils vary from place to place. In view of this, efforts should be made to take the samples in such a way that they are fully representative of the field. Only 1 – 10 g of soil is used for each chemical determination and this sample needs to represent as accurately as possible the entire surface 0 – 22 cm of soil, weighing about 2 million kg/ha.

Sampling Tools and Accessories

Depending on the purpose and precision required, the following tools may be needed for taking soil samples:

- Soil auger – it may be a tube, post hole or screw type auger or even a spade for taking sample
- Clean bucket or a tray or a clean cloth for mixing the soil and sub-sampling
- Cloth bags of a specific size
- Pencil for markings, and tags for tying cloth bags
- Soil sample information sheet.

Selection of a Sampling Unit

A visual survey of the field should precede the actual sampling. Note the variation in slope, colour, texture, management and cropping pattern by traversing the field. Demarcate the field into uniform portions, each of which must be sampled separately. Where all these conditions are similar, one field can be treated as a single sampling unit. Such a unit should not exceed 1–2 ha and it must be an area to which a farmer is willing to give separate attention. The sampling unit is a compromise between expenditure, labour and time on the one hand, and precision on the other.

Sampling in Crop Land

Prepare a map of the area to be covered in a survey showing different sampling unit boundaries. Enter a plan of the number of samples and manner of composite sampling on the map, designating different fields by letters (A, B, C, etc.). Traverse each area separately. Cut a slice of the plough layer at intervals of 15–20 steps or according to the area to be covered. Generally, depending on the size of the field, 10–20 spots must be taken for one composite sample. Scrape away surface litter to obtain a uniformly thick slice of soil from the surface to the plough depth from each spot. Make a V-shaped cut with a spade to remove a 1–2 cm slice of soil. Collect the sample on the blade of the spade and put it in a clean bucket. In this way, collect samples from all the spots marked for one sampling unit. In the case of hard soil, take samples with the help of an auger from the plough depth and collect them in the bucket. Between 10 and 20 sub-samples should be composited from each area. Sub-samples should be small enough that the composite sample will be of a size that can be completely processed for analysis.

The depth of the sampling is determined by the crop, the elements of interest and existing knowledge about the soil profile. Samples for cultivated crops are taken from the plow layer at 15-20cm. For pasture and sod crop, soil samples should be collected from the top 10cm. For deep rooted crops like sugar cane, horticultural and forest crops or under dry farming systems, samples from different depths/layers may be needed. For mobile nutrient forms like nitrate and sulphate, sample should be taken to a depth of 60 cm and when the biological activity is low. Samples for nitrate, soluble salts and available micronutrients should be taken at the root depth.

Pour the sampled soil onto a piece of clean paper or cloth and mix it thoroughly. Spread the soil evenly and divide it into quarters. Reject two opposite quarters and mix the rest of the soil again. Repeat the process until left with about 500g of the soil. Collect it and put in a clean cloth bag. Mark each bag clearly in order to identify the sample.

The bag used for sampling must always be clean and free from any contamination. If the same bag is to be used a second time, turn it inside out and remove the soil particles. Write the details of the sample on the information sheet (Annex 4 provides a suggested format). Put a copy of this information sheet in the bag. The duplicate copy of the same shall be tied the mouth of the bag carefully.

Precautions in Sampling

When sampling a soil, bear in mind the following:

- Do not sample unusual areas, such as unevenly fertilized areas, marshy areas, old paths, old channels, old bunds, areas near trees, sites of previous compost piles, and other unrepresentative sites.
- For a soft and moist soil, the tube auger or spade is considered satisfactory. For harder soil, a screw auger may be more convenient.
- Where crops have been planted in rows, collect samples from the middle of the rows in order to avoid the area where fertilizer has been band placed.
- Avoid any type of contamination at all stages. Soil samples should never be stored with fertilizer materials and detergents. Contamination is likely when the soil samples are spread out to dry in the vicinity of stored fertilizers or on floor where fertilizers were stored previously.
- Before putting soil samples in bags, they should be examined for cleanliness as well as for strength.

- The information sheet should be filled in clearly with a copying pencil.

Sampling in Salt-Affected Soils

Salt-affected soils may be sampled in two ways. Surface samples should be taken in the same way as for soil fertility analysis. These samples are used to determine the gypsum requirement of the soil. For reclamation purpose, it is necessary to know also the characteristics of lower soil depth. Therefore, such soils are sampled down to a depth of 1 m. The samples may be removed from one to two spots per 0.4 ha where the soil is uniformly salt-affected. Where patches are conspicuous, then all large patches should be sampled separately. Soil is sampled separately for soil depths (about 500 g from each depth) of 0–15, 15–30, 30–60 and 60–100 cm.

If a stony layer is encountered during sampling, such a layer should be sampled separately and its depth noted. This is very important and must not be ignored. Soil samples can be removed by a spade, or if the auger is used, then care should be taken to note the depth of "concretion" (stones) or other impermeable layer (hardpan). If the soil shows evidence of profile development or distinct stratification, samples should be taken by horizon. If a pit is dug and horizons are absent, then mark the vertical side of the pit at depths of 15, 30, 60 and 100 cm from the surface and collect about 500 g soil from each layer, cutting uniform slices of soil separately. In addition to the above sampling, one surface soil sample should be taken as in the case of normal soil sampling for fertilizer recommendation. Pack the samples and label the bags in the same way as for normal soil sampling, giving additional information about the depth of the sample.

Sampling in Forest Ecosystem

In general, soil sampling is done in two levels viz., level - I (extensive soil survey in larger area) and level -II (intensive soil survey in smaller area). The objectives of level - I sampling are assessment of basic information on the chemical status of the soil and its changes over time, and assessment of soil properties which determine the forest soil's sensitivity to air pollution and evaluation of the (quality of) forest soils at national level. Besides providing soil data for the study of atmospheric deposition effects at the broader scale, it will serve other purposes such as studies related to climate change (e.g. inventory of carbon storage) and sustainable forest management (e.g. in addition to acidification status, also nitrogen studies and nutrient imbalances).

The level-II studies are conducted in selected areas on permanent plots, where other measurements for the analysis of the forest ecosystem are concentrated. The objectives of the special forest ecosystem analysis are the verification of hypotheses and in-depth analyses of damage mechanisms and the derivation of fundamental knowledge of forecasting future developments.

Geo-referencing of Sample

One common datum, the World Geodetic System 1984 (WGS84) shall be applied and geographical lat/long coordinates (degrees, minutes & seconds). A GPS measurement (if technically possible) should be taken in the centre of the plot.

Pedological Characterization of the Plots

The pedological characterization is mandatory for Level - I and Level – II. It should be a general characterization, including a detailed site description with information on soil parent material and at least one profile description according to the FAO guidelines (FAO, 1990a). The soils should then be classified according to the most recent official version of the World Reference Base of Soil Resources (WRB) - classification system. The described soil profile(s) should be located at a location which is representative for the dominant soil type in the actual sampling area. For Level II, this should be in the buffer zone of the plot.

Sampling Time

In order to reduce temporal variations, especially in the organic layer, sampling activities should be confined to periods with low biological activity, e.g. winter or dry season, based on expert judgment. However, the countries that participated in the first survey, have to carry out the sampling activities in the same period (season) as for the first survey. The sampling dates should be recorded.

Sampling of Organic Layer

The organic layer at the soil surface, which may consist of one or more of the following organic horizons: litter (OL), fermentation horizon (OF) and/or humus (OH) in aerated organic layers is sampled separately from the underlying mineral soil. Buried organic layers are sampled in the same way as mineral layers. Material discarded for the representative sample can be used to refill bore holes or pits. The thickness of the different horizons OL, OF and OH constituting the organic layer.

The OL-horizon has to be sampled separately. The OH-horizon has to be sampled separately only if it is thicker than 1 cm; otherwise, it may be sampled together with the OF-horizon. Optionally, the individual horizons (OL, OF, OH) may be sampled and analysed separately.

In organic layer, a frame of 25 by 25 cm is recommended, but alternatives with a minimum total surface of 500 cm^2 are acceptable; for mor humus, an auger with a diameter of 8 cm can be used. In the field, the total fresh weight of each layer (OL, OF, OH or H) has to be determined, preferably together with the thickness of each organic layer (OL, OF, OH or H). Of each layer, a subsample is collected for determination of moisture content (weight %) in the lab. Based on the result of the moisture content, the total dry weight (kg/m^2) of each layer can be calculated.

Sampling in Mineral Layer

Where possible, the organic and mineral soil should be sampled at exactly the same locations, i.e. sample the mineral soil underneath the organic layer that has already been removed for sampling. Sampling should be done by fixed depth. The top of the mineral soil corresponds with the zero level for depth measurements. Mineral soil layers are designated as 'Mij', where "i" is the first number of the upper depth limit and j is the first number of the lower depth limit (e.g. MO1 corresponds to the 0-10 cm layer). Table 3.1 shows the layers that should be sampled.

Table 3.1 : Depth of layers to be sampled in level –I and Level -II

Sl. No	Level -I (1)	Level - II (1)
1	0-10 cm	0-10 cm
2	10-20 cm	10-20 cm
3	20-40 cm (2)	20-40 cm (3)
4	40-80 cm (2)	40-80 cm (3)

Where,

1. Note that the entire thickness of the predetermined depth should be sampled and not the central part of the layer only.
2. Optional, but recommended if big changes between topsoil and subsoil are to be expected
3. Only mandatory for a first assessment, not to be repeated (optional) for a second survey if all mandatory parameters are determined with the reference method.

Number of Samples

Level I

For every layer, mandatory 5 subsamples have to be taken (a composite of 5 is allowed) (e.g. if taken with an auger $\geq$ 8 cm diameter), but more subsamples are required according to the variability of the site. Mandatory one composite sample has to be analysed and reported, more can be analysed optionally to determine the variability of the site. In case of very stony soils where sampling by auger is not possible, one composite of at least 3 subsamples can be accepted for the optional depth layers (M24 and M48) only.

Level II

For every layer, mandatory a minimum of 24 subsamples has to be taken, to be combined in at least three composite samples (i.e. at least 3 composites of each 8 subsamples or 4 composite samples of each 6 subsamples). Mandatory at least 3 values have to be reported (1 from each composite), to obtain information on the sampling variability. The distance between 2 sampling points should be at least 5 meter in order to avoid autocorrelation. The subsamples have to be of equal weight, except for situations with a variable lower depth limit. In such a case (e.g. an indurated horizon within the depth range of the sampled layer), the weight of each subsample is function of the thickness of the actually sampled layer. The weight of the subsample taken should be a fraction equal to (65-40)/(80-40) of the normal weight.

Sample Size

The minimum weight of each sample should be large enough for all analyses (mandatory and optional parameters) and possible repetitions or reanalyses in time. It is also advisable to keep the sample in a store room. Normally, the recommended sample size of at least 500 g of fresh soil for each sample.

The sheet accompanying the sample must include information on

- Nature of the soil
- Hardness and permeability of the soil
- Cause and source of salinity (where known)
- Relief
- Seasonal rainfall

- Irrigation and frequency of water logging
- Water table
- Soil management history
- Crop species and conditions of plant cover and
- Depth of the hardpan or concretion.

As the salt concentration may vary greatly with vertical or horizontal distance and with moisture and time, it is necessary to keep an account of the time of irrigation and of the amount of irrigation or rain received prior to sampling.

Dispatch of Soil Samples to the Laboratory

Before sending soil samples to the testing laboratory, it is necessary to ensure that proper identification marks are present on the sample bags and labels placed in the bags. It is essential to use a copying pencil and not ink because ink can smudge and become illegible. The best system is to obtain soil sampling bags from the soil testing laboratory with most of the information printed or stencilled on them in indelible ink.

Compare the number and details on the bag with the dispatch list. The serial numbers of different places should be distinguished by putting the identification mark specific for each centre. This may be in letters, e.g. one for the district, another for the block/county and a third for the village.

Pack the samples properly. Wooden boxes are most suitable for long transport. Sample bags should be packed only in clean bags never used for fertilizer or detergent packing. Farmers may bring soil samples directly to the laboratory. However, most samples are sent to the laboratories through field extension staff. An organized assembly-processing-dispatch system is required in order to ensure prompt delivery of samples to the laboratory.

Preparation of Soil Samples for Analysis

Handling in the Laboratory

As soon as the samples arrive at the soil testing laboratory, they should be checked against the accompanying information list. If the laboratory personnel collected the samples themselves, then adequate field notes should have been kept.

All unidentifiable samples should be discarded. Information regarding samples should be recorded in a register, and each sample should be given a laboratory number, in addition to the sample number, to help to distinguish it where more than one source of samples is involved.

Drying of Samples

Samples received in the laboratory may be moist. They should be dried in woodener enamelled trays. Care should be taken to maintain the identity of each sample at all stages of preparation. During drying, the trays can be numbered or a plastic tag could be attached. The samples are allowed to dry in the air. Alternatively, the trays may be placed in racks in a hot-air cabinet, whose temperature should not exceed 35 °C and whose relative humidity should be 30–60 percent. Oven drying a soil can cause profound changes in the sample. This step is not recommended as a preparatory procedure despite its convenience. Drying has a negligible effect on total N content, but the nitrate content in the soil changes with time and temperature. Drying at a high temperature affects the microbial population. With excessive drying, soil K may be released or fixed depending on the original level of exchangeable K. Exchangeable K will increase if its original level was less than 1 methyl/100 g soil [1cmol(p+)/kg] and *vice versa*, but the effect depends on the nature of clay minerals in the soil. In general, excessive drying, such as oven drying of the soil, affects the availability of most of the nutrients present in the sample and should be avoided. Only air drying is recommended.

Nitrate, nitrite and ammonium determinations must be carried out on samples brought straight from the field. These samples should not be dried. However, the results are expressed on an oven-dry basis by estimating separately the moisture content in the samples.

Post-Drying Care

After drying, the samples are taken to the preparation room. Air-dried samples are ground with a wooden pestle and mortar so that the soil aggregate is crushed but the soil particles do not break down. Samples of heavy clay soils may have to be ground with an end-runner grinding mill fitted with a pestle of hard wood and rubber lining to the mortar. Pebbles, concretions and stones should not be broken during grinding.

After grinding, the soil is screened through a 2 mm sieve. The practice of passing only a portion of the ground sample through the sieve and discarding the remainder is erroneous. This introduces a positive bias in the sample as the rejected part may include soil elements with differential fertility. Therefore, the entire sample should be passed through the sieve except for concretions and pebbles of more than 2 mm. The coarse portion on the sieve should be returned to the mortar for further grinding. Repeat sieving and grinding until all aggregate particles are fine enough to pass the sieve and only pebbles, organic residues and concretions remain.

If the soil is to be analysed for trace elements, containers made of copper, zinc and brass must be avoided during grinding and handling. Sieves of different sizes can be obtained in stainless steel. Aluminium or plastic sieves are useful alternative for general purposes. After the sample has passed through the sieve, it must be mixed again thoroughly. The soil samples should be stored in cardboard boxes in wooden drawers. These boxes should be numbered and arranged in rows in the wooden drawers, which are in turn fitted in a cabinet in the soil sample room.

I. Analytical Methods for Physical Properties of Soil

Physical properties of soil greatly influence its use and behaviour towards of plant growth. Support to plant, root penetration, drainage, aeration, retention of moisture and plant nutrients are linked with physical properties. The physical properties also influence the chemical and biological properties of soil and *vice-versa*. It depends on the amount, size, shape, arrangement, mineral composition of its particles and organic matter content. The following are important physical properties of soil generally carried out in a service-oriented soil testing laboratory:

- Soil texture
- Soil structure
- Soil bulk density
- Porosity
- Volume of expansion
- Linear shrinkage of soil
- Water content of soil and
- Water holding capacity.

Determination of Soil Texture

Soil texture (particle size distribution) is a stable soil characteristic that influences the physical and chemical properties of the soil. The sizes of the soil particles have a direct relationship with the surface area of the particles. Soil particles remain aggregated owing to various types of binding forces and factors. These include the content of OM, other colloidal substances present in the soil, oxides of Fe and aluminium (Al), and the hydration of clay particles. To estimate the content of various sizes of soil particles, the soil sample has to be brought into a dispersed state by removing the various types of binding forces.

In the dispersed soil samples, the soil particles settle down at a differential settling rate according to their size. In the estimation of soil texture, particles of < 2 mm in diameter are determined separately and characterized as: coarse sand (2.0 – 0.2 mm); fine sand (0.2 – 0.02 mm); silt (0.02– 0.002 mm); and clay (< 0.002 mm).

The soil sample is dispersed by removing the binding force in soil particles. The settling rate of dispersed particles in water is measured. Large particles are known to settle out of suspension more rapidly than do small particles. This is because larger particles have less specific area and, hence, less buoyancy than smaller particles. Stokes' law (1851) is used to express this relationship. It stipulates that the resistance offered by the liquid to the fall of the particle varies with the radius of the sphere and not with the surface. Accordingly, the formula is:

$$V = 2 \div 9\,[(dp - d)/\eta]\; g \times r^2$$

Where,

V = veocity of the fall in centimetres per second;

g = acceleration due to gravity;

dp = density of the particle;

d = density of the liquid;

r = radius of the particle in centimetres,

η = absolute viscosity of the liquid.

The velocity of fall of the particles with the same density in a given liquid increases with the square of the radius. With the above principle in view, the particle size distribution is estimated by measuring the amount of different sizes of soil particles present at different calibrated depths in the cylinder containing the suspended soil sample. The two methods in general use for estimating particle size or soil texture are:

- The international pipette method and
- The Bouyoucos hydrometer method.

Pipette Method-Modified

The pipette method quantitatively determines the physical proportions of three sizes of primary soil particles as determined by their settling rates in a aqueous solution using a pipette. Proportions are represented by stated class sizes: sand ranging from 2000 - 50 μm; silt ranging from 50 - 2.0 μm and clay < 2.0 μm and those stated by the USDA Soil Survey and Canadian Soil Survey Committee. Settling rates of primary particles are based on the principle of sedimentation as described by Stokes' Law and measured using a pipette. For specific samples, the method may require the pre-treatment for removal of soluble salts, organic matter, carbonates and iron oxides with subsequent dispersion using sodium-hexa-metaphosphate (Day, 1965). Generally this method is more precise than the hydrometer method. The method has a detection limit of 0.2% sand, silt and clay (on dry basis) and is generally reproducible to within ± 5%.

Equipment

- 50 mL conical centrifuge tubes with caps
- Analytical balance: 100 g capacity, resolution ± 0.0001 g.
- Reciprocating horizontal mechanical shaker, capable of 180 oscillations per minute.
- Adjustable 5.0 mL pipette, pipette tip and stopper (place on pipette tip for accuracy of depth. Adjust tip to drop to a depth 2.5 cm below surface of centrifuge tube containing 40.0 mL of solution.
- Re-pipette dispenser, calibrated to 50.0 ± 0.2 mL.

Reagents

- Deionized water
- Sodium hexa-metaphosphate (HMP), 0.5% dispersing solution. Dissolve 5.0 g Na-hexa-meta-phosphate in 1.0 L.

Procedure

- Weigh 5 ± 0.003 g of air-dried soil pulverized to pass 10 mesh sieve (< 2 mm) into 40 mL centrifuge tube (see comments 1, 2, 3 and 4).
- Add 40 mL of HMP solution; cap and place on reciprocating horizontal shaker for sixteen (16) hours (see comment 5).
- Pre-weigh tins which have been in a desiccator and record tin tare weight to nearest 0.0001 g.
- After 16 hour shaking, hand shake centrifuge tubes to disperse soil allow to settle for the required time according to Table 3.2. Time begins once settling has started. Complete silt + clay fraction at time specified through entire sample set and return for clay fraction at time state in Table 3.2 for clay.
- Dispense 2.5 mL fraction of the solution in weigh tin and place in drying oven.
- Pre-weigh tins which have been in a dessicator and record tin tare weight to nearest 0.0001 g (see comment 7).
- Remove dried tins containing soil residue and allow to cool, desiccate and record dry weight to the nearest 0.0001 g.

Table 3.2 : Sampling times for silt + clay and clay pipette method.

Temperature °C	Sand 100% (Silt + Clay) time (sec)	Clay Time (min)
16	11.7	122.3
18	11.2	116.4
20	10.6	110.9
22	10.2	105.7
24	9.7	101.0
26	9.3	96.6

(Assumptions: Density of particles is 2.65 g cm^{-3}; sampling depth 2.5 cm below liquid surface; g = 9.8 ms^{-2}; clay = 0.002 μm).

Calculations

Sand % = 100 - (% silt + clay)

= 100 - [(((dry weight - tin weight) - blank) x 40 ÷ 2.5) ÷5) x 100]

Clay % = (((Dry Weight - tin weight) - blank) x 40÷ 2.5) ÷ 5) x 100

Silt % = (100 - % sand) - % clay

Comments

1. The exact sample size is soil texture dependent. For fine textured soils (silts or clays), 2- 4 g may be adequate. For coarse textured soils, 6 - 10 g will be needed in order to obtain reproducible results. For moist soils, dry overnight at 105°C and correct for moisture content.

2. For soils containing carbonates ($CaCO_3$ >2) and/or high in soluble salts (ECe > 2 dS m^{-1}), it is recommended soils be pre-treated. Place 5g of soil in 50 mL centrifuge tube; add 10 mL deionized water and 1mL of 1M sodium acetate (pH = 5). Mix and centrifuge for 10 min at 1500 rpm until the supernatant is clear. Decant and wash two more times with 50 mL of deionized water. Dry and determine particle sizes.

3. For soils containing organic matter content > 3.5%, after removal of carbonates, add 10 mL of water and add 5 mL of H_2O_2 to the suspension. If excessive frothing occurs, cool and add additional H_2O_2 when reaction subsides. Heat to 90°C when frothing ceases. Continue treatment until organic matter is oxidized (as judged by rate of reaction and bleached color).

4. For removal of iron oxides, add 20mL to the H_2O_2 treated sample of a solution 0.3 M sodium citrate and 84 g/L sodium bicarbonate. Shake for 30 minutes to disperse the soil and add 0.40 g of sodium dithionite ($Na_2S_2O_4$). Place in water-bath at 80 °C and stir intermittently for 20 minutes. Remove and add 1.5 mL of a 10% NaCl solution, centrifuge and decant. If sample is brownish in color repeat with the sodium citrate - sodium bicarbonate step. If sample is gleyed (gray), repeat with 10% solution of NaCl, and two deionized water rinses. Proceed with HMP addition.

5. It is recommended to use horizontal reciprocating shaking for the dispersing the samples. The use of electric stirrer at high rpm may result in significant grinding of sample primary minerals.

6. For determining sand fractions, quantitatively transfer the sediment suspension through a 270 mesh (53um) sieve and wash with deionized water using a wash bottle. Transfer the sand to a tared beaker, dry at 105° C and weigh. The dried sand may be placed in nested sieves to determine individual sand fraction size analysis.

7. For soils having clay particle density < 2.65 g cm^{-3}, settling time will increase and for soils > 2.65 g cm^{-3} it will decrease (Gee and Bauder, 1986).
8. An error of 0.001 ± g in the dry weight of the pipette sample results in an error of ± 0.32% for clay size fraction.
9. Using soil size fraction data, soil textural classification can be determined.

Bouyoucos Hydrometer Method

The bouyoucos hydrometer method is similar to pipette method except bouyoucos hydrometer. Settling rates of primary particles are based on the principle of sedimentation as described by Stokes' Law and measured using a hydrometer. The use of the ASTM 152H-Type hydrometer is based on a standard temperature of 20° C and a particle density of 2.65 g cm^{-3} and units are expressed as grams of soil per litre. For specific samples, this method too requires pre-treatment for removal of soluble salts, organic matter, carbonates and iron oxides with subsequent dispersion using sodium-hexa-meta-phosphate as in the pipette method. The hydrometer reading of a blank solution is used for corrections of temperature and solution viscosity (Gee and Bauder, 1986). Generally this method is of lower precision than the pipette or sedimentation methods. The method has a detection limit of 2.0% sand, silt and clay (on dry basis) and is generally reproducible to within ± 8%.

Equipment

- Analytical balance: 100 g capacity, resolution ± 0.01 g.
- Standard hydrometer with Bouyoucos scale in g L^{-1}.
- Reciprocating horizontal mechanical shaker, capable of 180 oscillations per minute.
- Sedimentation cylinder with 1.0 L mark 36 ± 2 cm from the bottom.
- Shaker bottle 200 mL and cap (polypropylene or glass).

Reagents

- Deionized water
- Amyl alcohol.
- Sodium hexa-meta-phosphate (HMP), 5% dispersing solution. Dissolve 50.0 g HMP in 1.0 L, deionized water.

Procedure

- Weigh 40 ± 0.05 g of air-dried soil pulverized to pass10 mesh sieve (< 2.0mm) into 200mL container (see comments 1, 2, 3 and 4).
- Determine oven dry soil moisture on a 2nd sample of soil.
- Add 100 mL of HMP solution, cap and place on reciprocating horizontal shaker for 16 hours (see comment 5).
- Quantitatively transfer the suspension to the sedimentation cylinder and add deionized water to bring to 1.0 L final volume.
- Allow the suspension to equilibrate to room temperature for 2 hours.
- Insert plunger and thoroughly mix contents, dislodging sediment from the bottom of the cylinder. Finish stirring with two or three smooth stokes.
- Add 2 mL of amyl alcohol to the surface to suspensions covered in foam.
- Repeat the process and determine hydrometer reading on a blank solution and to the nearest ± 0.5 g L^{-1} as R_{C1}.
- Lower the hydrometer carefully into the suspension after 30 seconds and take a reading after 40 seconds and record to the nearest ±0.5 g L^{-1} as R_{sand} (see comment 6).
- Remove the hydrometer carefully, rinse and wipe dry.
- After six (6) hours record temperature of the suspension to the nearest ± 1° C. Using the temperature correction values in Table 3.3 determine the settling time for the 2.0 *um* size fraction (see comment 7). Based on time after initiation of settling, re-insert the hydrometer carefully and take a reading and record as R_{clay} to the nearest ± 0.5 g L^{-1}. Repeat the process determining hydrometer reading on a blank solution and record as R_{C2} to the nearest ± 0.5 g L^{-1} (see comments 8).

Table 3.3 : Suspension temperature on the hydrometer determination of soil clay ($2 \mu m$) based on a particle density of 2.65g cm^{-3} and a solution density of 0.5 g L^{-1}.

Temperature °C	Settling time for clay(hours and minutes)
18	8:09
19	7:57
20	7:45
21	7:35
22	7:24
23	7:13
24	7:03
25	6:53
26	6:44
27	6:35
28	6:27

(Gee and Bauder, 1986)

Calculations

Sand % = {[(Oven dry soil mass) - (R_{sand} - R_{C1})]/ (oven dry soil mass)} x 100

Clay % = [(R_{clay} - R_{C2})/ oven dry soil mass)] x 100

Silt % = 100 - (Sand % + Clay %)

[*Note :* Report results to the nearest 0.1% content (see comment 9 and 10)]

Comments

1. The exact sample size is soil texture dependent. For fine textured soils, silts or clays, 10- 20 g may be adequate. For coarse textured soils, 60 - 100 g will be needed in order to obtain reproducible results. For moist soils dry overnight at 105° C and correct for moisture content.
2. For soils containing carbonates (>2.0%) and/or high in soluble salts (ECe > 2.0 dS m^{-1}) it is recommended soils be pre-treated. Place 40.0 g of soil in 250 mL centrifuge tube, add 100 mL deionized water and 10.0 mL of 1.0 M sodium-acetate (pH 5.0). Mix and centrifuge for 10 min. at 1500 rpm until the supernatant is clear. Decant and wash two more times with 50mL of deionized water.

3. For soils containing organic matter contents > 3.5%, after removal of carbonates, add 25mL of water and add 5mL of H_2O_2 to the suspension. If excessive frothing occurs, cool and add additional H_2O_2 when reaction subsides. Heat to 90° C, when frothing ceases. Continue treatment until organic matter is oxidized (as judged by rate of reaction and bleached color).

4. For removal of Iron oxides add 150 mL to the H_2O_2 treated sample of a solution 0.3M sodium citrate and 84 g/L sodium bicarbonate. Shake for 30 minutes to disperse the soil and add 3.0 g of sodium dithionite ($Na_2S_2O_4$). Place in water bath 80° C and stir intermittently for 20 minutes. Remove and add 10 mL of a 10% NaCl solution, centrifuge and decant. If sample is brownish in color repeat with the sodium citrate - sodium bicarbonate step. If sample is gleyed (gray), repeat with 10% solution of NaCl, and two deionized water rinses. Proceed with HMP addition.

5. It is recommended to use horizontal reciprocating shaking for the dispersing the samples. The use of electric stirrer at high rpm may result in significant grinding of sample primary minerals.

6. It may be advantageous to take a reading at 35 seconds and a 2nd at 45 seconds and record the average as the hydrometer value is dynamic.

7. The hydrometer procedure has been used by number of laboratories. Readings are frequently made at 40 seconds and 2 hour for the determination of sand and clay. Based on theoretical considerations, the 2 hour reading is an estimate of the 5.0 μm fraction and errors often exceed 10% by weight from that of actual clay (Gee and Bauder, 1979).

8. For determining sand fractions, quantitatively transfer the sediment suspension through a 270 mesh (53.0 *u*m) sieve and wash with deionized water using a wash bottle. Transfer the sand to a tared beaker, dry at 105° C and weigh. The dried sand may be placed in nested sieves to determine individual sand fraction size analysis.

9. For soils having clay particle densities < 2.65 g cm^{-3}, settling time will increase and for soils > 2.65 gcm^{-3} it will decrease (Gee and Bauder, 1986).

10. An error of 1 ± g L^{-1} in the hydrometer reading results in an error of ± 2.5% for clay size Fraction and on a percentage basis

translates to an error of ± 12.5% for 40g of soil containing 20% clay. For more accurate and precise measurement of silt and clay size fractions it recommended that the pipette method be used which has a precision of ±2-3%.

Determination of Soil Structure

Soil structure is defined as the arrangement of the soil particles. With regard to structure, soil particles refer not only to sand, silt and clay but also to the aggregate or structural elements that have been formed by the aggregation of smaller mechanical fractions. Therefore, the word "particle" refers to any unit that is part of the make-up of the soil, whether a primary unit (sand, silt or clay fraction) or a secondary (aggregate) particle.

The size, shape and character of the soil structure varies place to plance and within place. The prominent structures are prism-like, platy-like, cube-like and spherical. On the basis of size, the soil structure is classified as very coarse (> 10 mm), coarse (5–10 mm) and medium (2–5mm). According to proportions of sand, silt and clay, soil structural classes are fine (1–2 mm) and very fine (< 1 mm). Depending on the stability of the aggregate and the ease of separation, the structure is characterized as poorly developed, weakly developed, moderately developed, well developed and highly developed.

The soil structure or aggregate consists of an intermediate grouping of a number of primary particles into a secondary unit. The important factors that facilitate the aggregation of soil particles are clay particles and types of clay minerals, cations such as Ca, OM, colloidal matter such as oxides of Fe and Al, plant roots and soil microbes and their types (fungi being most effective).

Soil structure influences the extent of pore space in the soil, water holding capacity (WHC), aeration, root movement and nutrient availability. The better and more stable soil aggregates are considered a desirable soil property with regard to plant growth. Therefore, the determination of soil structure is an important exercise in a soil fertility evaluation programme. An aggregate analysis aims to measure the percentage of water-stable secondary particles in the soil anthem extent to which the finer mechanical separates are aggregated into coarser fractions.

The determination of aggregate or clod-size distribution involves procedures that depend on the disintegration of soil into clods and aggregates. The resulting aggregate-size distribution depends on the manner and condition in which the disintegration is brought about. As the measurements have practical significance, the disruptive forces causing disintegration should compare closely with the forces expected in the field. The field condition, particularly with respect to soil moisture, should be compared with the moisture condition adopted for soil disintegration in the laboratory. The sampling of soil and the subsequent disintegration of clods in regard to seed bed preparation for upland crops should be carried out under air-dry conditions for dry-sieve analysis. A rotary sieve shaker is ideal for dry sieving. Similarly, the processes of wetting, disruption of dry aggregates, and screening of aggregates should be compared with the disruptive actions of water and mechanical forces of tillage under wetland conditions.

Vacuum wetting of dry soil largely simulates the process of wetting *in situ*, particularly in the subsurface layers. However, the surface soil clods experience large scale disruption when they are immersed in water at atmospheric pressure. The reproducibility of the size distribution of clods should be the criterion for deciding the method of wetting by either vacuum wetting or immersion in water. Immersion wetting is closer to wetting of surface soil by irrigation. After wetting, aggregates of different sizes can be obtained through several methods, e.g. sedimentation, elutriation and sieving. However, sieving under water compares more closely with the disruptive actions of water and other mechanical forces as experienced during wetland rice field preparation.

Dry Aggregate Analysis

The size distribution of dry clods is measured by dry sieving analysis performed on an air-dried bulk soil sample, either manually or with the help of a rotary sieve shaker (Gupta and Ghil Dyal, 1998).

Apparatus required

- Nest of sieves, 20 cm in diameter and 5 cm in height, with screens having 25.0, 10.0, 5.0, 2.0, 1.0, 0.5 and 0.25 mm diameter round openings, with a pan and a lid
- Rotary sieve shaker
- Some aluminium cans
- Balance
- Spade
- Brush

- Polyethylene bags and
- Labels.

Procedure

1. Collect a bulk soil sample from the tilled field with the help of a 20cm diameter and 10cm height ring.
2. Place the ring on the tilled soil and press until level with the surface. Remove the loose soil within the ring and collect it in a polyethylene bag.
3. Put one label indicating the depth and soil profile inside the bag, and tie another label with the bag.
4. Take the soil sample to the laboratory and air-dry it.
5. Spread the soil on a sheet of paper and prepare the subsamples by "quartering". Cone the mixed soil material in the centre of the mixing sheet with care to make it symmetrical with respect to fine and coarse soil material. Flatten the cone and divide it through the centre with a flat metal spatula or metal sheet, moving one half to one side. Further divide each half into halves; separating the four portions into separate piles or "quarters".
6. Weigh the subsamples from two of these quarters and use them for clod-size and aggregate distribution analysis as duplicates.
7. Transfer the weighed soil sample to the top sieve of the nest of sieves with the 5.0, 2.0, 1.0, 0.5 and 0.25 mm-diameter round openings and a pan at the bottom.
8. Cover the top sieve with the lid, and place the nest of sieves on a rotary shaker.
9. Switch on the shaker for 10 minutes, and then remove the sieves.
10. Collect the soil retained on each screen in the pre-weighed aluminium cans (with the help of a small brush), and weigh the cans with the soil.
11. If the percentage of dry aggregates on the 5mm sieve exceeds 25%, transfer these aggregates to a nest of sieves with 25.0, 10.0 and 5.0mm sieves along with a pan.
12. Cover the top sieve containing the aggregates with a lid, and place the nest of sieves on the rotary sieve shaker.

13. Switch on the motor for 10 minutes, and proceed as above for the estimation of aggregate-size distribution.
14. Analyse the duplicate sample following the same procedure, and calculate the percentage distribution of dry aggregates retained on each sieve.
15. Dry the duplicate 100g sample in an oven for 24 hours at 105° C to calculate the oven-dry weight of the soil sample.

Calculation

The steps in the calculation are:

- Weight of aggregates in each sieve group = (wt. of aggregates + can) – wt. of can
- Percent distribution of aggregates in each size group

  = (weight of aggregates in each size group ÷ total soil wt.) x 100
- Oven-dry weight of aggregate (%)

  = (air - dry wt % x 100) ÷ 100 + Moisture %

Wet Aggregate Analysis

Apparatus required

For wet aggregate analysis, the following apparatus required

- Mechanical oscillator powered by a gear-reduction motor with an amplitude of oscillation of 3.8 cm and a frequency of 30 – 35 cycles per minute
- Two sets of sieves, each 20 cm in diameter and 5 cm high, with screen openings of 5.0, 2.0, 1.0, 0.5, 0.25 and 0.1 mm in diameter
- Two Buchner funnels, 15 cm in diameter, with rubber stoppers
- Two vacuum flasks of 1 litre capacity
- Suction pump or aspirator
- Rubber policeman
- Twelve aluminium cans
- Perforated cans
- Sand bath and Filter papers.

Reagents required

- Sodium hexa-meta-phosphate (5%)
- Sodium hydroxide (4%).

Procedure

Among the different procedures adopted, wetting the samples under vacuum is suggested because the rate of wetting influences the slaking of crumbs. The time of sieving ranges from 10 minutes to 30 minutes depending on the type of wetting. Baver and Rhodes (1932) suggest 10 minutes pre-shaking of the soil sample in a reciprocating shaker or end-to-end shaker for fine-textured soil.

The technique used by Yoder (1936) and subsequently improved by the Soil Science Society of America's Committee on Physical Analysis is generally used for determining the size distribution of water-stable aggregates.

1. Take the soil sample when it is moist and friable.
2. By applying mild stress, break it into smaller aggregates that can pass through an 8 mm screen.
3. Put the sieved soil sample on a watch glass for wetting by either vacuum soaking or the immersion method.
4. For vacuum wetting, place the sample in a vacuum desiccator containing de-aerated water at the bottom.
5. Evacuate the desiccator until the pressure inside drops to about 3 mm and water starts boiling. Now, allow water to enter through the top of the desiccator and to flow into the watch glass holding the sample.
6. Add enough water to cover the soil sample. Then, take the soil sample out of the desiccator.
7. Prepare four soil samples of 25 g each. Place a set of duplicate samples in an oven in order to determine the moisture content.
8. Transfer another set of saturated duplicate soil samples to the top sieve of the nest of sieves (5.0, 2.0, 1.0, 0.5, 0.25 and 0.1mm) and spread with the help of a glass rod and a slow jet of water.
9. Remove the bottom pan, and attach the nest of sieves to the Yoder-type, wet sieve shaker.

10. Fill the drum, which holds the set of sieves with salt-free water at 20–25°C to a level somewhat below that of the screen in the top sieve of the nest of sieves, when the sieves are in the highest position.
11. Then, lower the nest of sieves to wet the soil for 10 minutes.
12. Bring the nest of sieves to the initial position, and adjust the level of water so that the screen in the top sieve is covered with water in its highest position.
13. Now, switch on the mechanical oscillator to move the nest of sieves up and down with a frequency of 30 - 35 cycles per minute and a stroke of 3.8 cm. Sieve for 10 minutes.
14. Remove the nest of screens from the water and allow it to drain for some time.
15. Transfer the soil resting on each screen with a stream of distilled water, and brush it into a Buchner funnel having a pre-weighed filter paper and connected to a suction pump.
16. Transfer the soil along with the filter paper into an aluminium can and dry at 105° C for 24 hours. Weigh the soil to the nearest 0.01 g.
17. Transfer the oven-dry soil aggregates from all the cans of a set into the dispersion cup.
18. Add dispersing agent (10 ml of 5% solution of sodium-hexa-meta-phosphate for normal and calcium saturated soils, or 10 ml of 4 percent solution of sodium hydroxide for acid soil) and enough distilled water to fill the cup to within 4 cm of the rim, and then stir the suspension for 10 minutes.
19. Wash the suspension on an identical set of sieves as used previously by means of a stream of tap water and a brush, and transfer it to aluminium cans.
20. Weigh and oven dry the sand in each can in the same manner as above.

Calculation

Calculate the percentage distribution of soil particles (aggregates and the sand) and the sand particles retained on each sieve as follows:

Size distribution of soil particles (aggregate + sand):

- Soil particles in each size group (%) = [Wod (ag + s)i x 100] ÷ Wod
- Sand particle in each size group (%) = [Wod(s)i x 100] ÷ Wod

Where,

Wod is the oven dried weight of the aggregates (*ag*) and sand (*s*), and *i* is the size group.

Determination of Soil Bulk Density

Soil bulk density (D_b) is the ratio of the bulk or macroscopic volume of soil particles plus pore spaces in a sample. The mass is determined after drying to constant weight at 105^0 C and the volume is that of the sample as taken in the field. Bulk density is a widely used value. It is needed for converting water % by weight to constant by volume, for calculating porosity when the particle density is known, and for estimating the weight of a volume of soil too large to weigh conveniently, such as the weight of a furrow slice or an acre foot. The clod method, core method, excavation method, radiation method and Keen box method are employed for determination of bulk density of soil. These methods differ principally in the way the sample of soil is obtained. In most agricultural soils work, bulk density is expressed in g cm^{-3}. The term bulk density is preferred over the terms volume weight, bulk specific gravity or apparent specific gravity.

Particle density (D_p) of a soil is the mass per unit volume of the soil particles alone. Particle density for most mineral soils usually lies within a narrow limit of 2.60 and 2.75 g/cc. Sometimes it may exceed 2.75, if unusual minerals like magnetite, garnet, epidote, zircon, tourmaline and hornblende are present. On the other hand, D_p of some highly organic mineral top soils may drop as low as 2.4 g/cc or even below. The value of 2.65 is considered as standard value for most soils.

Bulk density of soil is influenced by soil texture, pore space, organic matter content, compactness and cultivation practices. D_b for fine textured (clay, clay loam, silt clay, silt) soil varies from 1.00 to 1.60g/cc D_b for coarse textured (sand, sandy loam) soil varies from 1.20 to 1.80 g/cc Db for very compact soil is 2.00 g/cc or more plough layer or furrow slice: The weight of 15cm (6inches) deep surface soil is required for fertilization, liming, etc. Considering D_b of 1.5g/cc, the weight of 1ha of land area comes to roughly 2.25 x 10^6 kg (2 x 10^6 lb $acre^{-1}$. It is known as Acre-furrow-Slice). The pore Space of a soil is that portion occupied by air and water. If we consider Vm^{-3} as bulk volume, D_b as bulk density and D_p as particle density then,

Weight of soil= V x D_b

Volume of soil particles (cm^{-3}) = V x $D_b \div D_p$

Total pore volume (v) = V- V x $D_b \div D_p$ = V (1-$D_b \div D_p$)

Percent pore volume or Pore Space = (v/V) x 100

= (1- $D_b \div D_p$) x100

= 100 - ($D_b \div D_p$) x 100

Thus, D_b and D_p and pore space of silt loam soil are 1.30, 2.65 g/cc and 50.9%, respectively. For a sandy soil, D_b and D_p and pore space are 1.50 and 2.65 g/cc, respectively. Sandy soils will have 35 to 50% pore space and medium to fine textured soils 40 to 60%. Soil texture, compactness, handling of soil etc. are the factors that influence pore pace of soil. The clod method, core methd and Keen box are described as follows.

Clod Method

The bulk density of clods, or coarse peds, is calculated from their mass and volume. The volume is determined by coating the clod with a water-repellent substance (paraffin) and by weighing it first in air, then again while immersed in a liquid of known density, making use of Archimedes' principle (see note 1).

Special Apparatus

- Balance.
- Fine thread (preferably synthetic fibre).
- Hard paraffin in a container kept at 60°C (or a few degrees above 60°C) into which the soil sample can be dipped.

Procedure

1. Select a representative air-dry clod or ped. It must be sufficiently stable to cohere during coating, weighing and handling. Carefully tie a length of thread around the clod, leaving about 20 cm free. Weigh the clod suspended in air.
2. Holding onto the end of the free thread, dip the clod momentarily in the melted paraffin.
3. Allow the excess to drain (see note 2.). When the adhering paraffin solidifies, weigh the clod and paraffin together.

4. Suspend the clod with paraffin coating in water and weigh it again (See note 3.) Record the water temperature.
5. To obtain a correction for moisture content of the soil, break open the clod, remove a sample of soil and determine moisture content.

Calculation

Bulk density (Mg m^{-3}) = $(D_w \times S_{od}) \div [S - SP + P - (P \times D_w \div D_{pf})]$

Where,

D_W = Density of water at temperature of determination (Mg/m^3)

S_{od} = Oven dry weight of soil sample (g)

S = Net weight of soil sample in air (g)

SP = Net weight of soil sample plus paraffin in water (g)

P = Weight of paraffin coating in air (g)

D_{pf} = Density of paraffin (Mg m^{-3})

Reporting results

- Report bulk density (Mg m^{-3}) to the nearest 0.01 Mg m^{-3}.

Notes

1. The clod method usually gives higher bulk density values than do other methods. One reason is that the clod method does not take the inter-clod spaces into account. A second reason is that the soil volume is the air-dry volume, which is likely to be slightly less than the volume of a field-moist sample used in other methods.
2. Paraffin is best used between 60°C and 70°C, a few degrees above the melting point, when clods are dipped. At this temperature, it quickly solidifies upon removal of the clod and is less likely to penetrate the pores of the clod than at higher temperatures. Furthermore at higher temperatures, pin-sized air leaks through the paraffin seal are more likely because of penetration of heat into the clod with consequent expansion of soil gases that continues after solidification of the paraffin.
3. If bubbles appear on the paraffin when the sample is weighed in water or if the weight in water increases with time, water is penetrating the clod and the sample must be discarded.

[Note: 0.1(ped with parafin weight-dry weight ped) – – corrects for the buoyant force of the wax 1.65(>2mm weight/2.65) – – corrects for the >2mm material assuming a density of 2.65 g/cm3 for that material].

Comments

The clod method typically yields higher bulk-density values than do other methods (Tisdall, 1951). The method mentioned here tries to reduce this error by removing the coating of each ped, thereby weighing each of the fractions. Care should be practiced to get naturally occurring peds. Peds on or near the soil surface are likely to be unrepresentative, due to tilling/plowing in agriculturally used soils. Peds should be sampled at other depths or from areas that may not be used for agricultural purposes. Should bubbles appear on the paraffin-covered ped while submerged in water, or if the weight in water increases with time, water is penetrating the clod, therefore the sample must be discarded. Precision in calculating the bulk density would require a correction for the difference of the weight of the wire in air and in water. However, the error is negligible with thread or a 28-gauge wire. In terms of overall accuracy, the greater number of samples used for each determination will significantly reduce the standard deviation. If paraffin is not available, rubber, saran, wax mixtures, and oils may be substituted (Blake and Hartge, 1986).

Core Method

Introduction

With this method, a cylindrical metal sampler is pressed or driven into the soil to the desired depth and is carefully removed to preserve a known volume of sample as it existed *in situ*. The sample is dried at 105^0C and weighed. Bulk density is the over-dried mass divided by the field volume of the sample. The core method is usually unsatisfactorily if more than an occasional stone is present in the soil.

Apparatus

Core samplers vary in design from a thin-walled metal cylinder to a cylindrical sleeve with removable sample cylinders that fit inside. A widely used and very satisfactory sampler consists of two cylinders fitted one inside the other. The outer one extends above and below the inner to accept a hammer or press at the upper end and to form a cutting edge at the lower. The inside cylinder is the sample holder. The inside diameters of the two cylinders when nested are essentially the same at the lower end, the inner being fitted against a shoulder cut on the inner surface of the outside cylinder.

Procedure

1. Drive/ press the sampler in to either a vertical or horizontal soil surface far enough to fill the sampler, but not so far as to compress the soil in the confined space of the sampler.
2. Remove the sampler with care and its contents so as to preserve the natural structure and packing of the soil as nearly as possible.
3. A shovel alongside and under the sampler may be needed in some soils to remove the sample without disturbance.
4. Separate the 2-cyliders, retaining the undisturbed soil in the inner cylinder. Trim the soil extending beyond each end of the sample holder (inner cylinder) flush with each end with a straight-edged knife or sharp spatula.
5. The soil sample volume is established to be the same the volume of the sample holder.
6. In some sampler designs, the cutting edge of the sampler has an inside diameter slightly less than the sampler holder, so as to reduce friction as the soil enters the holder. In these cases, determine the diameter of the cutting head and use this to calculate the sample holder volume. Transfer the soil to a container, place it in an oven at 105^0C until constant weight is reached, and weigh it.
7. The bulk density is the oven-dry mass of the sample divided by the sample volume.

Comments

- Core samples should not be taken in wet or dry soils. In wet soils, friction along the sides of the sampler and vibrations due to hammering are likely to result in viscous flow of the soil and thus in compression of the sample. When this occurs the sample obtained is unrepresentative, being more dense than the body of the soil.

- In dry or hard soils, another problem arises. Hammering the sampler into the soil often shatters the sample, and an actual loosening during sampling may occur. Samplers pressed into the soil usually avoid the vibration which causes shattering.

Keen Box Method

Soil physical properties such as bulk density / apparent specific gravity, pore space, true specific gravity, volume expansion, water holding capacity are most conveniently determined by the Keen-Raczkowski box experiment.

Materials required

- Keen box set : A circular brass box with perforated bottom and a split brass ring
- Filter paper

Procedure

1. Place a thin filter paper on the bottom and fix it by the split brass ring.
2. Weigh the box with filter paper (A). Transfer dry sieved soil to the keen box, tapping the box gently and smartly till full and level the top of the box with a spatula/scale and take the weight of dry soil with the keen box (B).
3. After properly packing of soil into the box, place the box in a Petri dish and pour water and allow the soil absorb water through the bottom of the Keen box overnight.
4. Remove the box with moist and expanded saturated soil, wipe out the outside and record the weight as box + saturated soil weight (C).
5. Weigh a dry watch glass (F) and remove the expanded soil from Keen box with spatula to the watch glass and record the weight of watch glass + moist soil (G).
6. Take the weight of Keen box with wet remaining moist soil (D).
7. Allow the watch glass and the Keen box with moist soil to be dry in an oven at 105°C. Collect the dry soil weight with Keen box (E) and with watch glass (H) until constant weights are attained.

8. After collection of all weight data, wash the Keen box and take measurements for determining height, diameter and volume (inner) of the box.

Calculation

Weight of Keen box + Filter Paper = A g

Wt. of Keen Box + Dry soil = B g

Wt. of Keen Box + Wet Expanded Soil = C g

Wt. of Keen Box + Wet remaining Soil = D g

Wt. of Keen Box + Dry remaining soil = E g

Wt. of Watch Glass = F g

Wt. of watch glass + wet soil = G g

Wt. of watch glass + Dry soil = H g

Diameter of keen box = d cm

Height of keen box = h cm

Volume of Keen box (inner) = $(d \div 2)^2 \times h$

Bulk Density (Db) = $(B - A) \div V$ g cm^{-3}

Particle Density (Dp) = $(E - A) \div \{V - (D - E)\}$ g cm^{-3}

Maximum Water Holding Capacity = $\{(C - B) \times 100\} / (B - A)$ cm^{-3}

% Pore Space = $\{(D - E) \times 100\} \div V$

Volume Expansion/100 g soil = $[(G - H) + \{(H - F) \times 100 \div D_p\}] \div V$ cm^{-3}

Determination of Soil Porosity

The geometry of the pore system of the soil is just as complex as that of the solid system. The pore system is described in relatively simple terms such as total porosity, volume % or pore size distribution. Characterizations of the pore system are important in investigations of the storage and movement of water and gases in soil. The principle on which the methods are based is very simple: bulk volume occupied by a given mass of soil can be divided into various kinds of space. Consider first a bulk volume of soil dried in an oven to constant weight at 105^0C. The mass in grams of a volume of 1cc can be taken as its density. The bulk density thus obtained is always lower than the average particle density. This means that only part of the bulk volume is occupied by solid particles; the remainder is occupied by a lighter material, air.

Principle

Determinations of total porosity yield the simplest partial characterization of the soil pore system. Calculating porosity from density simply involves converting data from densities to volumes. Since bulk density (D_b) is defined as $M_s \div V_b$, in which M_s is the mass of soil (oven dry) in bulk volume (V_b), then,

$$V_b = M_s \div D_b$$

Similarly, from the definition of D_p, the particle density, one obtains the relationship, $V_p = M_s \div D_p$, in which V_p is the volume occupied by solid particles having total mass M_s. But V_b is the whole volume of the space to be occupied by solid particles. From the above definitions, it follows that this fraction equals $D_b \div D_p$. The total porosity, S_t is defined as the percentage of the bulk volume not occupied by solids, that is,

$$S_t = 100\ [1 - (D_b \div D_p)] = 100\ ([(D_b - D_p) \div D_p].$$

Procedure

1. Determine the bulk density and particle density of soil with method described earlier.
2. Calculate porosity using the above-said equation.
3. In cases where great accuracy is not required, use the assumed the value of 2.65g cm^{-3} for particle density of mineral soils.

Determination of Volume Expansion of Soil

This method outlines the procedure for the determination of the free swell of a disturbed soil on wetting. Soils that shrink or fail to saturate are usually dispersible. This might mask the extent of volume expansion and a linear shrinkage test is recommended to indicate the likelihood of shrink-swell behaviour. This test is only performed for dispersive soil.

Principle

This test measures the free swelling of a disturbed soil (i.e. ground and sieved finer than 0.425 mm) on wetting from air-dry to saturation. The swell is calculated on a volumetric basis using a modification of the Keen-Raczowski method.

Special Apparatus

- Numbered circular boxes with perforated base, internal diameter 56 mm, internal depth
- 16mm, 20 gauge brass, fitted with brass circlip (see note 1.)
- 50 mm No 1 filter papers.
- Spatula with steel blade approximately 100 mm long and 20mm wide.
- Numbered aluminium weighing tins with tight-fitting lids.
- Two shallow trays (large plastic developing trays) approximately 300 x 250 x 40 mm.
- Balance readable and accurate to 0.1g.

Procedure

1. Obtain, by riffling or quartering, a representative sample of at least 150 g of the material passing a no 36BS sieve (0.425 mm) prepared according to the procedure for preparation of disturbed soil samples for testing.
2. Fit a filter paper to the volume expansion box and clamp it in place over the perforated base using the circlip. Weigh the box with filter paper to 0.1 g (W1).
3. Add about 10 g of soil to the box and carefully pack the soil to a uniform density by tapping the box on a flat surface. Turn the box frequently while tapping to ensure that the depth of soil is uniform around the edges. Adequate packing is indicated by migration of coarser particles to the perimeter. Add additional soil until the box is full to the sides. At this stage, the soil will form a mound in the centre.
4. Carefully level the soil to the sides of the box by drawing the spatula, with the blade on edge, across the top of the box. Return surplus soil to the container.
5. Place the full box in the shallow tray containing about 12mm depth of deionised water, cover the tray using the second tray in an inverted position and allow to stand overnight or until completely saturated (see note 2.) Saturation is indicated by the glisten of water on the surface of the sample (see note 3.)

6. Remove the box from the tray and trim off the expanded portion of soil by drawing the flat spatula blade across the top of the box. Transfer the wet soil to a weighing tin of known weight (W2) by scraping the spatula blade across the edge of the tin. Trim off any further expanded soil not collected on the first pass and transfer to the tin. Repeat if necessary. Cover the tin with the lid and weigh immediately to 0.1 g (W3).
7. Dry the outside of the box and weigh to 0.1 g (W4).
8. Perform another test and compare the results.

Calculations

Volume Expansion (VE %) = [(W3 - W2) ÷ (W4-W1)] x 100

Where,

W1 = weight of volume expansion box (g)

W2 = weight of weighing tin (g)

W3 = weight of wet expanded soil + tin (g)

W4 = weight of wet residual soil + box (g)

Reporting the results

Report the volume expansion to the nearest whole number. Report the shrinkage of the sample in the box if this occurs (See note 4.)

Notes

1. Some soils will wet up and swell so rapidly that dry surface soil falls out of the box. This might be prevented by wetting the soil around the perimeter with a few drops of deionised water.
2. The time for saturation varies according to the permeability of the sample. Some dispersible soils will never wet to saturation. If a soil is not saturated after 48 hours then the test is not appropriate. If the sample fails to saturate or dispersion percentage > 50%, report this fact and use Linear Shrinkage.
3. Shrinkage on saturation might occur in certain dispersible or silty soils. The occurrence of shrinkage on saturation might be relevant to the problem of saturation settlement in earthworks. If so, it should be reported and Linear Shrinkage should be used instead.

Determination of Linear Shrinkage of Soil

This test covers the determination of the linear shrinkage of a disturbed soil sample. It is a tedious and expensive test that is done only on soils (other than sands) when the dispersion percentage is >50 or volume expansion tests fail to saturate or shrink. This test is performed on dispersive soils only.

Principle

Linear shrinkage is the decrease in length of a soil sample when oven-dried, starting with a moisture content of the sample at the liquid limit.

Special Apparatus

- 100 mm spatula.
- Shrinkage moulds in the form of semi-cylindrical troughs 250 mm long and 25 mm diameter, with brazed-on square ends (see note 1.)
- A 300 mm steel rule graduated in mm.
- Enamel, plastic, glass or porcelain mixing bowl of about 150 mm diameter.
- A grooving tool
- Drying oven capable of maintaining from 105°C to 110°C.
- Petroleum jelly (vaseline) or silicone grease.
- Wash bottle containing deionised water.

Procedure

1. By riffling or quartering, obtain a sample of at least 300 g of the material passing the No 36 B.S. sieve (0.425 mm) prepared according with the procedure for the preparation of disturbed soil samples for testing. Place this sample in the mixing bowl and thoroughly mix with deionised water using the spatula, until the mass becomes a thick homogeneous paste. Add sufficient water to bring it to a consistency equal to or slightly wetter than the liquid limit (see note 3) When the sample is tested in the liquid limit machine, the groove should close with between 15 and 25 blows (see note 4).

2. Grease the inside of a clean shrinkage mould. Place the wet soil in the mould, taking care to thoroughly remove all air bubbles from each layer by lightly tapping the base of the mould. Slightly overfill the mould and then level off the excess material with the spatula. Remove all soil adhering to the rim of the mould.
3. Allow the specimen to dry at room temperature for about 24 hours until a distinct change in colour can be noticed. Transfer into an oven and dry at between 105°C and 110°C.
4. Allow the specimen to cool and then measure its longitudinal shrinkage (L_s) to the nearest millimetre. If the specimen cracks into pieces, firmly hold the separate parts together and measure the shrinkage Ls. If the specimen curls in the mould carefully remove it and measure the length of the top and bottom surfaces. Subtract the mean of these two lengths from the internal length of the mould to obtain the shrinkage (see note 5).

Calculation

Calculate the percentage linear shrinkage (L_s) of the specimen (see note 6):

$$L_s\ (\%) = (L_s \div L) \times 100$$

Where,

L = Length of the mould (mm)

L_s = Longitudinal shrinkage of the specimen (mm)

Reporting the results

Report the linear shrinkage (L_s) to the nearest 0.5% when determined with a 250 mm mould and to 1% with a 135 mm mould. Record the size of mould used and any unusual conditions or problems experienced.

Determination of Water Content in Soil

The method used for determination of the moisture content of a soil as a percentage of its oven-dried weight is employed for determination of water content. The method may be applied to fine, medium and coarse grained soils for particle sizes from 2 mm to >10 mm.

Principle

The method is based on removing soil moisture by oven-drying a soil sample until the weight remains constant. The moisture content (%) is calculated from the sample weight before and after drying.

Fine-grained Soils (maximum particle size 2 mm)

Special Apparatus

- A thermostatically controlled oven preferably of the forced-draught type, capable of maintaining a temperature between 105°C and 110°C.
- A balance readable and accurate to 0.01g (see note 1).
- Numbered aluminium weighing tins with close fitting numbered lids. A suitable size is 75 mm diameter and 25mm deep.
- A desiccator containing anhydrous self-indicating silica gel. A suitable size is 250mm diameter.

Procedure

1. Clean and dry the weighing tin + lid and weigh to 0.01g (W_1), (see note 2). Select a representative quantity of moist soil in the amount specified by a test. Where not otherwise specified use at least 30g. Place the sample in the weighing tin and replace lid. Weigh the tin and contents to 0.01 g (W_2) (see note 3).
2. Remove the lid and place the tin with contents and lid in the oven and dry to constant weight between 105°C and 110°C (see notes 4 and 5).
3. Remove the tin with contents from the oven, replace the lid and place the whole in the desiccator to cool (see note 6).
4. Weigh the tin and contents to 0.01g (W_3) (see note 7).

Medium-grained Soils (maximum particle size 10 mm)

Special Apparatus

- An oven as specified above.
- A balance readable and accurate to 0.2 g. (see note 1).

- Suitable air tight corrosion-resistant container of about 400g capacity.
- A scoop.

Procedure

1. Clean and dry the container and weigh to 0.1 g (W_1) (see note 2) Place a sample of about 300 g of soil in the container, replace the lid and weigh to 0.1g (W_2).
2. Remove the lid and place the container and lid in the oven and dry between 105°C and 110°C (see notes 3 and 4) to a constant weight (see note 5).
3. After drying, remove the container from the oven, replace the lid and allow to cool
4. Weigh the container with contents to 0.1 g (W_3).

Coarse-grained Soils (maximum particle size >10 mm)

Special Apparatus

- An oven as specified above.
- A balance readable and accurate to 1 g (see note 1)
- Suitable corrosion-resistant container of about 3.5kg capacity.
- A scoop.

Procedure

1. Clean and dry the container and weigh to 1 g (W_1). Place a sample of about 3 kg of soil in the container and weigh to 1 g (W_2).
2. Place the container in the oven and dry between 105°C and 110°C (see Notes 3 and 4) to a constant weight (See note 5).
3. After drying, remove the container from the oven and allow to cool
4. Weigh the container with contents to 1 g (W_3).

Calculation

Calculate the moisture content of the soil as a percentage of the dry soil weight.

$$MC\ (\%) = (W_2 - W_3) \div (W_3 - W_1) \times 100$$

Where,

W1 = Weight of tin (g)

W2 = Weight of moist soil + tin (g)

W3 = Weight of dried soil + tin (g)

Where chemical analyses are performed on moist (air-dry) samples, it is convenient to correct the results to an oven-dry basis by use of an appropriate Moisture Factor (MF) calculated as follows :

$$MF = W2-W1/W3-W1$$

(or)

$$= 1+MC/100$$

Reporting the results

Report the moisture content of the soil to three significant figures (see note 4)

Notes

1. The balance to be used in a particular test will depend on the size of the sample. The balance should be accurate to within 0.03% of the weight of the sample.
2. It is convenient to maintain a table of weighing tin weights. Weighing tins should be thoroughly cleaned and re-weighed at least every 6 months. If tins become dirty or tarnished, they should be thoroughly cleaned immediately and re-weighed.
3. The sample may be crumbled to assist drying but care is necessary to avoid loss of any soil.
4. Soils containing gypsum lose water of crystallisation on heating. Therefore, a moisture content determined by this method will be affected by approximately 0.1% for each 1% of gypsum. If it is suspected that gypsum is present in the soil, dry the moisture content samples at not more that 80°C, for a longer period and report the method used.
5. Checking every moisture content sample to determine that it is dried to a constant weight is impractical. In most cases, drying of a moisture content sample over-night (16 hours) is sufficient. In cases where there is doubt concerning the adequacy of overnight drying, drying should be continued until the difference in weight of the cooled sample after two

successive periods does not exceed 0.1% of the original sample weight. Samples of sand may often be dried to constant weight after 7 hours. Since dry soil may absorb moisture from wet samples, dried samples should be removed before placing wet samples in the oven. Drying time should be extended, if the oven is full.

6. If the lids of the tins fit well and it is unlikely that the samples are to be left for a considerable time before weighing, the samples need not be placed in the desiccators to cool.
7. Moisture content samples should be discarded and should not be used in any other test.

(In view of soil-plant relationship, it may be argued that for a number of soil parameters, it is relevant to express values on a soil volume basis (w/v) rather than on the usual soil weight basis (w/w). Soil weight can be converted to volume by means of the bulk density. Thus, for instance, a soil with a CEC of 10 cmol(p^+) kg^{-1} and a bulk density of 1.50 kg dm^{-3} would have a CEC of 15 cmol(p^+) dm^{-3}).*

Determination of Water Availability in Soil

The capacity of soils to absorb and retain water provides a reservoir from which water may be withdrawn by plants during periods between rainfalls and / or irrigations. The water retention properties of soils and the extraction of water from soils by plants have been studied and various soil-water constants have been defined and used as an index of the water holding capacity of soils. Of these, the properties defining the range of plant-available water have been the most universally used. The moist end of the range is defined by the **field capacity** and dry end by the **wilting point**.

Field Capacity of Soil

Field Capacity is defined as the amount of water, expressed as a percentage of the oven-dry soil, held in a soil after the excess of gravitational water has drained away, and the rate of downward movement of water has materially decreased (Veihmeyer and Hendrickson, 1931). The 1/3–bar percentage has been found to be closely correlated to the field capacity for many soils. It is measured on an undisturbed soil. There must be free drainage through the profile and there must be no water table near the horizons investigated.

Procedure

- Select a field site of the soil to be measured. Attempt to make the determination when the soil is in its normal driest condition.
- Place a raised border (a simple earthen band like structure is sufficient) around an area at least 8 x 8 feet.
- Add sufficient water (by flooding on level terrain and sprinkling, if terrain is not level) to wet the soil of the entire sampling area to the depth of interest (to the expected root depth).
- Cover the area with polyethylene plastic, or some similar material, to prevent evaporation.
- Allow the soil to drain for approximately 2 days, remove the protective cover and take soil samplings to determine the water percentage. Sample near the center of the plot, and take samples, by successive increments, to the depth of wetting.
- Make at least five separate borings if a gravimetric procedure is used. The water percentage at the time of sampling is defined as the field capacity.

Comments

Since the procedure is laborious, the usual procedures is to measure at one sample site for well-defiend soil. For practical use, the bulk density of the soil should be determined concurrently with the field capacity to convert the water percentage on an oven-dry basis to the more practical water percentage per unit volume basis, as follows:

$$W\ (\%) = (W_{od} \times D_b) \div D_w$$

Where,

W = water percent per unit volume

W_{od} = water percent per unit oven dry weight

D_b = bulk density, and

D_w = density of water.

Then the number of inches of water in a given depth is determined by

$$\text{Inches } H_2O = W\ (\%) \times \text{Depth}$$

Wilting Point of Soil

The evaluation of the water content of soils after permanent wilting of plants grown in them is one of the oldest techniques used in the determination of the lower limit of available water. Briggs and Shantz (1911) introduced the concept of the wilting point. The permanent wilting point (PWP) is defined as the water percentage of a soil when plants growing in that soil are first reduced to a wilted condition from which they cannot recover in an approximately saturated atmosphere.

There is a considerable range of water content between the inception and end point of permanent wilting. The inception wilting point (IWP) is defined as the water content in the soil at which the lowest pair of true leaves of a particular kind of plant at a particular stage of growth wilts and fails to recover in a saturated atmosphere. The elongation of plants ceases at about the same time that incipient wilting occurs. The concept of incipient wilting was first elucidated by Furr and Reeve (1945). The determination of the IWP and PWP can be made simultaneously. The 15-bar percentage has been found to be closely correlated with the PWP.

Procedure for IWP

- Place about 600g of air-dried 2mm soil in a weighed watertight container.
- Add nitrogen and other nutrients as needed to produce good plant growth without pronounced nutrient deficiencies.
- Plant several seeds of dwarf sunflower (*Helianthus annuus*).
- Moisten the soil to water content suitable for plant growth and re-weigh the container. The water content (%) corresponding to the 1/3 bar forms a convenient starting point. Each time the soil is watered, bring the average water content back to the starting point.
- After the seeds have germinated, cut off all but the best seedling at soil level, and discard the plants.
- Lead the remaining seedling out through a hole in the lid of the can.
- Grow the plant in a green house or under a cloth shade until the third pair of leaves is fully developed.
- Repeatedly check the soil water content to ensure an adequate supply of water during the plant development period.

- Never allow the plants to remain in an environment where daily wilting occurs at high water contents and at same time prevent water logging.
- After the third pair of leaves has developed, irrigate the soil with enough water to bring the water content to the moist starting point.
- Fill the space between the stem and the sides of the hole in the lid with cotton to reduce evaporation to a low level.
- When the lowest one or two pairs of true leaves wilt, transfer the container and plants to a dark, humid chamber. If the leaves regain turgidity during an overnight period (14 -16 hrs), return the experimental sample to the growth location.
- Repeat the process of wilting and humification until the lowest pair of leaves fails to recover in the humid chamber.
- When this stage of wilting has been reached, cut off the plant at soil level, and discard the plant. Then weigh the container and soil, and calculate the water content on the oven-dry basis.
- Alternatively, determine the water content of the soil by oven-drying a sample after removing the plant top and as many roots as can be taken out conveniently.
- The water percentage of soil at this stage of the wilting as the IWP.

Procedure for PWP

- Repeat the procedure as described in IWP up to point where wilting begins.
- Then follow the described procedure of alternating the experimental samples between the dark, humid chamber and the growth area until all leaves are wilted beyond recovery.
- Determine the water percentage at this stage, which is known as PWP.

Calculation

The determination of the water content of the soil after wilting point reached is most precise, if roots are removed. The water content is usually expressed as a weight percentage based on the oven-dry weight (110^{0}C). The computation procedure is as follows :

$$W(\%) = (W_w - W_{od}) \div (W_{od} - W_c) \times 100$$

Where,

W (%) = water percentage on dry weight basis

W_w = weight of container and contents after wilting

W_{od} = weight of container and contents after drying in oven at 110^0C

W_c = weight of container.

(*Note:* Available water (AWC) = *FC – PWP*

If bulk density is known, the percentage values can be converted to inches of water, as follows

Inches of water/ inch of soil = $(W_{od} \times D_b) \div D_w$

Where,

W_{od} = percent H_2O on oven- dry weight basis

D_b = bulk density

D_w = density of water).

II. Analytical Methods for Soil Chemical Properties

The chemistry of soil determines the availability of nutrients, the health of microbial populations, and its physical properties. In addition, soil chemistry also determines its corrosivity, stability, and ability to absorb pollutants and to filter water. It is the surface chemistry of clays and humus colloids that determines soil's chemical properties. In general, the following chemical parameters are carried out in the soil testing laboratories

- Cation exchange capacity (CEC)
- pH
- Lime requirement
- Electrical conductivity
- Gypsum requirement
- Organic C
- Total N
- Mineralizable N
- Inorganic N
- Total P
- Available P

- Total K
- Available K
- Available S
- Calcium (Ca)
- Calcium plus magnesium (Mg) and
- Micronutrients - available Zn, Cu, Fe, Mn, B and Mo.

Determination of Cation Exchange Capacity of Soil

Cation exchange is reversible reaction. The cations held on the surface of soil minerals and within the crystal frame work of some mineral species plus those which are part of certain organic compounds can be reversibly replaced by those of salt solutions and acids. Cation exchange capacity (CEC) usually expressed as milli-equivalents/me per 100g of soil and is defined as the sum of the exchangeable cations of a soil. Various methods proposed for determining CEC can be grouped into 4 categories:

- Those in which the soil is electro-dialyzed or leached with a dilute acid e.g. HCl and the H^+ and Al^{3+} saturated exchange material is titrated to pH 7.0 with $Ba(OH)_2$ or to about pH 8.5 with NaOH.
- Those in which exchange capacity is considered to be the sum of replaceable H^+ and replaceable bases.
- Those in which the exchangeable cations are replaced by the acetate of ammonium, barium, calcium or sodium and the amounts of the cation adsorbed are determined by appropriate means
- Those which involve equilibrating soils with dilute solution (100ppm Ca) of $Ca(NO_3)_2$ containing Ca^{43} and Ca^{40} (Blume and Smith, 1954).

Most investigators at present employ methods based on saturating the exchange complex with a given cation, and then determining the total of the absorbed cations by appropriate means. Three methods commonly used for this purpose are neutral 1N ammonium acetate (pH 7.0); alkaline, 1N sodium acetate and alkaline, 0.5N barium chloride plus 0.2N tri-ethanolamine solution (pH 8.2). The first two methods can be used on both calcareous and non-calcareous soils; third is used acid soils where it is desired to determine both exchange capacity and the amounts of exchangeable H^+.

Ammonium Saturation Method

Reagents

- *Ammonium acetate (NH_4OAc), 1N*: Dilute 114 ml of glacial acetic acid (99.5%) with water to a volume of approximately 1 litre. Then add 138 ml of concentrated ammonium hydroxide (NH_4OH) and add water to obtain a volume of about 1,980 ml. Check the pH of the resulting solution, add more NH_4OH as needed to obtain a reaction of pH 7 and dilute the solution to a volume of 2 litres with water.
- Isopropyl alcohol, 99%
- Ammonium chloride (NH_4Cl), 1N, adjusted to pH 7.0 with NH_4OH
- Ammonium chloride (NH_4Cl), 0.25N, adjusted to pH 7.0 with NH_4OH
- Ammonium oxalate [$(NH_4)_2C_2O_4.H_2O$], 10%
- Dilute ammonium hydroxide (NH_4OH): Add 1 volume of concentrated NH_4OH to an equal volume of water
- Silver nitrate ($AgNO_3$), 0.10N.

Procedure

- Place 10g of 2mm, air dried soil in a 500 ml Erlenmeyer flask and add 250 ml of neutral, 1N NH_4OAc. Use 25g of soil, if the exchange capacity is very low (3-5 me. per 100g soil).
- Shake the flask thoroughly. And allow it to stand overnight.
- Filter the soil with light suction using a 55 mm Buchner funnel. Do not allow soil to become dry and cracked.
- Leach the soil with the neutral NH_4OAc reagent until no test for calcium can be obtained in the effluent solution (for Ca test, add a few drops of 1N NH_4Cl, 10% into test tube, and heat the solution to near the boiling point. The presence of Ca is indicated by a white precipitate or turbidity).
- Save the leachate for determination of exchangeable bases, if required.

- Then leach the soil 4-times with neutral 1N NH_4Cl and once with 0.25N NH_4Cl.
- Washout the electrolyte with 150 to 200 ml of 99% isopropyl alcohol.
- When the test for Cl^- in the leachate (use 0.10N $AgNO_3$) becomes negligible, allow the soil to drain thoroughly. Determine the adsorbed NH_4 either by the action method or by the acid-NaCl method.

Comments

Some loss of ammoniated organic constituents occurs when ammoinium-saturated soil is leached with 95% ethyl alcohol/100% methyl alcohol to remove the residual electrolyte (Peechi *et al*, 1962), which leads to higher value of CEC. Therefore, it is desirable to use isopropyl alcohol, which causes less loss of ammoniated organic material.

Sodium Saturation Method

Reagents

- *Sodium acetate (NaOAc), 1.0N*: Disslove 136 g of Na $C_2H_3O_2.H_2O$ in water, and dilute it to 1000 ml. The pH of this solution should be 8.2. If needed, add a few drops of acetic acid or NaOH solution to bring the reaction of the solution to pH 8.2.
- *Ammonium acetate (NH_4OAc), 1N*: Dilute 114 ml of glacial acetic acid (99.5%) with water to a volume of approximately 1 litre. Then add 138 ml of concentrated ammonium hydroxide (NH_4OH) and add water to obtain a volume of about 1,980 ml. Check the pH of the resulting solution, add more NH_4OH as needed to obtain a reaction of pH 7 and dilute the solution to a volume of 2 litres with water.
- Isopropyl alcohol, 99%.

Procedure

- Weigh 4 g of medium or fine textured soil or 6 g of coarse textured soil and transfer the sample to a 50 ml, round -bottom, narrow-neck centrifuge tube
- Add 33 ml of 1N NaOAc solution, stopper the tube, shake it in a mechanical shaker for 5 minutes and centrifuge it until the supernatant liquid is clear

- Decant the liquid, and repeat the extraction three more times
- Then, wash the sample in an identical manner with three 33-ml portions of 99% isopropyl alcohol
- Using the shaking and centrifuge procedure replace the adsorbed Na with three 33-ml portions of NH_4OAc reagent, decanting each washing into a 100 ml volumetric flask
- Dilute the solution to volume with NH_4OAc reagent
- Determine the Na with flame photometer as per standard method
- Express the results in me/100 g of oven-dry soil

Summation Method

For distinctly acid soils, the summation method is suggested. This method works fairly well on acid soils, but is not as accurate with neutral, calcareous or saline soils; due to difficulties of making proper corrections for water-soluble bases and additional bases in the extract dissolved from silicates and carbonates.

In non-calcareous soils and particularly acid soils, the sum of the exchangeable hydrogen as determined by the $BaCl_2$ –tri-ethanolamine procedure has been discussed earlier and the exchangeable bases provide the most accurate estimate of CEC.

Determination of Soil Acidity (pH)

Perhaps the most important chemical property of soils as a medium for the plant growth is its pH (*Puissanco de Hydrogen*) value or hydrogen ion activity. The determination of pH is by far the most commonly made soil test. It is widely used by the soil scientists for estimating the lime requirement. Moreover, the activity of the 12 or more other ions that enter into plant nutrition is highly dependent up on the adjustment of the pH. Sorensen (1909) defined pH as the negative logarithm of the hydrogen ion concentration which in very dilute solution is expressed as g ions L^{-1} of g mol L^{-1}. The soil pH conventionally defined by the equation: Soil pH = $\log 1/aH^+ = -\log_{10} aH^+$. It is found that in aqueous system @ 22^0C. In soil -water system, some of the adsorbed H^+ dissociate from the surface of the soil colloids in to soil solution. The pH is a sort of voltage measurement and to cover the entire range of 0-14, a potential measurement in the range of +420 to -420mV is needed.

Factors affecting soil pH

As the soil pH varies widely with the method of preparation of a given soil (Reed and Cummings, 1945), the details of the preparation procedure must be carefully specified with any soil data. In the preparation of the soil system, the principle variables that affect the pH are:

- Drying
- Dilution
- Soluble salts content
- CO_2 content
- Amount of grinding and
- Field variation from core to core.

Effect of drying of sample

Measurement of the soil pH directly in the field moist condition may be considered the most valid. Measurement of air-dried soil samples is the most convenient and generally used, and perhaps could be considered the standard procedure since certain soil chemical reactions are hastened by drying and that dried samples are therefore more nearly at equilibrium (Jackson, 1973).

Effect of dilution

Within the entire range of soil water content from the moisture equivalent to the soil-to- water ratio of 1:5, the effect of dilution is to increase the pH of the soil suspension. The increase in pH upon dilution from the sticky point to soil- water of 1:5 may be over 1 pH unit (Chapman *et al.*, 1941). A soil- to-water ratio of 1:2.5 was adopted by the Soil Reaction Committee of the International Society of Soil science, where as a 1:1 ratio has been adopted in several states (Peech *et al*, 1947).

Effect of soluble salts

The pH of a soil suspension decreases with increasing concentration of neutral salts, e.g. NaCl, $CaSO_4$ in the suspension. The increase in pH of a soil suspension upon dilution is thus a direct corollary of the observed decrease in pH of the suspension upon addition of neutral salts. Seasonal variation in pH value of soils as measured in aqueous suspensions appears to be closely associated with fluctuations in amount of soluble salts such as sulfates and nitrates, which accumulate during the dry periods and thus lower the pH of the soil, but which are subject to leaching during the rainy season, when the pH returns to its maximum value. Some of the seasonal variation in the amount of soluble salts present in the soil is, due to addition of fertilizer salts (Black, 1965). European workers prefer to measure the pH of soils in 1N KCl (Puri and Asghar, 1938). The pH value of many soils in 1N KCl, however, may be as much as 1.5 to 2.0 pH units lower than that measured in aqueous suspension using the same soil to water ratio. Schofield and Taylor (1955) have proposed a method for the determination of soil pH in 0.01M $CaCl_2$ as it offers the following advantages:

- Independent of dilution ranges
- Independent of the initial amounts of soluble salts
- Provide more accurate value of pH of environment of plant roots and microorganisms
- Error of Liquid- junction potential is less.

However, the pH measured in 0.01M $CaCl_2$ is about 0.5 pH unit lower than that measured in water (1:2 of soil : water) and this should be keep in mind in interpreting the results of pH values (Black, 1965).

Methods of Measurement of Soil pH

Methods for determining soil pH may be divided into two groups viz., colorimetric and electrometric. The colorimetric method (Kolthoff and Laitinen, 1941) makes use of suitable dyes or acid - base indicators, the colour of which changes with H+ ion activity. As the use of colorimetric method is now primarily confined to field test kits only (Mason and Obenshain, 1939), the present discussion is confined with electrometric method alone.

Electrometric Method (Glass Electrode pH meter)

The glass electrode generally used for pH measurement. It consists of a glass membrane of appropriate composition blown into a small bulb sealed to a stem of pyrex glass. An internal reference electrode, consisting of either a silver-silver chloride or a calomel electrode, dips into a dilute solution of HCl placed inside the bulb, the potential of such an electrode is given by the Nernst equation: $E_g = E_0 + RT/F \ln aH^+$, where, R- Gas constant, T- absolute temperature, F–Faraday, E_0- constant. Many glass compositions are now used in the fabrication of glass electrode (soda lime glass is generally used). A saturated calomel electrode, which is a mercury- mercurous chloride electrode, is most commonly used as an external reference electrode.

Apparatus

- Glass electrode pH meter
- 50ml beakers
- Stirring rods
- Spatula and
- Wash bottle with distilled water.

Reagents

- *Potassium biphthalate* ($KHC_8H_4O_4$, mol wt. 204.14), 0.05M: Dry $KHC_8H_4O_4$ for 2 hours at 110^{0}C. Dissolve 61.2 g of $KHC_8H_4O_4$ in 1 litre of hot water, which results 0.3M stock solution. Three drops of toluene added to prevent mold growth. A dilution of 100 of the buffer with 500 ml of water results in a 0.05M solution.
- The pH 8.00 may be obtained by mixing 19.45 ml of 0.2M Na_2HPO_4 with 0.55 ml of 0.1M citric acid.
- *Phosphate buffer, 0.025 M KH_2PO_4 and 0.025M Na_2HPO_4*: Dry the two phosphate salts for 2hrs at 110^{0}C. Dissolve 3.44g of KH_2PO_4 and 3.55g of Na_2HPO_4 in distilled water, and dilute the solution to 1 litre with distilled water. Add 1.0 ml of chloroform/ thymol per litre of buffer solution as a preservative. This buffer solution has 6.90 at 15^{0}C., pH 6.88 at 20^{0}C., pH 6.86 at 25^{0}C and pH 6.85 at 30^{0}C.

  *(**Note:** Now days, pH tablets of pH 4.2, 7.0, & 9.0 are used for preparation of standard solutions directly).*
- Saturated KCl (about 40g per 100ml).

Standardization and Care of Glass Electrode pH Meter

- After zeroing the instrument in accordance with the directions supplied by the manufacturer, standardize the meter by immersing the glass and calomel electrodes into a standard buffer solution and setting the slide wire scale or the indicator needle to the pH of the buffer. This operation corrects for the symmetry potential of the glass electrode which may change slightly from day to day.

- Rinse the electrodes thoroughly with distilled water, and check the instrument with a second buffer solution differing in pH from the first buffer by 2 or 3 pH units.
- In subsequent measurements of pH of soils, use one of these standard buffer solutions to check the performance of the pH meter periodically.
- Clean the glass electrode periodically, if necessary, by soaking it in a solution of a mild detergent and wiping it with a piece of tissue paper to remove the film of soil that adheres to the electrode surface. A film of $CaCO_3$ that sometimes forms on the surface of the electrode during measurement of pH of calcareous soils may be removed by dipping the electrode for a second in dilute HCl and ringing it with water.
- At the beginning of a series measurement and before standardization of the pH meter, loosen the sleeve of the calomel electrode to flush the ground-glass joint with fresh saturated KCl solution. Then reset the calomel the sleeve firmly, and rinse it with distilled water. To fill the calomel electrode, use a solution standard with KCl and calomel (mercurous chloride). When not in use, keep the glass electrode and the calomel immersed in distilled water.

Procedure

- Take 10g of soil and add 25ml distilled water (1:2.5 :: soil: water ratio) in a 100ml beaker, shake it for 5 minutes by a magnetic stirrer.
- Let the soil suspension stand for about 20-30minutes to allow most of the suspended clay to settle out from the suspension.
- Adjust the pH meter with solutions of pH 4.0, 7.0 and/or 9.2 before immerging glass electrode into soil suspension.
- Then pH is measured with electrode, the suspension being stirred well just before the electrode is immersed, and report the results as "soil pH measured in water".

Precautions in using pH Meter

- The electrode is not allowed to remain in the test solution longer than necessary, especially if more alkaline than pH 9.2.
- Immediately after testing, the electrode is washed off with a strong stream of distilled water. If the system is alkaline, the electrode should be dipped for a few seconds in the acid pH buffer or dilute HCl to remove the film of $CaCO_3$
- After use, electrode is suspended in distilled water and the system is protected from evaporation. Drying out of the electrode is avoided.
- Failure of the electrode is indicated when, after standardization, it gives slow response to large pH changes. The glass electrode is immersed in an alkaline buffer, then in the original acid standard buffer (Jackson 1965).

Interpretation of Soil pH

Sl No	pH range	Rating	Remarks
1	< 4.5	Very strongly Acidic	Needs Liming
2	4.5 - 5.5	Strongly Acidic	
3	5.5 - 6.5	Slightly Acidic	
4	6.5 - 7.5	Neutral	Suitable for crop growth
5	7.5 - 8.5	Slightly Alkaline	....
6	8.5 - 10.0	Strongly Alkaline	Needs Gypsum application
7	>10.0	Very strongly Alkaline	

Determination of Lime Requirement

The term "lime requirement" is somewhat ambiguous. It refers the amount of lime that must be applied to soil to grow a certain crop. More often, however, it means the amount of $CaCO_3$ or its equivalent that must be applied to soil to increase the pH to 7 or some other desired value. The results obtained by a given lime-requirement method are often multiplied by a "liming factor". Different rapid lime-requirement methods are widely used. Most of the more rapid lime-requirement methods involve an equilibrium extraction of the soil with a highly buffered salt solution followed by determination of the exchange acidity in the extract either by direct titration or by measuring the pH change of the extract. More accurate lime requirement methods are based on exhaustive leaching of the soil with some buffered salt solution. The $BaCl_2$ - triethalamine solution is sufficiently well buffered to permit its use in routine determination of the lime requirement by a single equilibrium extraction of the soil. This modification of the $BaCl_2$ - triethanolamine method and an alternate method for estimating the lime requirement of soils from soil pH are described below.

Barium chloride - Triethanolamine Method

Principle

The exchange acidity is determined by a single equilibrium extraction of the soil using one part of soil to 25 parts of the extracting solution. In this method, the test is made on the soil sample screened through 2mm sieve and that the actual amount of lime necessary to bring 1-acre–furrow-slice of soil to pH 8.0 should be reduced by an appropriate factor depending upon the proportion of the soil from the field passing the 2-mm sieve. Another consideration that would lead to a lower lime requirement than that measured by this method is the fact that, for optimum crop production, soils are limed plowing the soil to a depth greater than 6 inches and using a lime stone that contains substantial amounts of slowly reacting coarse particles would tend to increase the line requirement as given by the method. In the absence of accurate evaluation of these factors, the maximum rate of application of lime stone in the field should not exceed 80% of the theoretical lime requirement as determined by this method.

Reagents

- *Extracting solution,* 0.5 N $BaCl_2$. H_2O -0.055N triethanolamine, adjusted to pH 8.0: Dissolve 1100 g of $BaCl_2.H_2O$ in CO_2 free water in a 5-gallon pyrex bottle. Add 500 ml of 2N triethanolamine and 72 ml of 6N HCl, and dilute the solution to 18 litres with CO2- free water. Mix well the solution and just the pH to 8.00 ± 0.02 with HCl or triethanolamine. This solution is 0.03N with respect to the free base. Prevent absorption of CO_2 by the solution a siphon and connecting a soda-lime tube to air inlet. In making up the above extracting solution, dilute cp. concentrated triethanolamine, which is about 7.5N, to 2N and standardize it against standard acid using the mixed indicator solution listed below.

- *Mixed indicator solution*: Dissolve 0.22 g of bromocresol green and 0.075 g of methyl red in 96 ml of 95% ethanol containing 3.5 ml of 0.1N NaOH.
- Standard HCl, 0.2N

Procedure

- Take 4 g of soil in 125 ml Erlenmeyer flask; add 100 ml of the extracting solution (0.5N $BaCl_2$ - 0.055N triethanolamine).
- Swirl the contents in the flask for about 30 seconds, stopper the flask, and allow it to stand over- night.
- On the following day, again swirl the soil suspension in the flask for about 30 seconds, and allow the soil particles to settle out about 2 hours.
- Pipette a 50 ml aliquot of the clear supernatant solution into a 125 ml. Erlenmeyer flask, add 3 drops of the mixed indicator, and titrate the aliquot with 0.2N HCl to a pink end point (pH 5.1).

Calculation

Calculate the lime requirement (LR) in pounds of $CaCO_3$, or its equivalent, required to bring 2 million pounds of soil to pH 8.0 as follows:

LR = N x (B- S) x 50,000

Where,

B = Amount of acid required to titrate 50 ml of the extracting solution

S = Amount of acid required to titrate 50 ml of the soil extract

N = Normality of the acid

Determination of Electrical Conductivity

Conductivity is a property of soil suspension that depends on its total ionic content. The conductivity of an electrolytic solution at any temperature depends only on the ions present and their concentration. When a solution of an electrolyte is diluted the conductivity will decrease, since fewer ions are present per cm^3 of solution to carry the current. If all the solution be placed between two electrodes 1 cm apart and large enough to contain the whole of the solution, the conductance will increase as the solution is diluted. This is due to largely to a decrease in inter-ionic effect for strong electrolytes and to an increase in the degree of dissociation for weak electrolytes. It expresses the resistance of a 1 cm cube of water to the passage of a current, usually at 25° C (Specific Resistance). Specific conductance, L, of solution is the conductance that would be measured at 25°C between electrodes 1 cm^2 in cross section and placed 1 cm apart. The specific conductance or conductivity is the reciprocal of the resistance (1/R) in Siemens (formerly mhos) or more exactly C/R for a given cell. Electrical resistance is defined by E = IR (E = electrical potential in volts, I is the current in amperes and R is resistance in ohms). The digital readout of modern conductivity meters is in C/R units recorded as $\mu S\ cm^{-1}$ or $mS\ cm^{-1}$.

Principle

Specific conductance is determined by an AC "salt bridge" or electrical resistance bridge. In a salt bridge 2 fixed resistances R1 and R2 and a variable resistance (Rv) are connected in a branched circuit with the conductance cell having resistance Rk. An AC potential is applied at C and D. The Rv is adjusted until there is no current passing in the phone circuit from A and B as indicated by a minimum sound or shift in the electric eye. Then A and B are at the same potential and the voltage drop IRk between BD must equal $I'R^2$, the voltage drop between AD.

$IRk = I'R^2$ and also $IRv = I'\,R1$

So, $IRk / IRv = I'R^2 / I'R1$

Therefore, $Rx = (R^2/R1) \times Rv$

Since R1 and R2 are fixed, the dial on Rv can be calibrated to read Rk, the resistance of the test sample. Or, the dial on Rv can be calibrated to read 1/Rk, that is directly in conductance of the solution. Specific conductance may be measured with a cell of various dimensions by means of a cell constant. Because the numbers obtained expressing specific conductance of soil solutions are generally small, it has been found convenient to express specific conductance as millimhos/cm (1000 times /cm) and this unit has been adopted widely. 1μ mhos/cm = 10^3 mmhos /cm = 10^6 mhos/cm. The most common unit of EC being followed is $dS\ m^{-1}$ (deci Siemen/ meter), which is equal to the older unit of millimhos/ min.

Percentage of soluble salts in soil = 0.064 x EC x SP/100

Where, SP - Saturation % of soil and EC is in $dS\ m^{-1}$.

Material required

- 0.02 M KCl and
- Distilled Water and Filter Paper

Procedure

- Take 10 g soil sample (2mm sieved) is weighed and transferred in to 50 ml beaker
- Add 50 ml distilled water (soil:water = 1:5) and the content mixed well with the help of glass rod or magnetic stirrer
- Allow the content to stand for 30 minutes
- Then, the cell of Conductivity Bridge is immersed into soil suspension and reading of specific conductance is recorded directly
- Before taking reading of the test sample, the instrument should be checked with 0.02 M KCl solution that gives conductance of 2.39 mmhos/cm at 18°C and multiplying it by the cell constant (specified with the instrument) will get the specific conductance (L mhos/cm) of the test solution/suspension
- Observed values of EC in the digital conductivity meter are multiplied by the cell constant (usually given on conductivity cell) and a temperature factor to express results at 25^0C.

Alternate procedure

- Place 40 g of soil in a 250 ml Erlenmeyer flask, add 80 ml of distilled water, stopper the flask, and shake on a reciprocating shaker for 1 hour. Filter through No. 1 filter paper.
- Wash the conductivity electrode with distilled water, and rinse with standard KCl solution.
- Pour some KCl solution into a 25 ml beaker, and dip the electrode in the solution. Adjust the conductivity meter to read 1.412 mS/cm, corrected to 25°C.
- Wash the electrode, and dip it into the soil extract.
- Record the digital display corrected to 25°C. The EC reading is a measure of the soluble salt content in the extract, and an indication of salinity status of the soil sample.

Calculation of Specific Conductance to Salt Concentration in solution and Osmotic Pressure of solution

Milli-equivalent (meq) of salt per litre = Equivalent per Million
= 12.5 L mmhos/cm (L = Specific conductance mmho/cm)

Content of salts (ppm) = 640 L mmho/cm

% salts in solution = 0.064 L mmho/cm

% salts in soil solution = 0.064L mmhocm^{-1} x % water in soil at extraction/100

Osmotic pressure of solution, atmosphere = 0.36 L mmho/cm

Salt index of a fertilizer:

= (Sp. cond. of solution when 1g of fert dissolve in 1 lit. of water) ÷ (Specific conductance of 0.1 % $NaNO_3$) x 100.

Determination of Gypsum Requirement

In the estimation of gypsum requirement of saline-sodic/sodic soils (Schoonover, 1952), the attempt is to measure the quantity of gypsum (calcium sulphate) required to replace the Na from the exchange complex. The Na so replaced with the Ca of the gypsum is removed through leaching of the soil. The soils treated with gypsum become dominated with Ca in the exchange complex.

When the Ca of the gypsum is exchanged with Na, there is a reduction in the Ca concentration in the solution. The quantity of Ca reduced is equivalent to the Ca exchanged with Na. It is equivalent to the gypsum requirement of the soil when "Ca" is expressed as $CaSO_4$.

Apparatus required

- a mechanical shaker
- a burette (50 ml) and
- some pipettes (100 ml and 5 ml).

Reagents required

- *Saturated gypsum (calcium sulphate) solution*: Add 5 g of chemically pure $CaSO_4$ $2H_2O$ to 1litre of distilled water. Shake vigorously for 10 minutes using a mechanical shaker and filter through No. 1 filter paper.

- *0.01N $CaCl_2$ solution*: Dissolve exactly 0.5 g of AR-grade $CaCO_3$ powder in about 10 ml f 1:3 diluted HCl. When completely dissolved, transfer to a 1 litre volumetric flask and dilute to the mark with distilled water. Do not use $CaCl_2$ salt as it is highly hygroscopic.
- *0.01N versenate solution*: Dissolve 2.0 g of pure ethylene-diamine-tetra-acetic acid (EDTA) – disodium salt and 0.05 g of magnesium chloride (AR-grade) in about 50 ml of water and dilute to 1litre. Titrate a portion of this against 0.01N of $CaCl_2$ solution to standardize.
- *Eriochrome Black T (EBT) indicator*: Dissolve 0.5 g of EBT dye and 4.5 g of hydroxylamine hydrochloride in 100 ml of 95 percent ethanol. Store in a stoppered bottle or flask.
- *Ammonium hydroxide-ammonium chloride buffer*: Dissolve 67.5 g of pure ammonium chloride in 570 ml of concentrated ammonium hydroxide and dilute to 1 litre. Adjust the pH to 10 using dilute HCl or dilute NH_4OH.

Procedure

- Weigh 5 g of air-dry soil in a 250 ml conical flask.
- Add 100 ml of the saturated gypsum solution. Firmly insert a rubber stopper, and shake for 5 minutes.
- Filter the contents through No. 1 filter paper.
- Transfer 5 ml of aliquot of the clear filtrate into a 100 or 150 ml porcelain dish.
- Add 1 ml of the ammonium hydroxide-ammonium chloride buffer solution and 2–3 drops of EBT indicator.
- Place 0.01N versenate solution in a 50 ml burette and titrate the contents in the dish until the wine red colour starts to change to sky blue. Volume of versenate used = B.
- Run a blank using 5 ml of saturated gypsum solution in place of sample aliquot. Volume of versenate solution used = A.

Calculation

Gypsum Requirement (in tonne per hectare) = $(A - B) \times N \times 382$

where,

A = millilitre of EDTA (versenate) used for blank titration;

B = millilitre of ETDA used for soil extract;

N = normality of EDTA solution.

Determination of Organic Carbon

Carbon occurs in soils in the elemental form (coal, graphite and so on), in the inorganic forms of carbonate, hydrogen (bi-) carbonate and carbon dioxide, and organically as plant and animal matter, their intermediate decomposition products and as the more resistant humus. The principle of total carbon analysis is to convert the element completely into CO_2, which is then determined gravimetrically or volumetrically.

The total organic matter content of a soil is estimated either from a knowledge of the total organic C content or from the loss in weight when the organic matter is destroyed by dry combustion (heating in presence of pure dry O_2 at 875 to 925°C and then absorbing S, halogen and water free CO_2 in soda lime) and wet combustion (heating with oxidizing agent and strong acid and absorbing purified CO_2 in NaOH) methods. The total organic matter is also determined by weight loss (ignition at 800 - 900°C).

Of all forms of C in soil, it is the chemically active form that is of most interest and this includes the immediate decomposition products of raw organic material and soil humus, i.e., the inorganically combined and elemental forms of C are to be excluded from the analysis. A method determining the oxidizatiable, or active organic carbon was introduced by Schollenberger (1927) and involves the partial oxidation of organic matter with chromic acid. Walkley and Black (1934) and Walkley (1935; 1947) modified the Schollenberger technique by using the heat of reaction between dilute dichromate solution and concentrated H_2SO_4 to effect oxidation. Silver sulphate or mercuric oxide is to be added to eliminate chloride interference and also excess H_3PO_4 of NaF was advocated after cooling to suppress ferric iron.

Principle

The determination of oxidizable matter is often termed the determination of "organic carbon". The oxidizable organic matter of soils is determined by chromic acid oxidation with heat applied. Organic matter in the soil is oxidized with a mixture of potassium dichromate ($K_2Cr_2O_7$) and concentrated H_2SO_4 utilizing the heat of dilution of H_2SO_4. Unused $K_2Cr_2O_7$ is back titrated with ferrous sulphate ($FeSO_4 . 7H_2O$).The milli-equivalent of chromic acid reduction may be measured by titration,

$4Cr^{6+} + 3Co \rightarrow 4Cr^{3+} + 3C4^{+}$

$2H_2Cr_2O_7 + 3C + 6H_2SO_4 \rightarrow 2Cr_2(SO_4)_3 + 3CO_2 + 8H_2O.$

Apparatus required

- Conical flask – 500 ml; 10 and 20 ml pipettes; Burette- 50 ml; Analytical Balance.

Reagent required

- Conc. H_2SO_4 (96%, Sp. Gr. 1.84)
- Orthophosphoric acid (H_3PO_4, 85%)
- *Standard 0.5 N $K_2Cr_2O_7$*: Exactly 24.52g of $K_2Cr_2O_7$ is dissolved in 1 litre of distilled water.
- *Diphenylamine indicator*: Approximately 0.5 g of reagent grade diphenylamine is dissolved in 20ml of water and 100 ml of conc. H_2SO_4.
- *Mohr Salt Solution* : A 0.5 N solution of ferrous is prepared by dissolving 196.1g of ferrous ammonium sulphate $Fe(NH_4)_2(SO_4)_2.6H_2O$ in 800 ml dist. water containing 20ml conc. H_2SO_4 and diluted to 1 litre.

Procedure

- Place 0.05 to 1.0 g air dried soil sample in 500 ml conical flask. Pipette out exactly 10ml of 0.5 N $K_2Cr_2O_7$ solution onto the soil and mix the two by swirling the flask.
- Add 20 ml of conc. H_2SO_4 and mix by gentle rotation for 1 minute. Allow the mixture to stand for 20 to 30 minutes
- Run a standardization blank (without soil) in parallel
- Dilute the mixture to 200 ml with water; add 10 ml of 85% H_3PO_4 and then 30 drops of diphenylamine indicator
- Back titrate the solution with Mohr's salt solution delivering from a burette
- Color is dull green with chromous ion at the beginning, and then will shift to a turbid blue
- At the end point, this colour will sharply shift to brilliant green.

Calculation

Standardization blank titration (ml ferrous solution), S = ...ml

Sample titration (ml ferrous solution), T = ...ml

Ferrous solution (Mohr's salt) consumed X = S - T ml

Strength of Mohair's salt (blank ÷ $K_2Cr_2O_7$ volume used) Y = ...N

Wt. of soil taken for analysis Z = ...g

$$\% \text{ Organic } C = \frac{XY}{Z} \times 100 \times 0.003 = \frac{XY}{Z} \times 0.3$$

% Organic Matter = % Organic Carbon x 1.724.

[The 1.724 is known as "Van Bemmelen factor" which is based on the assumption that soil organic matter has 58% C.].

Comments and Suggestions

- It is presumed that the OM contains 58% C and the recovery is 77%. However, both the carbon content and the extent of oxidation may vary considerably from soil to soil (Nelson & Sommers, 1982).
- Provision of external heat under reflex results in complete decomposition of organic compounds and give OC values equivalent to those obtained by wet or dry combustion. Hence, this does not require a factor to account for incomplete oxidation of OM (Mebius, 1960).
- If the sample tunes green color, add more $K_2Cr_3O_7$ and take less sample size, while adding $K_2Cr_2O_7$ to the sample.
- If the burette reading is 0-4 ml, repeat with less soil and if it is 17 or higher, repeat with more soil.
- Ferrous ammonium sulphate solution must be standardized daily because of slow oxidation of Fe^{2+} to Fe^{3+}.
- If high amounts of chloride are present in the sample, add 15g $AgSO_4$ to 1litre of H_2SO_4 to avoid over estimation of OM.
- Water-logged soils often contain large quantities of Fe, which cause positive errors but in most cases this can be oxidized by drying the soil sample prior to analysis.
- If H_2SO_4 readily absorbs water, use fresh reagent. Amounts of $K_2Cr_2O_7$ and H_2SO_4 added should be accurately (Nelson &

Sommers, 1982).

- For quality control, a minimum of one reference sample should be analyzed per batch of 20-25 samples (at least one reference daily). Duplicates may be done on 5% of samples.

Determination of Total Nitrogen in Soil

Most of the nitrogen in soils is in organic form. Relatively small amounts ordinarily occur in ammonium and nitrates, the available forms. Nitrogen determination has a long history in the area of analytical chemistry. Two general types of analytical procedures are widely used - the Kjeldhahl conversion of nitrogen to $(NH_4)_2SO_4$ and the Dumas conversion to nitrogen. John Kjeldahl first introduced the Kjeldahl nitrogen method in 1883. While studying proteins during malt production, he developed a method for nitrogen determination that was faster and more accurate than any method available at the time. His method used simple equipment and performed by an inexperienced technician. The Kjeldahl method has gained wide acceptance and is now used for a variety of applications, since 1883. It includes both organic and ammonium forms and, with modifications includes the nitrate form. Nitrate nitrogen should be included in the total nitrogen of soils.

Principles

Although the technique and apparatus have been altered considerably over the 100 years, the basic principles introduced by Johan Kjeldahl endure today. The Kjeldahl method may be broken down into three main steps viz. Digestion, Distillation and Titration.

Digestion: It refers the decomposition of nitrogen in organic samples utilizing a concentrated sulphuric acid. The end result is an ammonium sulfate solution. A general equation for the digestion of a organic sample is shown below as one basic example:

$$\text{Organic N} + H_2SO_4 \rightarrow (NH_4)_2SO_4 + H_2O + CO_2 + \text{other sample products}$$

Distillation: Adding excess base (NaOH) to the acid digestion mixture to convert NH_4^+ to NH_3, followed by boiling and condensation of the NH_3 gas in a receiving solution (BO_3/H_2SO_4).

Titration: to quantify the amount of ammonia in the receiving solution.

The amount of nitrogen in a sample can be calculated from the quantified amount of ammonia ions in the receiving solution. A number of interrelated digestion conditions determine the rate of reaction and completeness of the breakdown of nitrogen to ammonium sulfate. Among these are heat input, inorganic salt, reflux rate of H_2SO_4, length of digestion and catalyst addition.

Apparatus required

- Kjeldahl digestion manifold
- Kjeldahl distillation rack
- Kjeldahl flasks (500 or 800 ml)
- Conical flask (500ml)
- Analytical balance
- Pipette (25 ml)
- Burette (50ml)

Reagents required

- Concentrated sulphuric acid (H_2SO_4)
- Standard N/14 H_2SO_4
- *Digestion accelerators*: 1part (Approx. 20g CuSO4. 5H2O + 3g HgO + 1g Se, "Catalyst digestion mix") + 20 part Na_2SO_4 or K_2SO_4
- *NaOH (40%)*: First 50% NaOH solution is made up and impurities are allowed to settle out. To do this, 3kg of NaOH is dissolved in 3 litre of distilled water in a heavy-walled Pyrex flask or bottle. The solution is allowed to stand several days for the Na_2CO_3 to settle out. Then, the clear supernatant liquid is siphoned into 1.5kg of water; the solution is then mixed and placed in the 40% NaOH bottle with a glass delivery tube.
- *Mixed indicator solution*: Brom-cresol green (0.5%) and methyl-red (0.1%) mixed indicator is prepared by dissolving 0.5g of brom-cresol green and 0.1g methyl red in 100 ml of 95% ethanol, and adjusting the solution to the bluish purple midcolor at pH 4.5, with dilute NaOH or HCl. This indicator is pink at pH 4.2 or lower and bluish green as the pH rises to pH 4.9 and above.
- *Boric acid*: Approximately 40g of H_3BO_3 is dissolved in 1 litre of distilled water containing 5 ml of mixed indicator. This boric acid stock solution is adjusted by dilute H_2SO_4 or HCl titration

until the bluish color of the indicator weakens toward pink.

Procedure

The procedure of Kjeldahl distillation method includes three sequential steps viz., digestion, distillation and titration, which are discussed as under:

Digestion of Soils or Plant Tissue

- Take a soil sample of 5g (1g of muck or peat or 20g of sandy soil) that has been ground to pass 2mm sieve or 5g of dried plant tissue that has been ground to pass a 0.4mm screen is wrapped in a filter paper and dropped as a package into an 800 ml Kjeldahl digestion flask. Add about 20 ± 1g of the digestion accelerator mix (Na_2SO_4 + catalyst digestion mix) is added
- Add 35 ml concentrated H_2SO_4 and mix the contents by swirling the flask, with care not to throw the sample onto the sides. For medium and fine textured soils is to add 50 ml of water and to allow the sample to soak for 30 minutes and then add 35 ml of conc. H_2SO_4
- Digestion is then commenced with low flame for the first 10 to 30 minutes, until frothing stops, and then gradually more strongly until the sample is completely charred
- Heat gradually raised until the acid reaches a boil , and condensation of the acid reaches about 1/3 of the volume (Flame is not allowed to touch the flask above the part occupied by liquid; otherwise there may be loss of NH_3 in consequence of decomposition of $(NH_4)_2SO_4$ when temperature goes beyond 410^0C)
- Digestion flask is rotated at intervals and heating continued until the organic matter destroyed, best judged after the solution has cleared (light yellow or bluish grey colour)
- At end of the digestion, the heating is stopped, but the fume exhaustion is continued until fuming stops
- When the flasks are cooled just to the point where crystals start to form (not completely as salts re-dissolve slowly), add 300 ml of distilled water and this solution is cooled further

Note : *If soil nitrates are included, 35 ml of conc. H_2SO_4 containing 1g of salicylic acid is added to the sample. The flask is swirled until the acid is thoroughly mixed with soil and mixture allowed to stand for 30min. to react with the salicylic acid. Then add 5g of $Na_2S_2O_3$.*

$5H_2O$ and 50 ml of water and the mixture is slowly heated.

Digestion Procedure for Runoff Suspensions

- Take 250 ml aliquot (100 ml, if >5g of solids occurs in 100ml) in a 800 ml Kjeldahl flask after shaken thoroughly
- Add a few glass beads and about 20 ± 1 g of digestion accelerator mix (Na_2SO_4 + Catalyst mix)
- Add 35 ml of conc. H_2SO_4 to the flask and begin digestion.

Distillation

- Approximately 25 ml of 4% boric acid is pipette out into a 500ml conical flask.
- Add 4 drops of bromocresol green -methyl red indicator solution to it.
- A glass receiver tube is attached to the still and placed in the flask so that its end is below the surface of the boric acid in the flask.
- Cooling water is then started flowing in the condenser.
- Content of the Kjeldahl flask are mixed by rotation, and the flask is placed on the distillation stand and checked for a good fit with the condenser connection.
- Then, Kjeldahl flask held @ a 45° angle, about 125 ml (100ml, if bumping is a problem) of 40% NaOH to be poured so that it runs down the neck to the bottom of the flask without mixing.
- Burner is then lighted, the flask is attached to the still, and the solution is mixed by swirling.
- Immediately after this mixing, the flask is set to rest on the still support and heated to avoid the danger of sucking back. Flame is increased gradually.
- About 150 ml is distilled over and then the receiver flask and tube are disconnected to prevent sucking back.

The majority of NH_3 is distilled and trapped in the receiving solution (boric acid or H_2SO_4) within the first 5-10 minutes of boiling.

But depending upon the volume of the digestion mixture and the method being followed, 15 – 150 ml of condensate should be collected in the receiving flask to ensure complete recovery of nitrogen. Further, extension of the distillation time and volumes collected simply results in more water being carried over to the receiving flask. Excess water does not change the titration values. The rate of distillation is affected by condenser cooling capacity and cooling water temperature, but primarily by heat input. Typically the heating elements used for distillation have variable temperature controllers. A distillation rate of about 7.5 ml/ minute is most commonly cited in the accepted methods.

If the receiving solution is standardized HCl or H_2SO_4, it is desirable to have only a slight excess left after the NH3 is distilled and trapped in the receiving solution to minimize the back titration. Based on the anticipated amount of nitrogen in the sample, a target amount of standard acid can be calculated from the following formula:

Standard acid (ml) required to add to receiving flask

= {[(% nitrogen expected in sample) x (sample aliquot used) x gram sample wt.] + 2} ÷ (normality of Standard acid) x 1.4007 x digestion dilution volume).

Note: *When low levels of nitrogen are being determined, it is advisable to "pre-condition" the distillation apparatus prior to distillation. This can be done by distilling a 1:1 mixture of ammonia-free water and 50% NaOH for 5 minutes just before sample distillation to reduce contamination from atmospheric ammonia.*

If boric acid used as a receiving solution, the exact concentration is not needed because the titration directly measures the amount of ammonia in the distillate by neutralizing 1:1 complex formed by ammonia and boric acid.

Rapid Distillation Technique with Liquefied Petroleum Gas

A rapid LP-gas distillation technique developed by Dr. M.V. Durai, Institute of Forest Productivity, Ranchi is used for routine distillation in the Soil Laboratory, FRC, Mandar. With this technique, not only distillation time reduced by 83-85% but also uniform distillate would be collected. Further, there is scope to add as many as sample for distillation by adding more burners in the stove.

Figure 1 : Rapid distillation with LPG cylinder

Titration

There are two types of titration: back titration (commonly used in macro Kjeldahl) and direct titration. Both methods indicate the ammonia present in the distillate with a color change and allow for calculation of unknown concentrations of nitrogen in soil/ plant tissue.

Back titration

The ammonia captured by a carefully measured excess of a standard acid solution in the receiving flask. The excess of acid in the receiving solution keeps the pH low and the indicator does not change.

$$2NH_3 + 2H_2SO_4 \rightarrow (NH_4)_2\ SO_4 + H_2SO_4 \text{ (excess acid)}$$

The excess acid solution is exactly neutralized by a carefully measured standardized alkaline base solution such as NaOH. A color change is product at end point of the titration.

$$(NH_4)_2SO_4 + H_2SO_4 + 2\ NaOH \rightarrow (Na_2)SO_4 + (NH_4)_2SO_4 + 2H_2O.$$

Direct titration

If boric acid is used as the receiving solution instead of a standardized acid, the chemical reaction is: $NH_3 + H_3BO_3 \rightarrow NH_4$: $H_2BO_3^- + H_3BO_3$. The boric acid captures the ammonia gas, forming an ammonium - borate complex. As the ammonia collects, the color of the receiving solution changes: NH_4: $H_2BO_3^- + H_2SO_4 \rightarrow (NH_4)_2\ SO_4 + 2 \rightarrow H_3BO_3$. The boric acid method has two advantages viz. only one standard solution is necessary for the determination and the solution has a long shelf life.

Calculation

i) When standard acid is used as a receiving solution, the equation is

N % = {[(ml std. acid x N of acid) – (ml blank x N of base)] – (ml std. base x N of base) x 1.4007}/ weight of sample (g)

ii) When boric acid is used as a receiving solution, the equation is

N% = [(ml standard acid – ml blank) x N of acid x 1.4007] / weight of sample (g)

For soil or plant tissue, the percentage of nitrogen is calculated (based on the approximations) viz.

% N x 6.25 = % crude protein

% N x 20 = % organic matter in soil

% N x 20, 000 = pounds nitrogen per acre in soil.

For runoff, pounds N per acre inch of runoff (ppai) is calculated for a 250 ml sample of suspension analyzed as follows:

- N in runoff (ppai) = (T-B) x 0.906 (for N/14 H_2SO_4)
- N in runoff (ppai) = (T-B) x 1.27 (for 0.10N H_2SO_4)

Where, T – sample titration, ml standard acid

B – blank titration, ml standard acid

ppai – pounds N per acre inch runoff

Then, the nitrogen in the soil solids present in the runoff is calculated as follows:

- N in runoff (pp2ms) = (ppai nitrogen in run off/ ppai solids in runoff) x 2,000,000

Where, pp2ms – parts N per 2 million parts of soil solids in runoff.

Determination of Available/Mineralizable N

In most soils, the bulk of nitrogen is in organic forms and usually near the surface. The inorganic forms of nitrogen include nitrate (is soluble and easily leached or taken up by plants, nitrite (is usually a transitional stage between nitrate and ammonium), ammonium (occurs as the easily removed exchangeable ion and also in more unavailable fixed forms) and traces of gaseous forms such as di-nitrogen and nitrogen monoxides and elemental nitrogen. The bulk of plant-available nitrogen in soil is that present in mineral forms, the simple determination of nitrate and ammonia is of limited use for estimating available nitrogen. The usual chemical method (Subbiah and Asija, 1956) of estimating available nitrogen involves the distillation of soil in the presence of alkaline permanganate solution. Ammonia is quantitatively expelled and is absorbed in excess standard acid, which is then back-titrated.

Reagents required

- *0.32% potassium permanganate* ($KMnO_4$) solution: Dissolve 3.2 g $KMnO_4$ in distilled water and make up to 1 litre in volumetric flask.
- *2.5% sodium hydroxide* (NaOH): Dissolve 25g NaOH flakes in distilled water and make up to 1litre in volumetric flask
- Liquid paraffin
- 0.02N (N/50) standard sulphuric acid
- *Boric acid–indicator solution*: Dissolve 20g of pure boric acid (H_3BO_3) in about 700ml of hot water. Transfer the cooled solution to a 1 litre volumetric flask containing 200 ml of ethanol and 20 ml of mixed indicator. After mixing the contents of the flask, add approximately 0.05N NaOH cautiously until the colour is reddish purple. Then, dilute the solution to volume with water and mix it thoroughly.
- *Mixed indicator*: Dissolve 0.07 g methyl red with 0.1g bromocresol green in 100 ml of 95% ethanol.

Procedure

- Place 20g soil in 800 ml dry Kjeldhal flask
- To this, add 20 ml of water and swirl. Then add 1ml of paraffin and a few glass beads to prevent frothing and bumping, respectively during distillation. Then add 100 ml each of 0.32% $KMnO_4$ and 2.5% NaOH solutions
- Distill the contents in a Kjeldhal assembly at a steady rate and collect the liberated ammonia in an Erlenmeyer flask (250ml) containing 20ml boric acid solution (with mixed indicator). With the absorption of ammonia, the pink colour boric acid solution turns to green. Nearly 100 ml of distillate is to be collected in about 30 minutes

- Titrate the contents with 0.02N H_2SO_4 to the original shade (pink). Blank correction is to be made for the final calculations.

Calculation

Sample tire value = S ml of 0.02N H_2SO_4
Blank tire value = B ml of 0.02N H_2SO_4
Actual titre value (Z) = (S – B) ml of 0.02N H_2SO_4
Weight of soil taken = 20g
As per the law of equivalence or equilibrium
1g equivalent of H_2SO_4 = 1g equivalent of N
1000ml of 1N H_2SO_4 = 14g N
Z ml of 0.02N H_2SO_4 = (Z x 14 x 0.02)/ 1000 g of N
So, 20g of soil contains = (Z x 14 x 0.02)/ 1000 g of N
1g of soil contains = (Z x 14 x 0.02)/ (20 x 1000) g of N
1000g of soil contains = (Z x 14 x 0.02 x 1000)/ (20 x 1000) g of N
1 ha soil contains = (Z x 14 x 0.01 x 2.24 x 10^6)/ (20 x 1000) kg of N
= Z x 31.36 kg of N/ha.

Interpretation of Data

Sl No	Available N (kg/ha)	Soil Rating
1	<280	Low
2	280 – 560	Medium
3	>560	High

Comments and Suggestions

In order to include nitrate –N which forms 10 - 40% of available N in the soil test, add 1.5 g Devarda's alloy to the distillation flask in addition to alkaline permanganate. For these modifications, 2- stage distillation is recommended. It includes as in standard method until 50 ml distillate is collected, then addition of Devarda's alloy followed by further distillation until another 25ml is collected.

- Prepare 2.5% NaOH solution fresh as NaOH absorbs CO_2 and the strength of alkali comes down. Avoid blockade of mouth of the regent bottle by using rubber stopper in place of glass stopper.

- Check leakage in the distillation unit before use.
- Steam the apparatus with distilled water before use
- In the original method, it is recommended to collect 30ml of distillate. Other workers recommend 50-100 ml distillate in 30 minutes. It is preferable to specify the time and amount of distillate collected as the amount estimated would increase with time.

Determination of Total Phosphorus

The total P in the soil can be extracted and determined by several methods, of which major are $NaCO_3$ fusion method, perchloric acid digestion method and HF digestion method. Perchloric acid method has been widely used for total P in soils. The details of perchloric acid method are described as follows:

Reagents required

- 60% $HClO_4$, HNO_3

Procedure

- Take 2 g of soil (< 0.5mm size) into a 300 ml conical flask. If the sample contains high organic matter, 20ml of HNO_3 is added
- Then add 30ml of 60% $HClO_4$ is added and the digestion is carried out at 130^0 C in a special digestion apparatus
- $HClO_4$ digestion is carried out until the solution appears colourless, with a slight increase of temperature if necessary
- As the digestion completed, white dense fumes of $HClO_4$ appear and the silica becomes white
- Additional $HClO_4$ may be used to wash down any dark particles that stick to the sides of the flask
- When digestion is completed, the flask is removed and cooled sufficiently to avoid spattering, 50 ml of distilled water is added, and the solution transferred to a 200 ml volumetric flask through a filter
- Remaining residue is washed to bring the volume of solution to the mark

- An aliquot is taken for analysis by the vanadomolybdo phosphoric blue/yellow color method, which is described in the following text in this chapter.

Determination of Available Phosphorus

Phosphorus determinations for the soils have received extensive attention from soil chemist due to the importance of phosphorus in soil fertility. The extraction of phosphorus has received extensive study along lines viz,

A) Extraction of more active or available phosphate with high specific surface and

B) Fractionations of the total of each chemical class or species of phosphate.

Method of Phosphorus Determination

Phosphorus determination for soil is greatly expedited by the development of sensitive colorimetric methods. Osmond method involving molybdophosphoric blue color developed by selective reduction of heteropoly molybdophosphoric acid has been extensively adapted (Osmond, 1887). Four modification of this method are widely used viz,

1. Chlorostannous reduced molybdophosphoric blue color method (in H_2SO_4 system)
2. Chlorostannous reduced molybdophosphoric blue color method (in HCl system)
3. Molybdenum reduced molybdophosphoric blue color method (in H_2SO_4 system)
4. 1,2,4-amononaphthalsulphonic reduced molybdophosphoric blue color method (in $HClO_4$ or H_2SO_4 system) and
5. Unreduced vanadomolybdophosphoric heteropoly complex yellow color method

Each of these methods offers its respective advantages of sensitivity, tolerance to interfering substances, speed or stability of the color. The choice of the method for given phosphorus analysis depends on the amount of phosphorus available for the determination, the acid system involved and the concentration of the interfering substances. However, all above-said methods except 3rd method are described in detail in the proceeding text. The characteristics of above - said spectrophotometric methods given in the Table 3.4.

Table 3.4 : Characteristics of spectrophotometric methods (I to V) for phosphorus

Particulars	Molybdophosphoric blue color method* reductant consisting of				Vanadomolybd ophosphoric
	Chlorostannous acid		Reduced molybdate system	1,2,4-amononaphthal sulphonic acid	
	In H_2SO_4 system	In HCl system			
	I	II	III	IV	V
P concentration at 50% transmission, ppm P#	0.4	0.8	0.9	2.2	6
%Transmission, 1ppmP,660nm	18	36	50	75	-
Range of confirmatic to Beer's law, ppm P	0-1	0-2.5	0-4	0-10	0-20
Working range ppm P	0.02-1	0.05-2	0.1-5	0.2-10	0.8-20
Time to develop color	5min	5min	30min	15min	5min
Temperature of the color develop	20-25^{0}C	25	100	25	25
Stability	15min	20min	24hrs	Changes**	Infinite
Final conc. of acid, N	0.39	0.7	0.44	0.9	0.2-1.6
Final conc. of molybdate %	0.1	0.3	0.0506	0.4	0.5
Effect of excess molybdate acid reaction	Slightly decrease	Slightly decrease	Slightly decrease	None	None
Effect of excess reductant	Slightly increase	Slightly increase	Slightly increase	Slightly increase	Nil
Sensitivity	Greatest	-	relatively	Less	Much less
Positive aspects Choice of Phosphorus method	Suitable for Infertile soil	Suitable for Soils with for High chloridethe	Eliminates the arsenic effect	Determination at 200ppm Fe^{3+}, moderate sensitive for acidity variation, Eliminates the arsenic effect	Stable color, no reduction step, free from contamination (glassware) and interference

Note

* After Woods and Mellon, 1941, Ind. Eng. Chen. a. e., 13760

** Measurement must be made at a definite time

1cm cell at 700nm for the methods I to IV evelyn tube at 440nm for method V

General Principle

The heteropoly complexes is thought to be formed by coordination of molybdate ions with phosphorus as the central coordinating atom (Boltz *et al.*, 1949), the oxygen of molybdate radical is being substituted for that of PO4:

$$H_3PO_4 + 12H_2MoO_4 \quad --------\rightarrow H_3P(Mo_3O_{10}) + 12H_2O$$

Ions besides (P^{5+}) which act as a central coordinating atom to form 12 fold heterpoly acid with molybdate include arsenic (As^{5+}) Silicon (Si^{4+}) Germanium (Gr^{4+}) and in some condition Molybdium (Mo^{3+}) and Boron (B^{3+}). The heteropoly complexes, before reduction, give a yellow hue to the water solution. With high P concentration a yellow precipitate is formed. In the solution of low enough concentration to be suitable for determination by reduction to form the blue color, yellow color is so faint that it is not notice. At about 100 times this concentration the yellow color is suitable for spectrophotometry. The vanadomolybdophosphoric yellow color is greatly intensified by vanadium component. A characteristics blue color is produced when either molybdate or its heteropoly complexes are partially reduced. The spectrophotometic absorption curve for blue colored molybdenum blue in the presence or absence of heteropoly complexes of phosphorus shows two wavelengths (660nm and 830nm) for characteristics light absorption.

Phosphate Standards

Primary phosphate standard (50ppm P)

Potassium dihydrogen phosphate (KH_2PO_4) is dried at 40^0C and 0.2195g is dissolved in 400ml of distilled water in a 1000ml volumetric flask. Then, 25ml of 7N H_2SO_4 is added and the solution is made to 1000ml and mixed, giving 50ppm of P. Thus, preserved with H_2SO_4, the solution keeps indefinitely, but it should be stored in a soft-glass bottle. This solution is diluted directly for the yellow coloured solutions of the vanadomolybdophosphoric acid (Method V, Table 2)

Secondary standards, 2 and 20ppm of P

For the 2ppm standard, 20 ml of 50ppm stock solution is diluted to 500ml. For the 20ppm standard, 200ml is diluted to 500ml. They are used in making the blue colored solutions (Methods I, II, III, & IV, Table 2).

Working standards and blank

All reagents including the extraction solution and sample processing chemicals must be included in each of the standard solutions and in the blank employed for any of the calibration curves (Table 3.5). A slight color in the blank does not interfere, since the photometer is set with the blank reading, G = 100 (L = 0). The blank transmission % usually will be > 95% of a similar but uncoloured solution.

Table 3.5 : Appropriate concentration ranges of phosphorus standard solutions for various analytical methods

Volume of stock solution taken	Concentration obtained when stock solution is diluted to 50ml final volume					% Transmission
	2ppm stock		20ppm stock		50ppm stock	
	I	II	III	IV	V	
ml	ppm	ppm	ppm	ppm	ppm	
0 (Blank)	0	0	0	0	0	100.0
0.50	0.02	-	0.2	0.2	-	-
1.00	0.04	0.04	0.4	0.4	1.0	-
2.50	0.10	0.10	1.0	1.0	2.5	-
5.00	0.20	0.20	2.0	2.0	5.0	-
7.50	0.30	-	3.0	-	7.5	-
10.00	-	0.40	-	4.0	10.0	-
12.5	0.50	-	5.0	-	12.5	-
15.0	0.60	0.60	-	6.0	15.0	-
20.0	-	0.80	-	8.0	20.0	-
25.0	-	1.0	-	10.0	-	-

Chlorostannous - Reduced Molybdophosphoric Blue Color Method in Sulphuric Acid System (Bray and Kurtz, 1945)

Methods for determining phosphorus in soil have been discussed in the literature for more than a century. The purpose of these methods has been to characterize the phosphorus in the soil system. The selection of suitable methods requires a clear understanding of objectives that necessitate the measurement of the soil P. Other considerations are the properties of the soil involved, accuracy and reproductivity needed and the facilities and personal available. Most soil P determination has two district phases viz., the preparation of the solution containing the soil P or fraction thereof and the quantitative determination of the P in the solution. The choice of chlorometric method for determining P depends on the concentration of P in the solution, concentration of interfering substances in the solution to be analyzed, and the particular acid system involved in the analytical procedures.

The molybdenum blue methods are the most sensitive and as results widely used for soil extract containing small amount of P as well as for total P in soils. These methods are based on the principle that in an acid molybddate solution containing orthophosphate ions, a phosphomolbdate complex that can reduce by stannous chloride and other reducing agents to a molybdenum blue colour. The intensity blue colour varies with P concentration but it affected also by others factors such as acidity, arsenic, silicate and substances, which influences oxidation reduction conditions of the system (Jackson, 1958).

Method

The two most widely used methods for extracting the total P from the soils are digestion with HClO4 and fusion with Na_2CO_3. The recommended procedure involved $HClO_4$ digestion of soil followed by a chlorimetric determination of the P in the digest. The digestion procedure is differ because of it's simplicity and adaptability as a routine procedure. However it is recognized that some laboratory deemed the use of the $HClO_4$ has unsafe or ill-advised, and in such instance the Na_2CO_3 fusion method described by Jackson (1958, Pp. 175- 176) is recommended.

Reagents

- Phosphoric acid ($HClO_4$), 60%
- *Sulfomolybdic acid*: Ignite reagent - grade MoO_3 in a porcelain dish at a dull red heat, but below the melting point, in muffle furnace for about 1hr. cool the MoO_3, and weigh 7.2 g into an 800 ml, Kjeldahl flask. Add 250 ml of conc. H_2SO_4 and a few glass beads, and boil the mixture until solution is completes or until only a slight cloudiness remains after extended boiling. Cool the solution, and preserve it in a glass stopper bottle.
- *Standard phosphate solution*: Dilute 0.4393 g of oven dry KH_2PO_4 to 1 litre in a volumetric flask with distilled water. 1 ml of this

solution contains 100 μg of P. Prepare solution containing 10 μg and 1 μg of P per ml by diluting suitable aliquots of the solution with distilled water.

- *Sodium bisulphate* ($NaHSO_3$) solution: Dissolve 5.2 g of reagent grade $NaHSO_3$ in 100 ml of 1.0N H_2SO_4. Prepare the solution weekly and stopper the flask.
- Quinaldine red, 0.01% aqueous solution
- *Metol*: Dissolve 0.42g method (p- methylaminophenol sulfate) and 6.3 g of Na_2SO_3 in distilled water, and dilute this solution to 100 ml. Prepare fresh a solution every 3 or 4-days
- Sodium carbonate (Na_2CO_3), 2N
- Sulfuric acid (H_2SO_4), 2N

Procedure

- Mix 2.0 g of finely ground soil (0.5mm) with 30ml of 60% $HClO_4$ in a 250 ml volumetric flask.
- Digest the mixture at the temperature a few degrees below the boiling point on a hot plate in hood until the dark colour due to organic matter disappears.
- Then continue heating at the boiling temperature 20 minutes longer. At this stage, heavy white fumes of $HClO_4$ appear, and the insoluble material become like white sand, if necessary, add 1 or 2 ml of $HClO_4$ to work down any black particles that stick to the sides of the flask. Occasionally shake the flask.
- Cool the mixture, add distilled water to obtain a volume of 250 ml, and mix the contents.
- Allow time for the solid material to settle before taking an aliquot.
- Pipette an aliquot (< 25 ml) of the solution in to a 50 ml volumetric flask.
- Add 1 drop of the quinaldine red, and adjust the pH with 2N Na_2CO_3 and 2N H_2SO_4 to the point where the red color just disappears.
- Add water to make a volume of 25 ml; then add 5 ml of $NaHCO_3$ solution, and digest the contents in a water bath for

30 minutes with the flasks partly immersed in the water. Carefully pipette 0.5 ml of the sulfomolybdic acid reagent in to the flask, letting it run down the side of the neck.

- Pipette 2.0 ml of metol reagent into the flask, and wash down the neck with water.
- Continue the digestion in the bath for 1 hour, cool the solution, and adjust the volume of 50 ml with distilled water.
- Mix the contents, and measure the transmission photometrically with 660μ incident light. Plot the transmittances of the standards against the μg of P per ml on semi-logarithmic graph paper, the reading range being 0 to 1μg of P per ml.

Comments

Heating of the digestion mixture should be continued until heavy white fumes of $HClO_4$ appear. Otherwise, the digestion will be incomplete, and some of the P may remain in the solids. The $NaHSO_3$ reduces arsenic acid to arsenious acid and ferric iron to the ferrous form. These reduced forms of arsenic and iron do not interfere should be limited to 25 ppm and iron 2 ppm. The color is stable for 24 hrs.

Chlorostannous – Reduced Molybdophosphoric Blue Color Method in HCl System

This method has been used widely as an index of available P in soils. It is commonly referred as Bray- Kurtz method (1945). The combination of HCL and NH_4F is designed to remove easily acid- soluble forms of P, largely calcium phosphates, and a portion of the aluminium and iron phosphates. The NH_4F dissolves aluminum and iron phosphates by its complex ion formation with these metal ions in acid solution. However, two different methods are employed for phosphorus estimation according to nature of soils:

- Bray- Kurtz method (1945) for acid soils
- Olsen (et al) method (1954) for calcareous, alkaline or neutral soils

Bray- Kurtz Method (1945) for Acid Soils

Reagents

- *Ammonium fluride* (NH_4F), 1N: Dissolve 37 g of NH_4F in distilled water and dilute the solution to 1 litre. Store this solution in a polythene bottle.
- *Hydrochloric acid (*HCl), 0.5N: Dilute 20.2 ml of concentrated HCl to volume of 500 ml with diluted water.
- *Extracting solution:* Add 15 ml of 1.0 N NH_4F and 25 ml of 0.5 N HCl to 460 ml of distilled water. This gives a solution 0.03 N in NH_4F and 0.025 N in HCl. It will keep in glass more than 1 year.
- *Stannous chloride* ($SnCl_2$. $2H_2O$), stock solution: dissolve 10 g of reagent -grade $SnCl_2.2H_2O$ in 25 ml of concentrated HCl. Keep the solution in the black, glass-stoppered bottle in a refrigerator in a polythene bottle to lengthen in the life of the reagent.
- *Ammonium molybdate* [$(NH_4)_6Mo_7O_{24}$. $4H_2O$]: Dissolve 15 g of reagent- grade $(NH_4)_6Mo_7O_{24}$. 4 H_2O in 350 ml of distilled water. Add water to obtain a volume of 1 litre. Store the solution in a black, glass- stoppered bottle. Prepare a fresh solution for every 2 months.
- *Stannous chloride, dilute solution*: Mix 1 ml of $SnCl_2$ stock solution with 333 ml of water. Make a fresh solution for every 3 hours as needed.

Procedure

- Weigh 1 g of soil into an extraction bottle or tube and add 7 ml of the extracting solution. Shake the container for 1 minute and filter the contents through Whatman No. 42 paper. If the filtrate is not clear, pour the solution back through the filter.
- To 2 ml of the filtrate, add 5 ml of distilled water. Add 2 ml of the ammonium molybdate solution, and mix the contents well.
- Add 1 ml of the $SnCl_2$ dilute solution and mix again.
- After 5 or 6 minutes and before 20 minutes, measure the colour photometrically using 660 μ incident light.
- Prepare a standard curve including the 2 ml of extracting solution in the range of 0.1 to 1 μg of P per ml. Plot the

transmittances of the standards against the μg of p per ml on semi-logarithmic graph paper.

Calculation

P in soil (ppm) = ppm of P in solution x 35

Available P in soil (kg/ha) = (R x volume of extract x 2.24 x 10^6) ÷ (volume of aliquot x wt. of soil x 10^6)

Where,

R = μg P in the aliquot obtained from standard curve

Available P_2O_5 Kg/ha = Available P Kg/ha x 2.29

Precautions to be taken during P Estimation

The glassware to be used for P estimation must be free of contamination with phosphorus. Clean the glassware with sulphuric acid – dichromate solution and wash them thoroughly with tap water followed by rinsing with distilled water.

Comments

The ratio of soil to extracting solution and the shaking time are not the same at various labs (Jackson, 1958). Some modifications use more extracting solution per unit weight of soil, and others increase the shaking time up to 5 minutes. Boric acid eliminates possible interferences of fluorides in the color development (Kurtz, 1942), but its necessity for the analysis of most soils has not been established. Some acid, sandy soils may show some interference from fluorides. The soil values are interpreted in general as follows: < 3 ppm = very low, 3 to 7 ppm = low, 7- 20 ppm = medium and >20 ppm = high.

- This method is more appropriate for acid soils than the Olsen's method. It can be used for soils that contain less than 2% calcite/ dolomite. It is not appropriate for calcareous soils because $CaCO_3$ rapidly neutralizes the acid, resulting in low estimates of available P (Kalra and Maynard, 1991).
- Although the original ratio of soil (air-dry) to extractant was 1:10, ratios of 1:10 to 1:50 have also been advocated. The originally advocated shaking time was 1 minute but periods up to 5 min. have been tried and long periods preferred (Dewis and Freitas, 1984).
- While P1 extracts mainly the 'adsorbed' P, Bray and Kurtz P2 removes both the adsorbed and the acid-soluble P as it has

0.10N HCl. The P1 has also been found suitable for extracting exchangeable K in acid -neutral soils (Frageria *et al.*, 1991).

- An extractant known as Mehlich No. 3 was introduced as a universal extractant for acid soils (Mehlich 1984). This is a mixture of 0.2N acetic acid, 0.25N ammonium nitrate, 0.015N NH_4F, 0.013N HNO_3 and 0.001M EDTA. It is being adopted by laboratories, which have been using neutral normal ammonium acetate for determination of major cations K, Ca and Mg and Bray P1 for P. For storing and extracting vessel with Mehlich 3, must be plastic and not use glass (Jones, 1990).
- Amount of P extracted increases with increase in speed and shaking time. If one minute is chosen, it is preferable to use wrist action shaker which accommodates 2-samples at one time.
- Owing to the effect of the F^- ion on the molybdenum blue color development, not more than 5 ml of extract should be taken for color development. If the soils have high P, reduce the aliquot to 2 ml and add 3ml extractant (Dewis and Freitas, 1984).
- Some acid, sandy soil may show interference from fluoride (Olsen and Sommers, 1982).
- Boric acid can be added to eliminate the fluoride interference if larger amount of aliquot has to be taken for analysis in case of low -P soils.

Olsen Method (1954) for Calcareous, Alkaline or Neutral Soils

Phosphorus is extracted from the soil with 0.5M $NaHCO_3$ at a nearly constant pH of 8.5. In calcareous, alkaline (pH = 7.0) or neutral soils containing calcium phosphates decreases the concentration of Ca in solution by causing precipitation of Ca as $CaCO_3$; as a result, the concentration of P in solution increases. In the presence of solid-phase calcite, the concentration of Ca in the extracting solution an equilibrium is $6X10^{-7}$ M (Olsen *et al*, 1954). In acid soil containing Al and Fe phosphates such as variscite and strengite, P concentration in solution increases as the pH rises (Lindsay and Moreno, 1960). Secondary precipitation reactions in acid and calcareous soils are reduced to a minimum because the concentration of Al, Ca, and Fe remains at low level in this extractant.

Reagents

- *Chlormolybdic acid-* Dissolve 15g Ammonium molybdate in 300ml water by slow heat at 50°C. Add 410 ml 10.0 (N) HCl slowly by cooling and make the total volume 1000ml. Keep it in cool and dark place.
- *Standard Phosphorus solution* – Dissolve 0.2195 g of potassium dihydrogen orthophosphate in 975 ml water in a 1000ml volumetric flask. Add 25 ml 0.1(N) H_2SO_4 to it and mix it well. The strength of the solution will be of 50ppm. Prepare 0.1, 0.2, 0.4, 0.8, 1.0, 1.2 ppm phosphorus solution from the above solution by dilution.
- *Olsen's extractant* - Dissolve 42.0 g of Sodium bicarbonate ($NaHCO_3$) in 1000 ml dist. water and adjust the pH to 8.5 with NaOH solution.
- *Stanous chloride solution* - Dissolve 2.0 g stannous chloride in 5 ml conc. HCl . Add 1 ml of this solution to 330 ml dist. water and shake it well. Prepare this solution freshly for taking reading each time.

Procedure

- Take 10 g soil and add 100 ml Olson's reagent and 1 tea spoon of carbon black (P free). Shake it for 30 min. and filter with Whatman No.40/42 filter paper.
- Take 10 ml aliquot in 50 ml volumetric flask and add 10ml chlormolybdic acid and add 20 ml dist. water.
- Then add 0.25 ml clorostanous acid (0.1M) and make the volume to 50 ml and read the OD or % T (Transmission) in colorimeter (660 μ).

Standard Curve of P

Take standard solution of P at different concentration and develop colour as mentioned above and prepare a standard curve. Determine the ppm P of the aliquot and then of soil from the standard curve.

Calculation

Phosphorus in soil (ppm) = 50 x A

Where,

A - ppm of phosphorus in the coloured solution.

Interpretation of results

Sl No	Available P (Kg/ha)	Soil Rating
1	< 10	Low
2	10 - 19	Medium
3	> 20	High

Comments and Suggestions

- Olsen's method is suitable for neutral, alkaline and calcareous soils. It is normally used for alkaline soils of semiarid regions which have high CEC and high base saturation and very often free $CaCO_3$. The extractant ($NaHCO_3$) has two disadvantages. It dissolves organic matter, producing coloured extracts, which have to be carified with Dargo-60 or activated carbon.
- These days there is an interest in universal extraction reagents which can be used to determine major elements and micronutrients (Jones, 1990). The ammonium bicarbonate - DTPA extractant (AB-DTPA) was introduced for use on alkaline soils (Sultanpour and Schwab, 1977). AB-DTPA (1M NH_4HCO_3 - 0.005 M DTPA: pH 7.6) can substitute for Olsen's method on alkaline soils whose water pH exceeds 7.5 but are not excessive in their Ca or Na content. It can be used as an extractant for K and NO_3-N, in addition to several micronutrients. One of the main problems with this reagent is that it is unstable in its pH and must be made either before use or kept stored under mineral oil.
  - To obtain P free Dargo-G-60 or activated charcoal, 80g material as a slurry in distilled water is leached overnight with 1 litre of 6 M HCl in 60mm diameter columns (250 ml capacity) and then with deionized water till the leachate is free of chloride. The material is then dried at 110^0C (Sarirullah *et al.* 1990).
  - Before P estimation is carried out, take 5 ml of the extractant in a separate 25 ml beaker and determine the volume of acid required to bring the pH of the solution to 5.0 using p-nitrophenol indicator, the yellow colour of

which disappears at this pH. The requisite volume of acid can be added to aliquots and kept aside for sufficient time with occasional shaking by hand to neutralize the bi-carbonate and allow the CO_2 bubbles to escape.

- Prepare a fresh solution of $NaHCO_3$, if solution has been standing over 1 month in a glass bottle. Its pH tends to increase in glass bottle. Use polythentene bottle for periods longer than 1 month but check ph every month (Olsen and Sommers, 1982).
- The ascorbic acid method has proved to be reliable and less subjected to interferences in color development than the $SnCl_2$ method. The colour is stable for 24 hours.
- Temperature and shaking speed increases the P extracted by $NaHCO_3$. Therefore, room temperature and shaking speed have to be regulated to obtain precise estimates of the Olsen's P. A shaking time of 30 minutes, and speed of 180 + oscillations/minute should be used.

Nelson Method for Fixed P Estimation

Solutions such as acetic acid and sodium acetate extract very small quantities of P from the soils, which fix P strongly. The mixed acids are more effective than HCl alone as a P extractant on these soils and the correlate better with plant response. Relatively greater amounts of iron phosphate dissolve in the mixed acid than in HCl alone.

Reagents

- *Extracting solution*: Add 12 ml of concentrated H_2SO_4 and 73 ml of concentrated HCl to 15 litre of distilled water. Dilute the solution to 18 litre with distilled water. This extracting solution is approximately 0.05N HCl and 0.025N H_2SO_4.
- *Molybdate-vanadate solution*: Dissolve 25g of ammonium molybdate $[(NH_4)_6Mo_7O_{24}\cdot 4H_2O]$ in 500 ml of distilled water. Dissolve 1.25 g of ammonium vanadate (NH_4VO_3) in 500 ml of 8N HNO_3. Mix equal volumes of these solutions. Prepare a fresh mixture each week.
- *Standard phosphate solution*: Dissolve 0.1098 g of monobasic potassium phosphate (KH_2PO_4) in 500 ml of extracting solution and dilute the solution to 1 litre with the extracting solution. This solution contains 25ppm of P.

Procedure

- Add 5g of soil and about 200 mg of charcoal (Dargo G 60 quality) to a 50 ml flask and then add 20 ml of the extracting solution.
- Shake the flask for 5 minutes in a mechanical shaker, and filter the mixture through Whatman No. 42 filter paper.
- Measure 4 ml of the extract in to a glass vial and add 1 ml of distilled water.
- Add 1 ml of reagent 2 and allow the tube to stand 20 minutes. Use 420mμ incident light in the photoelectric colorimeter.
- Adjust the galvanometer to 100% transmission, using a tube containing all the reagents except P.
- Prepare a standard curve from aliquots of reagent 3 in the range of 0.5 to 4 ml. concentrations of P in the extract equal to 1 and 4 ml of reagent 3 give 25 and 100 ppm of P in the soil, respectively.

Molybdenum-Reduced Molybdophosphoric Blue Color Method

Molybdenum-Reduced molybdophosphoric blue color method is employed for estimation P in forest soil. This procedure covers the extraction and analysis of plant available phosphorus (P) in forest soil. Plant available phosphorus (P) is extracted from the soil with 0.002 N sulfuric acid. The extracted P is reacted with a sulfuric-molybdate to form a blue phosphomolybdate compound in the presence of a reducing agent.

Apparatus and Materials

- Erlenmeyer flasks (500 ml)
- Pipette banks
- Time-controlled oscillating shaker (Eberbach) set at 160 excursions per minute.
- Filter paper (9 cm Whatman No. 2 or equivalent).
- Funnel tubes (15 ml).
- Matched colorimetric tubes (10 ml).
- UV-Vis spectrophotometer

Reagents

- N/10 sulfuric acid
- Sulfuric acid extracting solution: Dissolve 3 g of $(NH_4)_2SO_4$ in approximately 0.5 L of deionized water. Add 20 ml of N/10 sulfuric acid and dilute to 1 L with deionized water.
- Standard phosphate solution : Weigh out 0.4394 g of KH2PO4, bring to 1liter with extracting solution. This solution contains 100 ppm of phosphorus. Prepare a second stock solution by taking 50 ml of 100 ppm Phosphorus and diluting to 1 liter with extracting solution; this solution contains 5 ppm of phosphorus. Pipette 4, 8, 12, 16, and 20 ml of the second stock solution into 100-ml volumetric flasks and bring to volume with extracting solution. These solutions contain 0.2, 0.4, 0.6, 0.8, and 1.0 ppm of phosphorus.
- Sulfuric-molybdate solution (Dissolve 8.5716 g ammonium molybdate, $(NH_4)_6Mo_7O_{24}.4H_2O$, in 500 ml of deionized water. Dissolve 0.1959 g of antimony potassium tartrate, $K(SbO)C_4H_4O_6 \frac{1}{2} H_2O$, in the above solution. Slowly add 100 ml of H_2SO_4 and mix well). Let cool and dilute to 1 liter. Store in a brown polyethylene or Pyrex bottle in a refrigerator.
- Ascorbic acid solution : Dissolve 0.528 g of ascorbic acid in 30 ml of deionized water. Prepare fresh each day.
- Color reagent : Add 30 ml of ascorbic acid solution to 70 ml of sulfuric-molybdate stock solution. This solution should be made fresh daily.

Procedure

- Place a 1.5 g scoop of soil into a 500-ml Erlenmeyer flask.
- Add 150 ml of 0.002 N sulfuric acid.
- Shake the suspension on shaker for 30 min.
- After shaking, immediately filter suspension through filter paper.
- Filtrate should be discarded until clear.
- Place 5 ml of filtrate into a clear 10-ml tube and add 1 ml of sulfuric-molybdate and ascorbic acid solution.

- Shake tube and wait 15 minutes.
- Transfer solution to a colorimeter tube.
- Percent transmittance is determined by a spectrophotometer set at 882 nm by a filter colorimeter at 660 nm, and concentration of P is determined using a standard curve.

Note

Color development is complete in 15 minutes but will continue at a slow rate. For this reason, samples should be read within two hours. Arsenic forms a blue molybdate complex but is usually present in very low amounts unless a special arsenical pesticide has been applied in the past. Very high soil pH interferes with phosphorus by this extraction method.

Calculations

In lieu of direct calibration of the colorimetric scale,

Extractable P in soil (PPM) = ppm P in solution x 150 ml ÷ 1.5 g
= ppm P in solution x 100.

Vanadomolybdophosphoric Yellow Color Method in HNO_3 System (Method -V)

This method has been long used in steel analysis (Mission, 1908) and biological materials (Koenig and Johnson, 1942). The advantages of this method are extreme simplicity, lower sensitivity (1-20ppm of P), stability of colour, freedom from interferences of ions up to 100ppm.

Apparatus

- Burette (50 ml)
- Volumetric flask (1000 ml)
- Colorimeter

Reagents

- Standard P solution
- *HNO_3 - vanadate-molbdate reagent*: Solution A is prepared by dissolution of 25g of ammonium molybdate in 400 ml of water. Then, solution B is prepared by dissolving 1.25g of ammonium metavanadate in 300 ml of boiling water. Solution B is cooled and then 250 ml of conc. HNO_3 is added and the solution is

again cooled to room temperature. Finally solution A is poured into solution B and mixture is diluted to 1 litre.

Procedure

- *Preparation of test solution*: An aliquot of the phosphorus solution (standard/test sample) that contains 0.05 to 1.0 mg of P, in acid not exceeding the equivalent of 0.2N in the final 50ml is placed in 50ml volumetric flask not exceeding 35ml.

  Note: *the acid concentration should be lies between 0.5N and 1.0N for full color development.*

- *Vanadomolybdophosphoric yellow color*: To the P solution (sample aliquot) in a 50 ml volumetric flask, 10 ml of the vanadomolybdate reagent is added and the solution is diluted to 50ml with distilled water and mixed well. The color develops rapidly but is usually read after 10 minutes to assure full strength. A blank must be prepared and read with the sample. The color is read in the colorimeter with a light maximum from 400 to 490mu, according to the sensitivity needed. The light maxima, 400, 440, 470 and 470 is required for concentration ranges, 0.75 - 5.5, 2.0 -15.0, 4.0-17.0 and 7.0-20.0 ppm P, respectively.

Determination of Total Potassium in Soil

A large portion of the potassium (K) in soils is present as a part of the crystalline structure of primary and secondary minerals such as micas, feldsfars and micaceous minerals of the clay fraction. A small portion is found as exchangeable ions and an extremely small part is present as a soluble salt. The total K in soils is of the order of magnitude of 1 to 2%, the exchangeable K varies from <100 ppm to several thousand ppm and the soluble K is usually a few ppm of the dry weight of the soil. The total K in soils is of no value as an index to the availability of K to plants nor is it always of value in tracing the movement/ accumulation of applied fertilizer K. However, the total K can be determined by chemical method of Wilcox (1937) as presented below with a precision of ±0.05mg of K (Jackson, 1958)

Estimation of Total K

Standard potassium chloride (KCl) solution, 0.01N: Dissolve 0.7456g of dry KCl in water, and dilute the solution to a volume of 1 liter.

Procedure

- If a flame photometer is to be used for K determination, decompose 0.1g of finely ground soil in a 30ml platinum crucible.
- Wet the soil with a few drops of water, and add 5ml of HF and 0.5ml of $HClO_4$.
- With organic soils, add 3ml of HNO_3 and 1 ml of $HClO_4$ to the crucible, heat the soil-acid mixture on a hot plate until fumes of $HClO_4$ appear, cool the crucible, and then add 5 ml of HF.
- Place the crucible in a sand bath and cover about nine-tenths of the crucible top with a platinum lid.
- Heat the crucible to 200 - 225^{0}C., and evaporate the contents to dryness. Cool the crucible, and add 2ml of water and a few drops of $HClO_4$.
- Replace the crucible in the sand bath, and evaporate to dryness. If organic matter stains are still present on the sides or lid of the crucible, direct the flame of a Meker burner onto the sides and lid the organic matter is oxidized. A faint red heat is sufficient.
- Remove the crucible, and cool, add 5 ml of 6N HCl and about 5ml of water.
- Heat the crucible on a hot plate or over a burner until the solution boils gently.
- If the sample does not dissolve completely, evaporate the solution to dryness; repeat the procedure, starting with 5ml of HF and $HClO_{4.}$
- When the residue completely dissolves in HCl, transfer the sample to a 50 ml volumetric flask, filter into a 100ml volumetric flask.
- Wash the filter paper with water, and dilute the solution to volume.
- Filtration is desirable to keep the solution free of solid particle which cause clogging of burner capillaries of flame photometers.
- Compare the solution with standards of 0, 5, 10, 20, and 40 ppm K made in the same HCl concentration as the samples.

Comments

Potassium usually occurs in low concentrations in soil-water extracts, while Na ranges from low to very high concentrations. Sodium interferes, to some extents, with the flame-photometric determination of K, but the interference can be reduced or eliminated by proper calibration. This involves the preparation of calibration curves for K in the absences of Na and in the presence of Na in the concentration encountered. The instrument should be set up in a room free from drafts, dust, or fumes, and smoking should not be permitted.

Estimation of Exchangeable K

The exchangeable potassium is by definition that which is free to exchange with cations of salt solutions added to soils. But, since the amount of K exchanged from the soil depends on the nature of the replacing solution, the exchangeable K is defined more specifically as that which is extracted with neutral 1N NH_4OAc minus the water soluble K; in non-saline soils the amount of water soluble potassium is so small that no appreciable error is made by including it as part of the exchangeable K in saline soils, however, the water-soluble K should be determined and subtracted from the total K in the NH_4OAc extract. The removal of soluble salts by leaching with water before extraction with NH_4OAc is not recommended, because as the salt content is decreased, the adsorption of divalent cations in solution increases. Thus, the correlation for soluble K or Na should be made by subtracting the soluble constituents in a saturation extract of soils from the total extracted by NH_4OAc (Black, 1965)

Reagents

- Hydrochloric acid, 2N
- Hydrochloric acid, 1N
- *Ammonium acetate* (NH_4OAc), 1N adjusted to pH 7: For each liter of solution desired, add 58 ml of glacial acetic acid to about 600 ml of water, and then add 70 ml of concentrated NH_4OH, specific gravity 0.9. The NH_4OH is best added under a fume hood through a long stemmed glass funnel so that it is introduced into the bottom of the acid solution. Cool the solution and adjust the pH to 7 with acetic acid or NH_4OH using a pH meter or bromothymol blue indicator. Dilute the solution to volume, mix it and store it in a pyrex bottle.

- *Standard potassium solution*: Dissolve 0.9533g of dried Kcl in water, dilute the solution to 500ml and mix it. This solution contains 1,000 ppm K.

Procedure (by Flame photometer)

- Place 10g of soil (use 5 g if it contains >500 ppm, extractable K) in a 50ml centrifuge tube. Add 25 ml of NH_4OAc and shake the tube for 10minutes.
- Centrifuge until the supernatant liquid is clear. Decant the supernatant liquid into a 100 ml volumetric flask.
- Make three additional extractions in same manner.
- Dilute the combined extract to 100 ml with NH_4OAc.
- Mix the solution and determine K on a flame photometer by comparing the emission with that from standards made 0,10,20,40, and 60 ppm K.
- NH_4OAc extract can be put directly into flame photometers. If care is taken to avoid solid particle that may clogged the atomizer. If solid particles appear in the extract, filter small portion of the extract using Whatmann No 40 or equivalent quality filter paper before putting to flame photometer.
- Most prominent lines of K and radiations most usable for flame analysis in soil work are the doublets at 766 and 769 nm for K. The alkali elements are easily exited by a flame and to avoid the some of the interference a low flame temperature is recommended.

Comments

- Do not use the soil that has been oven-dried.
- If the water content is to be determined use separate sample for this.
- In most soils, the exchangeable K changes with drying. When the exchangeable K is relatively high following application of K fertilizer, there is likely to be K fixation or decreased with drying and when a given soil is relatively low the exchangeable K there is usually a release of K from non- exchangeable forms during drying. Thus if an accurate estimate of the exchangeable K is to be made for soil as it occurs in the field, the soil should

not be air-dried but a separate sample should be used for determining the water content, so that the result can be calculated to a air dry basis or oven dry basis.

Method for Estimation of Available K

Probably the most universally employed index to K availability in soils is available K i.e., the sum of exchangeable and water soluble K which is extracted by neutral 1N NH_4OAc. As an index to K availability for rapidly growing annual and perennial food crops, the exchangeable K is perhaps is best expressed as quantity such as ppm or meq/100 g. However with some other crops such as fruit trees and forest trees the exchangeable K is perhaps is best calculated as a % of cations exchangeable capacity (Black, 1965). The extraction with cold H_2SO_4 also provides a reliable index of K (Hunter and Pratt, 1957). The extraction with cold H_2SO_4 in a short period of time removes the same amount of K from most soils as extraction does with NH_4OAc.

Available K along with Ca and Mg are usually determined in neutral ammonium acetate (1N NH_4OAc) extract of soil. The extraction is carried out by shaking followed by filtration or centrifugation. The K is estimated by using a flame photometer and Ca and Mg either by EDTA- titration or by using atomic absorption spectrophotometer. In soils with appreciable amount of soluble K, Ca, and Mg, these cations are estimated in a saturation extract (Jackson, 1958) and deducted from 1N NH_4OAc extractable K, Ca, and Mg to obtain respective exchangeable cations.

The extraction of soil with boiling HNO_3 (1N) has been used successfully as an index to release of K from non exchangeable forms (Wood and De Turk, 1941). Essentially the same amount of K can be extracted by H_2SO_4 (Hunter and Pratt, 1957). In the later procedure the heat is applied by adding 10ml concentrated H_2SO_4 to a mixture of 10g of soil and 25 ml of water and the sample is allowed to stand for 30minutes before filtration and washing with 1N H_2SO_4.

Ammonium Acetate Extraction Method for Calcareous Soils

Reagents and Standard Curve

- Ammonium acetate (1N, pH 7.0): To 700 ml of distilled water, add 57 ml 99.5% glacial acetic acid (CH_3COOH) and then 69 ml of conc. ammonium hydroxide (NH_4OH). Dilute to a volume of 900 ml and adjust pH to 7.0 by the addition of more of 3N NH_4OH or 3N CH_3COOH and make upto 1 litre. Alternatively, dissolve 154 g ammonium acetate 7.0 with dilute NH_4OH or HOAc as required and make to 2 litre.

- Potassium chloride standard solution: make a stock solution of 1000 ppm K by dissolving 1.908 g of potassium chloride dried at 60^0C for 1 hr) in distilled water and diluting up to 1 litre. Prepare 100 ppm standard by diluting 100 ml of 1000 ppm stock solution to one litre with extracting solution.
- Standard curve: Pipette 0, 5, 10, 15, and 20 ml of 100 ppm solution into 100 ml volumetric flasks and bring the volume to mark with extracting solution. The solutions contain 0, 5, 10, 15 and 20 ppm K, respectively.

Procedure

Shaking and filtration can be done by the method of Schollenberger and Simon (1945) or shaking and centrifugation as described by Knudsen *et al.* (1982).

Shaking and Filtration

- Place 5 g soil in a 150 ml Erlenmeyer flask and pour in 25 ml of neutral 1N ammonium acetate (pH 7.0).
- Shake on a reciprocating shaker (180 + oscillations/min) for 5 minutes and immediately through Whatman No. 1 filter paper. First few ml of the filtrate may be rejected.
- Centrifuge the tube at 2000 rpm for 10 min until the supernatant liquid is clear.
- Decant the supernatant liquid into a 100 ml volumetric flask.
- Make three additional extractions in the same manner. Dilute the combined extracts to 100 ml with NH_4Ac
- Mix the solution and determine K in the flame photometer using K filter after necessary setting and calibration of the instrument (use 0 and 20 ppm working K concentrations).

Shaking and Centrifugation

- Place 10 g of < 2 mm air-dried soil (or use 5 g if the soil contains greater than 500 ppm K) in a 50 ml centrifuge tube
- Add 25 ml of NH_4OAc, stopper and shake the tube for 10 min.

- Read similarly the different concentration of K in flame photometer and obtain the standard curve by plotting the reading against the different concentrations of K.

Calculation

$$\text{Available K (Kg/ha)} = \frac{R \times \text{volume of extract} \times 2.24 \times 10^6}{\text{Wt. of soil}}$$

Where, = PPM K × 11.2

R – ppm of K in the extract (obtained from standard curve)

Available K_2O Kg/ha = Available K Kg/ha x 1.2

Interpretation of results

Sl No.	Available K (kg/ha)	Rating
1	< 108	Low
2	108 - 280	Medium
3	> 280	High

Cold H_2SO_4 Extraction Method (Hunter and Pratt, 1957)

This index to the available K has been used with acid and neutral soils. This method is described as follows:

Reagents

1. Concentrated, H_2SO_4
2. H_2SO_4, 0.1N

Procedure

- Place 10 g of (acidic/neutral) soil in a 100 ml of beaker, add separately 25 ml of water and 1N of concentrated H_2SO_4 in that order and stir the mixtures with a small glass rod.
- Allow it for 30 minutes. Transfer it to an ordinary 60^0 funnel and receive the filtrate in 100 ml volumetric flask.
- Wash soil and filter with 50 ml portion of 0.1N H_2SO_4 until the filtrate is brought to volume. Mix the solution and determine K on flame photometer. The most prominent lines of K and radiations most usable for flame analysis in soil work are the doublets at 766 and 769 μ for K.

Comments

This index to the available K has been used with acid and neutral soil. However, the NH_4OAc extraction is a safer index for K availability in calcareous soil.

Determination of Exchangeable Calcium and Magnesium

Exchangeable Ca and Mg are normally determined in ammonium acetate extracts of soils (obtained as discussed above under K) by direct titration with EDTA. The presence of ammonium acetate does not interfere with the titration, if this is carried out by the procedure suggested below (Hesse, 1971). The amount of organic matter dissolved is usually too small to affect the colour change of the indicator. This procedure permits the determination of Ca and Mg in the same solution.

Reagents

- *Standard calcium solution*: Weigh 0.5005 g of $CaCO_3$ dried at 150^{0}C into a 1 litre volumetric flask. Add 200 ml of water and then 150 ml of 1M HCl slowly and with shaking. Dilute the solution to litre. This solution is 0.01N in Ca.
- *EDTA solution*: Dissolve 2.0 g of ethylene-diamine- tetraacetic acid (di-Na salt) in water and dilute to 1 litre.
- Sodium hydroxide aqueous solution (10% w/v)
- *Buffer solution*: Dissolve 67.5 g NH_4Cl in 400 ml of water; add 570 ml of conc. NH_4OH and dilute to 1litre.
- Hydroxylamine - hydrochloride aqueous solution (5% w/v, prepare fresh each week.
- Potassium hexacyanoferrate (II) aqueous solution (potassium ferrocyanide, 4% w/v).
- Potassium ferrocyanide (1% w/v).
- Triethanolamine (commercial reagent)
- *Calcon solution*: Dissolve 0.2 g reagent in 50ml methanol. Prepare fresh every 2-week.
- *Eriochrome Black T solution*: Dissolve 0.2 g reagent in 50 ml methanol; prepare fresh every 2-weeks.

Procedure

Standardization of EDTA

Pipette 5 ml of standard calcium solution into a graduated, tall-form, 100 ml beaker. Dilute to 10 ml and add 15 ml of ammonium chloride - hydroxide buffer solution. Add 10 drops each of potassium cyanide, hydroxylamine-hydroxide, potassium hexacynoferrate (II), triethanolamine and Erichrome Black T solutions. Place the beaker on magnetic stirring plate and commence stirring. Prepare a blank solution in exactly the same manner, taking 5 ml of water instead of calcium solution. Usually the blank will be blue in color, but if not, it should be titrated with EDTA solution until blue and the bank titre value noted. Keep the blue blank solution alongside the standard calcium solution and titrate the standard with EDTA solution, stirring all the time to permanent blue color matching the blank. Dilute the blank with water now and again to equalize the volumes of the two solutions as the titration proceeds.

Repeat the standardization using Calcon as indicator. In this case add to the diluted calcium solution 10 drops each of potassium cyanide, hydroxylamine hydroxide, and triethanolamine solutions. Then, add 2.5 ml NaOH solution and 1 ml of Calcon solution. Prepare a reagent blank and titrate both solutions with EDTA solution until blue.

Determination of Ca in the NH_4OAc extract

Pipette an aliquot of the extract containing upto 3 mg Ca in a 100 ml tall-form beaker and dilute to 10 ml. For soils, containing < 10 m.e. Ca per 100 g or solutions containing <1 mg Ca/ 10 ml, it is necessary to take larger aliquots in a 250 ml beaker. Add 10 drops each of potassium cyanide, hydroxylamine-hydrochloride and triethanolamine solutions. Add 2.5 ml NaOH solution and 1 ml of Calcon solution. Titrate with EDTA until blue.

Determination of Ca + Mg

Pipette an aliquot containing upto about 3mg (Ca+Mg) into a beaker. Dilute to 10ml, add 15 ml of ammonium chloride- hydroxide buffer solution and then 10 drops each of potassium cyanide, hydroxylamine-hydrochloride, potassium hexacynoferrate (II) and triethanolamine solutions while gently warming the solution on the magnetic stirrer. When all reagents have been added, continue warming for 3 minutes, cool and add 10 drops of Erichrome Black T solution. Titrate with EDTA.

Determination of Mg

For most purposes, Mg is calculated from the difference between the (Ca + Mg) and the Ca determinations.

Calculation

$$\text{Ca or (Ca +Mg), meq/litre} = \frac{\text{T} \times \text{volume of EDTA} \times 1000}{\text{Vol. of Aliquot (ml)}}$$

Where,

T = volume in (ml) of standard EDTA used in titration (or) m.e.q. Ca or (Ca + Mg) per 100 g soil = [(100/soil weight (g)] x (Extract volume/1000) x meq Ca or (Ca + Mg)/litre.

Comments and Suggestion on K, Ca, and Mg

Ammonium acetate method is suitable for nearly neutral and non-calcareous soils. Since Ca and Mg carbonates dissolve to a large extent in ammonium acetate at pH 7.0, the contents of these cations are over-estimated in calcareous soils. Exchangeable K, Ca, and Mg in saline and calcareous can be estimated by lithium chloride- acetate method (Yaalon, 1962, Dewis and Freitas, 1984) with extraction at pH 8.2 but can be used on all types of soils by adjusting pH of the saturating and replacing solutions. The use of pH 8.2 solutions could be restricted to soils having pH values (1:5 w/v in water) of 7.6 and above, while pH 7.0 solutions for soils up to pH 7.5.

Neutral salt solutions other than ammonium acetate or dilute / weak acids can also be tried equally well. The Bray P1 extractant has been used to extract K at the same time. Similarly while estimating exchangeable Al or acidity in un-buffered 1N KCl extract, Ca and Mg can also be estimated as is being done in Brazil. Silver thiourea (AgTU) at 0.01M concentration or hot H_2SO_4 (30%) extracts more exchangeable K from kaolinite soils containing vermiculite clay mineral than M NH4)Ac (Pleyier *et al*, 1988) indicating its superiority over the latter. In soils with appreciable amounts of micaceous minerals, it is desired to obtain a measure of non-exchangeable K by employing a procedure like boiling 1n HNO_3 method (Wood and de Turk, 1940).

- Exchangeable K, Ca and Mg determination after extraction on Buchner funnel filtration (Knudsen et al, 1982) or leaching columns (Hesse, 1971) is recommended only when simultaneously CEC has also to be estimated.

- An equilibrium extraction at 1:5 to 1:10 soil solution ratio is commonly used rather than repeated extraction on a centrifuge. This extracts 80-90% exchangeable K. A wider ratio of 1: 20 and shaking time of ½ hr removes 90-95% of exchangeable K and water soluble K. This may be used as an alternative to centrifugation method if exact values of exchangeable cations are not needed or for comparative purposes.
- In soils with < 200 ppm K, calibrate the flame photometer with standards in the range of 0 -10 ppm. For K content in the range of 200- 500 ppm, calibration in 0-20 ppm range is preferred. If the soil K content is more than 500 ppm, the soil to solution ratio can be widened to 1:40 - 1:50.
- During drying, when exchangeable K is relatively high, there is likely to be K fixation or a decrease in K and when exchangeable K is low there is usually a release of K from non-exchangeable forms. Therefore, it is preferable to estimate K on field moisture samples and calculate K content on air dry or oven dry basis.
- Use AAS to determine Ca and Mg separately, if the instrument is available.
- Take extra care in the handling of potassium cyanide. Discard all solutions containing it immediately after analysis and wash thoroughly the drain and do not allow acid to come in contact with the cyanide solutions (Dewis and Fruitas, 1984).
- Add hydroxylamine - hydrochloride to reduce Fe and Mn interference in the determination of Ca and Mg. Add excess potassium ferrocyanide to precipitate manganese ferrocyanide. Addition of hydroxylamine - hydrochloride, potassium cyanide and potassium ferrocyanide may not always be necessary but it is advisable to include them as a precautionary, measure.
- Murexide can be used in place of Calcon. Mix 0.2 g murexide with 40 g dry potassium sulphate powder and store it in a dark bottle, away from light. However, Calcon is preferred to murexide.

Determination of Available Sulphur

For estimating plant-available sulphur (S) in soils, heat -soluble S and 0.15% $CaCl_2$ extractable S methods (Williams and Steinbergs, 1959) are usually recommended.

Heat- soluble S

In-organic sulphate -S (SO_4 -S) and a portion of organically held SO_4 - S are mobilized by special heat treatments and extraction with 1.0 % sodium chloride. Sulphate -S is converted into $BaSO_4$ suspension using $BaCl_2$ crystals and a special conditioning reagent. The resulting turbidity is determined by a spectrophotometer (Cottenie *et al.* 1979).

Reagents

1. *1% sodium chloride (NaCl)*: dissolve 10 g of NaCl in 700 ml of distilled water and make to 1litre with distilled water.
2. *Barium chloride dehy*drate: $BaCl_2.H_2O$ crystals, 20-30 mesh.
3. *Conditioning agent:* Dissolve 75g NaCl in 275 ml of distilled water in a 500 ml volumetric flask, stirring with magnetic stirring bar, add 30 ml of conc. HCl 100 ml of absolute ethanol and 50 ml of glycerol. Rinse glycerol into flask. Continue stirring until NaCl dissolves. Remove stirring bar and make to volume with distilled water.
4. *Standard sulphate solution*: Dissolve 0.5434 g K_2SO_4 in 1 litre of distilled water. This contains 100 mg S/ml. Dilute 10 times to obtain 10ppm. Transfer 0, 5, 10, and 20 ml (containing 0, 50, 100, 150, 200 µg SO4 -S) to Erlenmeyer flask of 150 ml, brining the volume with distilled water to 30 ml.

Procedure

- Weigh 5 g soil into a silica basin and add 20 ml distilled water.
- Place the basin on a gently boiling water-bath and evaporate to dryness.
- Then, heat it in a hot -air-oven at 102^0C for 60 min.
- After cooling, transfer the soil to a 50 ml centrifuge tube and extract it with 33 ml of 1% NaCl.
- 25 ml of aliquot is pippeted into a silica basin and evaporated to dryness with 2 ml of 3% H_2O_2. This is done to remove interfering organic matter. The basin is then heated in a hot air-oven at 102^0C for 60 min. to ensure the removal of excess H_2O_2. After cooling, the residue is taken up in 25 ml water, transferred to a centrifuge tube and centrifuged to remove suspended matter. Sulphur is then determined by taking a suitable aliquot.

- Pipette 10 or 20 ml extract in a 150 ml Erlenmeyer flask and add 20 or 10 ml of H_2O_2, thus bringing the volume to 30 ml.
- Add 2.5 ml of stabilizing solution and 0.2 -0.3 g of $BaCl_2$ crystals by a spatula to the standards and extract.
- Shake the flasks for 1 minute each at constant rate.
- After 1-3 minutes, measure the turbidity in a colorimeter using a blue filter. Turbidity can be more accurately measured at 340 nm on a spectrophotometer. The turbidity remains constant during 3-10 min.

Calculation

SO_4 -S (mg/kg) = [S (mg/l) in the aliquot x vol. of extract (ml)] ÷ [Volume of aliquot (ml) x oven-dry soil (g)]

Comments and Suggestions

Heat soluble- S measures the amount of water soluble -S released during gentle hydrolysis as a result of sequential wet and dry heating of soils (Williams and Steinbergs, 1959). An autoclave method developed by Fox et al (1964) as an alternative to heat -soluble S extracts more S than the heat-soluble method. As heat -soulble method is laborious; this method is not adopted for routine soil testing. An alternative to this is sodium bicarbonate method: 0.5M $NaHCO_3$ at 1:4 soil solution ratio, 60 min. equilibrium (Kilmer and Nearpas, 1960). It extracts water - soluble, adsorbed and labile organic sulphate -S.

$CaCl_2$ - Extractants S

In this method, S is extracted with 0.15% $CaCl_2$ and the soluble sulphate estimated turbidimetrically on a colorimeter using blue filter or spectrophotometer at 340 nm.

Reagents

- Calcium chloride dehydrate ($CaCl_2 . 2H_2O$) 0.15%: Dissolve 1.5 g of $CaCl_2$. 2H2O in about 700 ml of water and make to 1 litre with distilled water.
- Reagents 2 to 4 of heat -soluble S method.

Procedure

- Transfer 5 g soil into an 150 ml Erlenmeyer flask
- Add 25 ml 0.15% $CaCl_2$ to it
- Shake for 30 min on a reciprocating shaker (180 + oscillations/min.)
- Filter the suspension through Whatman No. 42 filter paper.
- Analyze 10- 20 ml extract turbidimetrically as described for heat - soluble S.

Calculation

SO_4-S in soil (mg/kg) = [S (mg/l) in the aliquot x vol. of extract (ml)] ÷ [Volume of aliquot (ml) x oven-dry soil (g)].

Determination of Micronutrients in Soil

For the estimation of micronutrients in soils, it is the plant-available form that is critical and not the total content. The major objective of soil testing for micronutrients, as with macronutrients, is to determine whether a soil can supply adequate micronutrients for optimal crop production or whether nutrient deficiencies are expected in crops grown on such soils. The most commonly studied micronutrients are Zn, Cu, Fe, Mn, B and Mo, and the same are dealt with here.

Micronutrients are present in different forms in the soil. Among the most deficient ones is Zn, which is present as the divalent cation Zn^{2+}. Maize, citrus, legumes, cotton and rice are especially sensitive to Zn deficiency. Iron is present mostly in sparingly soluble ferric oxide forms, which occur as coatings of aggregate or as separate constituents of the clay fraction. Soil redox potential and pH affect Fe availability. The Fe form that is predominantly taken up by plants is Fe^{2+}. The uptake of Fe is inhibited by phosphate levels caused by the formation of insoluble iron phosphate. Chemically, Mn behaves in soil in the same way as Fe.

Soil Mn originates primarily from the decomposition of ferromagnesian rocks. It is taken up by the plants as Mn^{2+} ions although it exists in many oxidation states. Manganese and phosphate are mutually antagonistic. Copper, as zinc, exists in soils mainly as divalent ions, Cu^{2+}. It is usually adsorbed by clay minerals or associated with OM although they have little or no effect on its availability to crops. High phosphate fertilization can induce Cu deficiency. Molybdenum usually occurs as MoO_3, MoO_5 and MoO_2. These oxides are transformed slowly to soluble molybdates (MoO_4), which is the form taken up by plants. Boron deficiency occurs mostly in the light-textured acid soils when they are leached heavily through irrigation or heavy rainfall.

There are different extractants for assessing plant-available nutrient (element) content in soils. The elements so extracted can be estimated quantitatively through chemical methods or instrumental techniques. Table 3.6 lists commonly used extractants for different elements.

Table 3.6 : List of commonly used extractants for different elements

Element	Extractants
Zinc	EDTA + ammonium acetate, EDTA + ammonium carbonate DTPA + $CaCl_2$, HCl, HNO_3 and dithiozone + ammonium acetate
Copper	EDTA, EDTA + ammonium acetate, ammonium bicarbonate + DTPA, HCl and HNO_3
Iron	EDTA, DTPA, EDTA + ammonium acetate, HCl and HNO_3
Manganese	Hydroquinone, ammonium phosphate, DTPA and EDTA + ammonium acetate
Boron	Hot water and mannitol + $CaCl_2$
Molybdenum	Ammonium oxalate, ammonium acetate, ammonium fluoride and water

Determination of Zinc, Copper, Iron and Manganese

Ethylenediamine tetraacetic acid (EDTA) with ammonium acetate is commonly used for the extraction of many elements. Diethylenetriamine pentaacetic acid (DTPA) is another common (universal) extractant and it is widely used for the simultaneous extraction of elements such as Zn, Cu, Fe and Mn (Lindsay and Norvell, 1978). Although a specific extractant for an element that has a higher correlation with plant availability may be preferred, the universal or common extractant saves on the cost of chemicals and the time involved in estimation, especially in a service laboratory where a large number of samples need to be analysed in a short period.

The estimation of elements in the extract is done with the help of an AAS. The critical limits for DTPA-extractable micronutrient elements is given in the Table 3.7 (Lindsay and Norvell (1978).

Table 3.7 : Critical limits for DTPA-extractable micronutrient elements

Availability	Micronutrients (ig/g soil)			
	Zn	Cu	Fe	Mn
Very low	0–0.5	0–0.1	0–2	0–0.5
Low	0.5–1	0.1–0.3	2–4	0.5–1.2
Medium	1–3	0.3–0.8	4–6	1.2–3.5
High	3–5	0.8–3	6–10	3.5–6
Very high	> 5	> 3	> 10	> 6

DTPA is an important and widely used chelating agent that combines with free metal ions in the solution to form soluble complexes of elements. To avoid excessive dissolution of $CaCO_3$, which may release occluded micronutrients that are not available to crops in calcareous soils and may give erroneous results, the extractant is buffered in slightly alkaline pH. Triethanolamine (TEA) is used as buffer because it burns cleanly during atomization of extractant solution while estimating on an AAS. The DTPA has a capacity to complex each of the micronutrient cations as 10 times of its atomic weight. The capacity ranges from 550 to 650 mg/kg depending on the micronutrient cations.

Preparation of DTPA 0.005M, 0.01M $CaCl_2.2H_2O$ and 0.1M TEA extractant

- Add 1.967 g of DTPA and 13.3 ml of TEA in 400 ml of distilled water in a 500 ml flask.
- Put 1.47 g of $CaCl_2.2H_2O$ in a separate 1000 ml flask. Add 500 ml of distilled water and shake to dissolve.
- Add DTPA + TEA mixture to the $CaCl_2$ solution and make the volume up to 1 litre. Adjust the pH to 7.3 by using 1M HCl before making the volume.

The extracted elements can be estimated by various methods, including volumetric analysis, spectrometry and atomic absorption spectroscopy. Volumetric methods such as EDTA and $KMnO_4$ titrations are used for estimating Zn and Mn, and Fe, respectively. Copper can be estimated by titration with $Na_2S_2O_3$.

Spectrometric methods are used in the estimation of a specific colour developed because of the presence of an element that forms coloured compounds in the presence of specific chemicals under a definite set of conditions. The colour intensity has to be linear with the concentration of the element in question. The interference caused by any other element has to be eliminated. Such methods are:

- Dithiozone method for Zn
- Orthophenonthroline method for Fe
- Potassium periodate method for Mn
- Carbamate method for Cu.

These methods are generally cumbersome and time-consuming. Therefore, the most commonly employed method is atomic absorption spectrometry. Here, the interference by other elements is almost nil or negligible because the estimation is carried out for an element at a specific emission spectra line. In fact, in atomic absorption spectrometry, traces of one element can be determined accurately in the presence of a high concentration of other elements.

The procedure is based on flame absorption rather than flame emission and on the fact that metal atoms absorb strongly at discrete characteristic wavelengths that coincide with the emission spectra lines of a particular element. The liquid sample is atomized. A hollow cathode lamp (which precedes the atomizer) emits the spectrum of the metal used to make the cathode. This beam traverses the flame and is focused on the entrance slit of a monochromator, which is set to read the intensity of the chosen spectra line. Light with this wavelength is absorbed by the metal in the flame, and the degree of absorption being the function of the concentration of the metal in the flame, the concentration of the atoms in the dissolved material is determined. For elemental analysis, a working curve or a standard curve is prepared by measuring the signal or absorbance of a series of standards of known concentration of the element under estimation. From such a curve, the concentration of the element in the unknown sample is estimated.

Atomic absorption spectroscopy can be applied successfully for estimating Zn, Cu, Fe and Mn. For specific estimation with an AAS, hollow cathode lamps are specific to specific elements are used (Table 3.8).

Table 3.8 : Parameters for estimation of micronutrients using an AAS

Specifications	Zn	Cu	Fe	Mn
Lamp current (mA°)	5	3	7	5
Wavelength (nm)	213.9	324.8	248.3	279.5
Linear range (mg/litre)	0.4–1.5	1.0–5.0	2.0–9.0	1.0–3.6
Slit width (nm)	0.5	0.52	0.2	0.2
Integration time (seconds)	2.0	2.0	2.0	2.0
Flame		Air acetylene		

The software provided with the equipment manual details the operating parameters that are specific to a particular model. Accordingly, the current supply, wavelength of hollow cathode lamp, integration time and anticipated estimation ranges are fixed. Hollow cathode and deuterium lamps need to be aligned properly before starting the equipment. After proper alignment and adjustment, standard curves are prepared to ensure that the concentration of the elements in solutions relates perfectly to the absorbance.

Ready-made standard solutions of 1000 µg/ml or 1mg/ml (1000 ppm) of dependable accuracy are supplied with the AAS and are also available from suppliers of chemical reagents. Where the standard solutions are to be prepared in the laboratory, either metal element foils of 100.percent purity or the standard chemical salts can be used. The details the quantities of chemical required to make 1 litre of standard solution of 100 µg/ml for different elements (Table 3.9).

Table 3.9 : Specifications for preparing micronutrient standard solutions

Element	Concentration of stock Solution (µg/ml)	Salt to be used	Quantity of salt required*(g/litre)*
Zn	100	Zinc sulphate($ZnSO_4.7H_2O$)	0.4398
Cu	100	Copper sulphate ($CuSO_4.5H_2O$)	0.3928
Fe	100	Ferrous sulphate ($FeSO_4.7H_2O$)	0.4964
		or Ferrous ammonium sulphate	0.7028
Mn	100	Manganese sulphate ($MnSO_4.H_2O$)	0.3075

In the case of Zn, Cu and Fe, 1000 μg/ml (1000ppm), standard solutions are preferably prepared by dissolving 1.0 g of pure metal wire and making the volume up to 1 litre as per the method described under each element. The solution is diluted to obtain the required concentration. In the case of Mn, $MnSO_4.H_2O$ is preferred.

Preparation of Standard Curve for Zinc

Reagents Required

- *Standard Zn solution*: Weigh 1.0 g of pure zinc metal in a beaker. Add 20 ml of HCl (1:1). Keep for a few hours, allowing the metal to dissolve completely. Transfer the solution to a 1litre volumetric flask. Make up the volume with glass-distilled water. This is 1000 μg/ml Zn solution. For preparing the standard curve, refer to the 1000 μg/ml solution as solution A. Dilute 1 ml of standard A to 100 ml in order to obtain a 10 μg/ml solution, to be designated standard B.
- *Glass-distilled or demineralized acidified water* of pH 2.5 ± 0.5: Dilute 1 ml of 10 percent sulphuric acid to 1 litre with glass-distilled or mineralized water and adjust the pH to 2.5 with a pH meter using 10 percent H_2SO_4 or NaOH. This solution is called acidified water.
- *Working Zn standard solutions*: Pipette 1, 2, 4, 6, 8 and 10 ml of standard B solution in 50.ml numbered volumetric flasks and make the volume up with DTPA solution to obtain 0.2, 0.4, 0.8, 1.2, 1.6 and 2.0 μg/ml zinc. Stopper the flasks and shake them well. Fresh standards should be prepared every time when a fresh lot of acidified water is prepared.

Procedure

- Flaming the solutions: Atomize the standards on an AAS at a wavelength of 213.8 nm (Zn line of the instrument).
- Prepare a standard curve of known concentrations of Zn solution by plotting the absorbance values on the y-axis against their respective Zn concentration on the x-axis.

Special points to keep in mind

- Weighing must be done on an electronic balance.

- All the glass apparatus to be used should be washed first with dilute hydrochloric acid (1:4) and then with distilled water.
- The pipette should be rinsed with the same solution to be measured.
- The outer surface of the pipette should be wiped with filter paper after use.
- After using the pipette, place it on a clean dry filter paper in order to prevent contamination.

Preparation of Standard Curve for Copper

Reagents required

- *Standard Cu solution*: Weigh 1 g of pure copper wire on a clean watch glass and transfer it to a 1 litre flask. Add 30 ml of HNO_3 (1:1) and make up to the mark by glass-distilled water. Stopper the flask and shake the solution well. This is 1000 μg/ml Cu solution and it should be stored in a clean bottle for further use. Dilute 1 ml of 1 000 μg/ml solution of Cu to 100 ml to obtain 10 μg/ml of standard Cu solution.
- Glass-distilled or demineralized acidified water of pH 2.5 ± 0.5: Same as that for Zn (above).
- *Working Cu standard solutions*: Pipette 2, 3, 4, 5, 6 and 7 ml of 10 μg/ml of standard Cu solution in 50.ml numbered volumetric flasks and make the volume up with DTPA solution to obtain 0.4, 0.6, 0.8, 1.0, 1.2 and 1.4 μg/ml Cu. Stopper the flasks and shake them well. Prepare fresh standards every fortnight.

Procedure

- Flame the standards on an AAS at a wavelength of 324.8 nm (Cu line of the instrument).
- Prepare the standard curve with the known concentration of Cu on the x-axis by plotting against the absorbance value on the y-axis.

Preparation of Standard Curve for Iron

Reagents required

Standard Fe solution: Weigh accurately 1 g of pure iron wire, put it in a beaker, and add about 30 ml of 6M HCl and boil. Transfer it to a 1 litre volumetric flask through a funnel, giving several washings to the beaker and funnel with glass-distilled water. Make the volume up to the mark. Stopper the flask and shake the solution well. This is 1000 mg/ml iron solution. Glass-distilled or demineralized acidified water of pH 2.5 ± 0.5 same as that of Zn (above).

Working Fe standard solutions: Pipette 10 ml of Fe stock solution in a100.ml volumetric flask, and dilute to volume with DTPA solution. This is 100 µg/ml iron solution. Take 2, 4, 8, 12 and 16 ml of 100 µg/ml solution and dilute each to 100 ml to obtain 2, 3, 8, 12 and 16 µg/ml of Fe solution.

Procedure

- Flame the standards on an AAS at a wavelength of 248.3 nm (Fe line of the instrument).
- Prepare the standard curve with the known concentration of Cu on x-axis by plotting against the absorbance value on the y-axis.

Preparation of Standard Curve for Manganese

Reagents required

- *Standard Mn solution*: Weigh 3.0751 g of AR-grade manganese sulphate ($MnSO_4.H_2O$) on a clean watch glass and transfer it to a 1litre flask through a funnel, giving several washings to the watch glass and funnel with acidified water, and make the volume up to the mark. This solution will be 1000 µg/ml Mn. A secondary dilution of 5 ml to 100 ml with acidified water gives a50 µg/ml solution.
- *Glass-distilled or demineralized acidified water* of pH 2.5 ± 0.2: Same as that for Zn (above).
- *Working Mn standard solutions*: The standard curve is prepared by taking lower concentrations of Mn in the range of 0.10 µg/ml. Take 1, 2, 4, 6 and 8 ml of 50 µg/ml solution, and make the volume up with DTPA solution to 50 ml to obtain 1, 2, 4, 6 and 8 µg/ml working standards.

Procedure

- Flame the standards on an AAS at a wavelength of 279.5 nm (Mn line of the instrument).
- Prepare the standard curve with the known concentration of Mn on the x axis by plotting against the absorbance value on the y-axis.

Procedure for Extraction by DTPA

Once standard curves have been prepared, proceed for extraction by DTPA as follows:

- Put 10 g of the soil sample in a 100 ml narrow-mouthed polypropylene bottle.
- Add 20 ml of DTPA extracting solution.
- Stopper the bottle, and shake for 2 hours at room temperature (25°C).
- Filter the content using filter paper No. 1 or No. 42, and collect the filtrate in polypropylene bottles.
- Prepare a blank following all steps except taking a soil sample. The extract so obtained is used for estimation of different micronutrients.

For extraction of a more accurate quantity of an element that has a higher degree of correlation with plant availability, there are element-specific extractants. An extractant standardized/recommended for a given situation in a country may be used. However, the estimation procedure on an AAS remains unchanged.

Method of Estimation on an AAS

Procedure

- Select an element-specific hollow cathode lamp and mount it on the AAS.
- Start the flame.
- Set the instrument at zero by using blank solution.
- Aspirate the standard solutions of different concentrations one by one and record the readings.

- Prepare the standard curve, plotting the concentration of the element concerned and the corresponding absorbance in different standard samples(as described above).
- When the operation is performed accurately, a straight line relationship is obtained between the concentration of the element and the absorbance on the AAS with a correlation coefficient that may be nearly as high as 1.0.
- Aspirate the soil extractant obtained for estimation of the nutrient element in the given soil sample and observe the readings.
- Determine the content of the element in the soil extract by observing its concentration on the standard curve against its absorbance

Calculation

Micronutrient in the sample (mg/kg) = C μg/ml x 2 (dilution factor)

where,

- Dilution factor = 2.0 (soil sample taken = 10.0 g and DTPA used = 20 ml);
- Absorbance reading on AAS of the soil extract being estimated for a particular element = X
- C = concentration of micronutrient as read from the standard curve for the given absorbance (X).

Available Boron

The most commonly used method for available B is hot water extraction of soil as developed by Berger and Truog (1939). A number of modified versions of this method have been proposed but the basic procedure remains the same.

Water-soluble B is the available form of B. It is extracted from the soil by water suspension. In the extract, B can be analysed by colorimetric methods using reagents such as carmine, azomethine-H, and, most recently, by inductively coupled plasma (ICP) and atomic emission spectrometry. However, the colorimetric method is preferable owing to the fact that as B is a non-metal, the use of an AAS for its estimation poses some limitations. The estimation of B includes two steps viz. (i). Extraction and (ii). Estimation.

Extraction procedure

- Put 25 g of soil in a quartz flask or beaker.
- Add about 50 ml of double-distilled water (DDW) and about 0.5 g of activated charcoal.
- Boil the mixture for about 5 minutes, and filter through No. 42 filter paper.

Estimation by AAS

The specifications/relevant parameters for estimation of B on an AAS are:

- Lamp current: 20 m°A
- Wavelength: 249.7 nm
- Linear range: 1.10 µg/ml
- Slit width: 0.2 nm
- Integration time: 2.0 seconds
- Flame: acetylene nitrous oxide.

The software provided with the equipment manual gives the operating parameters that are specific to a particular model. Accordingly, the current supply, wavelength of hollow cathode lamp, integration time and anticipated estimation ranges are fixed. Hollow cathode and deuterium lamps need to be aligned properly before starting the equipment. After proper alignment and adjustment, standard curves are prepared in order to ensure that the concentration of the element in solutions relates perfectly to the absorbance.

Reagents required

- *Standard B solution*: Dissolve 8.819 g of $Na_2B_4O_7.10H_2O$ in warm water. Dilute to 1 litre to obtain 1000 µg/ml B stock solution. Dilute 1 ml of standard to 100 ml to obtain 10µg/ml B.
- *Working standards*: Take 1, 2, 3, 4, 5, 6, 7 and 10 ml of 10 µg/ml solution and dilute each to 50 ml to obtain 0.2, 0.4, 0.6, 0.8, 1.0, 1.2, 1.4 and 2.0µg/ml B.

Procedure

- Atomize the working standards on an AAS using acetylene nitrous oxide as fuel instead of air acetylene fuel (as used for other micronutrients) at a wavelength of 249.7 nm.
- Prepare a standard curve of known concentration of B by plotting the absorbance values on the y-axis against their respective B concentration on the x-axis. Measure the absorbance of the soil sample extract and determine the B content in the soil from the standard curve.

Calculation

Content of B in the sample (mg/kg) = C μg/ml X 2 (dilution factor)

where,

- C = concentration of B in the sample, as read from the standard curve for the given absorbance;
- Dilution factor = 2.0 (soil sample taken = 25 g and water used = 50 ml).

Estimation by Colorimetric Method

The extracted B in the filtered extract is determined by the azomethine-H colorimetric method.

Apparatus required

- An analytical balance;
- A flask or beaker;
- A volumetric flask;
- Some funnels;
- Some No. 42 filter paper;
- A spectrophotometer.

Reagents required

- *Azomethine-H*: Dissolve 0.45 g of azomethine-H and 1.0 g of L-ascorbic acid in about 100 ml of deionized or double-distilled water. If the solution is not clear, it should be heated gently in a water-bath or under a hot water tap at about 30°C until it dissolves. Every week, a fresh solution should be prepared and kept in a refrigerator.

- *Buffer solution*: Dissolve 250 g of ammonium acetate in 500 ml of deionizedor double-distilled water, and adjust the pH to about 5.5 by adding slowly about 100 ml of glacial acetic acid, stirring continuously.
- *EDTA solution* (0.025 M): Dissolve 9.3 g of EDTA in deionized or double distilled water, and make the volume up to 1 litre.
- *Standard stock solution*: Dissolve 0.8819 g of $Na_2B_4O_7.10H_2O$ (AR-grade) in a small volume of deionized water, and make the volume up to 1000 ml to obtain a stock solution of 100 μg B/ml.
- Working standard solution: Put 5 ml of stock solution in a 100 ml volumetric flask and dilute it to the mark. This solution contains 5 μg B/ml.

Procedure

- Put 5 ml of the clear filtered extract in a 25ml volumetric flask and add 2 ml of buffer solution, 2 ml of EDTA solution and 2 ml of azomethine-H solution.
- Mix the contents thoroughly after the addition of each reagent.
- Let the solution stand for 1 hour to allow colour development. Then, make the volume up to the mark.
- Measure the intensity of colour at 420 nm. The colour thus developed has been found to be stable for 3 - 4 hours.
- *Preparation of the standard curve*: Put 0, 0.25, 0.50, 1.0, 2.0 and 4.0 ml of 5 μg B/ml solution (working standard) in a series of 25 ml volumetric flasks. Add 2 ml each of buffer reagent, EDTA solution and azomethine-H solution. Mix the contents after each addition and allow to stand at room temperature for 30 minutes. Make the volume up to 25 ml with deionized or double-distilled water, and measure absorbance at 420 nm. This will give reading for standard solution with B concentration of 0, 0.05, 0.10, 0.20, 0.40 and 0.80 μg B/ml.

Calculation

Content of B in the soil (µg/g or mg/kg) = C x dilution factor (10)

Where,

- C (µg/ml) = concentration of B as read from the standard curve against the absorbance reading of the soil solution on the spectrophotometer;
- Dilution factor = 10, which is calculated as follows:

  Weight of the soil taken = 25 g;

  Volume of extractant (water) added = 50 ml;

  First dilution = 2 times;

  Volume of the filtrate taken = 5 ml;

  Final volume of filtrate after colour development = 25 ml;

  Second dilution = 5 times;

  Total dilution = 2 x 5 = 10 times.

Important points to keep in mind

- The use of azomethine-H is an improvement over that of carmine, quinalizarin and curcumin because the procedure involving this chemical does not require the use of concentrated acid.
- The amount of charcoal added may vary with the OM content of the soil, and it should be just sufficient to produce a colourless extract after 5 minutes of boiling on a hotplate. Excess amounts of charcoal can result in a loss of extractable B from soils.

Available Molybdenum

Molybdenum is a rare element in soils, and it is present only in very small amounts in igneous and sedimentary rocks. The major inorganic source of Mo is molybdenite (MoS_2). The total Mo content in soils is perhaps the lowest of all the micronutrient elements.

In the soil solution, Mo exists mainly as $HMoO_4$ ion under acidic condition, and as MoO_{42}- ion under neutral to alkaline conditions. Because of the anionic nature of Mo, its anions will not be attracted much by the negatively charged colloids, and therefore, tend to be leached from the soils in humid region. Molybdenum can be toxic owing to greater solubility in alkali soils of the arid and semi-arid regions, and deficient in acid soils of the humid regions. In plants, a deficiency of Mo is common at levels of 0.1 µg/g soil or less. Molybdenum toxicity (molybdenosis) is common where cattle graze forage plants with 10 - 20 µg Mo/g.

The extraction of Mo usually uses ammonium acetate and/or ammoniumoxalate. Estimations can be done both by the AAS and colorimetric methods, with preference for the latter owing to the formation of oxide in the flame in the case of estimation by AAS. Ammonium oxalate is considered a better extractant. However, for estimation on an AAS, ammonium acetate is preferred as the oxalates pose a limitation on the AAS unless removed by digesting with di-acid (below).

Estimation by AAS

The specifications/relevant parameters for estimation of Mo on an AAS are:

- Lamp current: 7m AU
- Wavelength: 313.3 nm;
- Linear range: 1.4µg/ml;
- Slit width: 0.2 nm;
- Integration time: 2.0 seconds;
- Flame: acetylene nitrous oxide.

The software provided with the equipment manual gives the operating parameters that are specific to a particular model. Accordingly, the current supply, wavelength of hollow cathode lamp, integration time and anticipated estimation ranges are fixed. Hollow cathode and deuterium lamps need to be aligned properly before starting the equipment. After proper alignment and adjustment, standard curves are prepared in order to ensure that the concentration of the element in solutions relates perfectly to the absorbance.

Apparatus required

- A centrifuge and some 50 ml centrifuge tubes
- An automatic shaker
- An AAS.

Reagents required

- Ammonium acetate solution (NH_4OAc) 1.0M: Dissolve 77.09 g of ammoniumacetate in 1 litre of distilled water, and adjust the pH to 7.0.
- Glass-distilled acidified water of pH 2.5: Same as that for Zn estimation (above).
- Standard molybdenum solution: Dissolve 0.15 g of MoO_3 (molybdenumtrioxide) in 100 ml of 0.1M NaOH. Dilute to 1 litre to obtain 100 μg/ml Mo stock solution. Dilute 10 ml of the standard to 100 ml to obtain 10μg/mlMo.
- Working standard solutions: Take 1, 2, 3, 4, 5, 6, 7 and 10 ml of 10 μg/ml Mo standard solution and dilute each to 50 ml. This will give 0.2, 0.4, 0.6, 0.8, 1.0, 1.2, 1.4 and 2.0 μg/ml Mo, respectively.

Procedure

1. Weigh accurately 5 g of soil, and transfer it to a 50ml centrifuge tube.
2. Add 33 ml of 1M ammonium acetate solution to the tube, stopper, and shake in a mechanical shaker for 5 minutes.
3. Centrifuge at 2 000 rpm for 5 minutes or until the supernatant is clear.
4. Decant the solution into a 100.ml volumetric flask.
5. Repeat steps 2 - 4.
6. Make up the volume to 100 ml with ammonium acetate.
7. Atomize the working standards on an AAS at a wavelength of 313.5 nm.
8. Prepare a standard curve of known concentration of Mo by plotting the absorbance values on the y-axis against their respective Mo concentration on the x-axis.
9. Measure the absorbance of the soil sample extract and determine the Mo content in the soil from the standard curve.

Calculation

Content of Mo in the sample (mg/kg) = C μg/ml x 20 (dilution factor).

Where,

- C = concentration of Mo in the sample, as read from the standard curve for the given absorbance
- Dilution factor = 20.0 (soil sample taken = 5 g and volume made to 100 ml).

Estimation by Colorimetric Method

Apparatus required

- A spectrophotometer
- A hotplate
- A refrigerator
- A water-bath.

Reagents required

- *50 % potassium iodide solution*: Dissolve 50 g in 100 ml of DDW.
- *50 % ascorbic acid solution*: Dissolve 50 g in 100 ml of DDW.
- *10% sodium hydroxide solution*: Dissolve 10 g of NaOH in 100 ml of DDW.
- *10% thiourea solution*: Dissolve 10 g in 100 ml of DDW and filter.
- *Toluene-3, 4-dithiol solution* (commonly called dithiol): Place 1.0 g of AR grade melted dithiol (51°C) in a 250 ml glass beaker. Add 100 ml of the 10 percent NaOH solution and warm the content up to 51°C with frequent stirring for 15 minutes. Add 1.8 ml of thioglycolic acid, and store in a refrigerator (prepare a fresh solution on the same day of use).
- *10 % tartaric acid*: Dissolve 10 g in 100 ml of DDW (prepare a fresh solution on the same day of use).
- Iso-amyl acetate Ethyl alcohol.
- *Ferrous ammonium sulphate solution*: Dissolve 63 g of the salt in about 500 ml of DDW and then make the volume up to 1 litre.

- Nitric-perchloric acid mixture (4:1).
- *Extracting reagent*: Dissolve 24.9 g of AR-grade ammonium oxalate and 12.6 g of oxalic acid in water, and make the volume up to 1 litre.
- *Standard stock solution* (100 µg/ml Mo): Dissolve 0.150 g of AR-grade
- MoO_3 in 100 ml of 0.1M NaOH, make slightly acidic with dilute HCl, and make the volume up to 1 litre.
- Working standard solution (1µg/ml Mo): Dilute 10 ml of the stock solution to 1 litre.

Procedure

- Weigh 25 g of air-dry soil sample in a 500 ml conical flask. Add 250 ml of the extracting solution (1:10 ratio) and shake for 10 hours.
- Filter through No. 50 filter paper. Collect 200 ml of the clear filtrate in a 250ml glass beaker and evaporate to dryness in a water-bath.
- Heat the contents in the beaker at 500°C in a furnace for 5 hours to destroy OM and oxalates. Keep overnight.
- Digest the contents with 5 ml of $HNO_3.HClO_4$ mixture (4:1), followed by10 ml of 4M H_2SO_4 and then with H_2O_2, each time bringing to dryness.
- Add 10 ml of 0.1M HCl and filter. Wash the filter paper, first with 10 ml of 0.1M HCl and then with 10 ml of DDW, until the volume of the filtrate is 100 ml.
- Run a blank side by side (without soil).
- Put 50 ml of the filtrate in 250 ml separatory funnels, add 0.25 ml of ferrous ammonium sulphate solution and 20 ml of DDW, and shake vigorously.
- Add excess of potassium iodide solution and clear the liberated iodine by adding ascorbic acid drop by drop while shaking vigorously.
- Add 1 ml of tartaric acid and 2 ml of thiourea solution, and shake vigorously.
- Add 5 drops of dithiol solution, and allow the mixture to stand for 30 minutes.

- Add 10 ml of iso-amyl acetate, and separate out the contents (green colour) in colorimeter tubes/cuvettes.
- Read the colour intensity at 680 nm (red filter).
- Preparation of standard curve: Measure 0, 2, 5, 10, 15 and 20 ml of the working standard Mo solution containing 1 mg/litre Mo in a series of 250 ml separatory funnels. Proceed for colour development as described above for sample aliquots. Read the colour intensity and prepare the standard curve by plotting Mo concentration against readings.

Calculation

Content of Mo in the soil (μg/g or mg/kg) = C μg/ml x dilution factor (0.5)

Where,

- C (μg/ml) = concentration of Mo as read from the standard curve against the absorbance reading of the soil solution on the spectrophotometer
- Dilution factor = 0.5, which is calculated as follows

  Weight of the soil taken = 25 g; Volume of extract = 250 ml
  First dilution = 10 times

  Volume of the filtrate taken = 200 ml

  Filtrate digested (concentrated) to 100 ml.

  Volume of concentrated filtrate taken = 50 ml

  Second dilution = 0.25 times

  Volume of solvent (iso-amyl acetate) used for extraction = 10 ml

  Third dilution (50 ml extracted by 10 ml) = 0.2 times

  Total dilution = 10 x 0.25 x 0.2 = 0.5 times.

4

Methods for Plant Analysis

Introduction and Scope

Plant and soil testing enable scientific assessment of the needs of the plant for nutrient elements and of the capacity of the soil to supply them. The nutrient elements enter the plant in ionic form from the soil solution. Ion transport to the root surface may take place through ion diffusion and bulk transport (mass flow). Mass flow is the sweeping along of ions as water moves to the root. It is particularly important for ions that are not absorbed on soil colloids such as nitrates and sulphates. Because of mass flow, a plant deficient in N can extract all the nitrates from the soil. Potassium, phosphate and the micronutrient cations are absorbed on soil colloids with various degrees of affinity and are greatly retarded in movement with the soil water. Diffusion (movement along a concentration gradient) is the main mode of transport from the solid phase to the root surface for these non-mobile ions. There is also a possibility that some of them are absorbed by a direct exchange of an ion, usually hydrogen, between the root surface and ions absorbed on soil colloids. Most ions are sorbed by the root against a concentration gradient and, thus, the process involves the use of metabolic energy. The fact that nutrient uptake is an active process explains some of its peculiarities. Plants not only accumulate nutrients against a concentration gradient, they are also able to select from the nutrients at the root surface according to their requirements (preferential uptake).

The understanding of the mechanism of nutrient uptake by plants explains why a chemical solvent for non-mobile elements does not extract the same amount of nutrient as does the root, and any attempt to match the value is futile. The root can contact only a part of the soil, while a chemical solvent can contact all but some internal surfaces. Plant analysis generally provides more current plant-based information than soil testing but it is more costly and entails more effort in terms of sampling, sample handling and analysis. Ideally, both tools should be used as they complement each other.

Unlike soil analysis where the amounts of available nutrients are of importance, in plant analysis, the total content of nutrients is relevant. The available nutrients taken from the soil or fertilizer source are assimilated by the plants and, thus, they become part of crop composition.

Knowledge of nutrient concentration in growing plants can serve as a tool for correcting any deficiencies where carried out early enough to safeguard yield. The nutrient uptake by a healthy crop, which has attained its growth and yield potential, is taken as the effective requirement for the crop. It can also be used to evaluate the efficacy of a recent application. The information it provides can help to plan nutrient application in subsequent crops on that field or to compute nutrient removals in relation to productivity and nutrient balance sheets.

Although the nutrient contents vary from one species to another, the composition of a particular species is generally considered to be indicative under optimal nutrient supply and growth conditions. General guidelines of optimal nutrient content in crops can be used for understanding the probable deficiency of nutrients (Table 4.1).

Whole plant analysis is conducted in order to determine the total nutrient uptake (which is usually carried out on the shoot). For plant analysis to be meaningful as a diagnostic tool, the collection of particular plant parts (tissue) at the right stage of growth for analysis is very important. Plant leaves are considered the focus of physiological activities. The concentrations of leaf nutrients appear to reflect changes in mineral nutrition. As an example, Table 4.2 shows the specific parts, as identified by various researchers, to be sampled from different plant species. Their concentrations are expected to reflect the true nutrient status of a growing plant (deficiency, sufficiency or excess).

Table 4.1 : General sufficiency/ optimal range of nutrients in plants

Nutrients	Sufficiency/optimal range (%)
Macro Nutrients	
N	2.0-5.0
P	0.2-0.5
K	1.0-5.0
Ca	0.1 -1.0
Mg	0.1 -0.4
S	0.1-1.3
Micro-nutrients	**(ppm)**
Zn	20-100
Fe	50-250
Mn	20-300
Cu	5-20
Mo	0.1-0.5
B	10-100

Table 4.2 : Typical plant parts suggested for analysis

Crop	Part to be sampled with age or growth stage
Wheat	Flag-leaf, before head emergence
Rice	3rd leaf from apex, at tillering
Maize	Ear leaf before tasselling
Barley	Flag -leaf at head emergence
Pulses	Recently matured leaf at bloom initiation
Groundnut	Recently matured leaf at maximum tillering stage
Soya bean	3rd leaf from top, 2 months after planting
Cotton	Petiole, 4th leaf from apex at imitation of flowering
Sugar cane	3rd leaf from top, 3-5 months after planting
Tea	3rd leaf from tip of young shoots
Potato	Most recent, fully developed leaf (half-grown)
Tomato	Leaves adjacent to inflorescence (mid-bloom)
Onion	Top non-white portion (1/3 to 1/2 grown)
Beans	Uppermost, fully developed leaves
Pea	Leaflets from most recent, fully developed leaves, atfirst bloom
Apple, Pear	Leaves from middle of terminal shoot growth, 8–12weeks after full bloom, 2–4 weeks after formation ofterminal buds in bearing trees

Contd.

Cherry	Fully expanded leaves, mid-shoot current growth in July–August
Peach	Mid-shoot leaves, fruiting or non-fruiting spurs, midsummer leaves
Strawberry	Fully expanded matured leaf without petiole, at peak or harvest period
Banana	Petiole of 3rd open leaf from apex, 4 months after planting
Papaya	3–5-month old leaves from new flush
Pineapple	Middle third portion of white basal portion of 4th leaf from apex, at 4–6-month stage

The interpretation of plant analysis data is usually based on the total concentrations of nutrients in the dry matter of leaves or other suitable plant parts compared with standard values of "critical nutrient concentrations" ("critical values"). Between the nutrient concentrations of the deficiency range and those of adequate supply, there is the critical nutrient range. The critical level is that level of concentration of a nutrient in the plant that is likely to result in 90 percent of the maximum yields. The main advantage of critical values, once properly established, is their wide applicability for the same crop. Their disadvantage is that they only provide yes or no type of information and do not cover the entire range over which nutrient supplies need to be managed. Table 4.3 presents some critical values for a range of crops.

Table 4.3 : Critical nutrient concentrations for 90-percent yield for various crops

Element	Wheat & Rice	Oilseed rape	Sugarcane	Alfalfa	Grass*	Citrus
N (%)	3.0	3.5	1.5	3.5	3.0	2.5
P (%)	0.25	0.3	0.2	0.25	0.4	0.15
K (%)	2.5	2.5	1.5	2.0	2.5	1.0
Mg (%)	0.15	0.2	0.12	0.25	0.2	0.2
S (%)	0.15	0.5	0.15	0.3	0.2	0.15
Mn (µg/g)	30.0	30.0	20.0	30.0	60.0	25.0
Zn (µg/g)	20.0	20.0	15.0	15.0	50.0	20.0
Cu (µg/g)	5.0	5.0	3.0	5.0	8.0	5.0
B (µg/g)	6.0	25.0	1.5	25.0	6.0	25.0
Mo (µg/g)	0.3	0.3	0.1	0.2	0.3	0.2

* Not critical but optimal concentrations for cows producing 15 litres of milk per day.

Critical values determine whether immediate action such as foliar spraying is needed to correct a deficiency. Conclusions can also be drawn as to whether the amount of fertilizer applied at sowing time was sufficient or should be increased for the next crop. Where the concentration is in the toxicity range, special counter measures are required but no application is called for. For some nutrients, e.g. Ca and Fe, the "active" (mobile) nutrient content of plants should be considered because immobilization can make the total concentrations misleading. The nutrient concentrations of green (fresh) material or of plant sap can be used as a suitable basis for interpretation in some situations.

Collection and Preparation of Plant Sample for Analysis

Representative sampling should be done of specific plant parts at the growth stage that is most closely associated with critical values as provided by research data. Sampling criteria and procedures for individual samples are similar to those of soil testing in that the sample should be representative of the field. A predetermined, representative number of plants from a homogenous sampling unit contribute to the composition of bulk sample. The composite sample should be about 200-500g fresh weight. Factors such as the desired precision of recommendation, the nature of the crop (seasonal or perennial) and economic considerations should be taken into account. The following procedure is suggested:

- For analysis of seasonal crop plants, pick a few representative plants at random from each plot. Remove the shoot (aerial part) with the help of a sharp stainless steel cutter for whole shoot analysis or the desired part for analysis of specific plant parts.
- If roots are to be included, uproot the whole plant carefully from wet soil, retaining even the fine/active roots. Dip the plant roots gently in water several times to remove adhering soil.
- Wash with water several times.
- Wash the samples with about 0.2 percent detergent solution to remove the waxy/greasy coating on the leaf surface.
- Wash with 0.1M HCl followed by thorough washing with plenty of water. Give a final wash with distilled water.
- Wash with DDW if micronutrient analysis is to be carried out.
- Soak to dry with tissue paper.
- Air-dry the samples on a perfectly clean surface at room temperature for at least 2-3 days in a dust-free atmosphere.

- Put the samples in an oven, and dry at 70^0C for 48 hours.
- Grind the samples in an electric stainless steel mill using a 0.5.mm sieve. Clean the cup and blades of the grinding mill before each sample.
- Put the samples back in the oven, and dry again for constant weight. Store in well-stoppered plastic or glass bottles or in paper bags for analysis.

Digestion of Plant Tissue

The plant sample can be brought into solution form through digestion with acids that dissolve the solid plant parts and bring the plant nutrient in liquid form for estimation. This is called wet digestion. The plant sample can also be heated at high temperatures to destroy OM, and the ash so obtained can be dissolved in acids to bring the sample into liquid form for estimation. This method is called dry ashing.

Wet digestion

A mixture of HNO_3, H_2SO_4 and $HClO_4$ in the ratio of 9:4:1 is used for sample digestion. It is known as tri-acid digestion. When only two acids, viz. HNO_3 and$HClO_4$ (9:4), are used, it is known as di-acid digestion. Perchloric acid ($HClO_4$) is used primarily for increasing the efficiency of oxidation of the sample as $HClO_4$ dissociates into nascent chlorine and oxygen at high temperature, which increases the rate of oxidation or the digestion of the sample. At times, perchloric acid causes an explosion when it comes into direct contact with the plant sample. Therefore, pre-digestion of the sample with HNO3 is considered desirable, followed by treatment with the di-acid or tri-acid mixture.

Generally, 1 g of ground plant sample is taken for analysis. It is placed in a 100 ml volumetric flask, and 10 ml of acid mixture is added and the contents are mixed by swirling. The flask is placed on a hotplate in the fumehood and heated, starting at 80-90^0C and then the temperature is raised to about 150-200^0C. Heating continues until the production of red NO_2 fumes ceases. The contents are further heated until the volume is reduced to 3-4 ml and becomes colourless, but it should not be dried. After cooling the contents, the volume is made up with the distilled water and filtered through No. 1 filter paper. This solution is used for nutrient estimation.

Di-acid digestion is used for determination of most of the elements (P, K, Ca, Mg, S, Fe, Mn, Zn and Cu). However, tri-acid digestion is preferred for P and K estimations. It cannot be used for S estimation owing to the presence of H_2SO_4. Sulphuric acid also contains many trace elements as contaminants. Therefore, micronutrients should preferably be estimated through di-acid digestion or by using a dry-ash sample solution.

Wet digestion can also be accomplished by using H_2O_2 to destroy OM followed by digestion with H_2SO_4 to dissolve the sample. In such digestion, N estimation can be carried out as per the Kjeldahl method of total N estimation as described in Chapter III.

Dry ashing

High-temperature oxidation destroys the OM. The plant sample is ashed at 500-600^{0}C by placing a suitable weight (0.5 - 1.0 g) of the sample in a silica crucible and heating it in a muffle furnace for 4 - 6 hours. The ash residue is dissolved in dilute HNO_3 filtered through acid-washed filter paper in a 100ml volumetric flask, and the volume is made up to the mark. The estimation of K, Ca, Mg and micronutrients (including B and Mo) is carried out in the dry-ashed sample solution.

Dry ashing is a preferred method for the analysis of P, K, Ca, Mg and trace elements, especially B and Mo. It is a relatively simple method and requires very little operational attention. It does not involve the use of perchloric acid. It also avoids the use of boiling acids. However, at times, incomplete recovery of some elements may be caused by:

- Volatilization of elements such as S (also Se and halogens). To avoid loss of S, $Mg(NO_3)_2$ should be mixed with plant samples while dry ashing.
- Retention of elements such as Cu on the walls of silica crucibles. Hence, platinum crucible should be used.
- Formation of compounds that are not completely soluble in the acid used for digestion.

A blank should always be carried out to account for any contamination through the acids used in the digestion.

Analytical Methods for Plant Tissue Analysis

Total Nitrogen Estimation

Total N in plants is estimated by the Kjeldahl method as described in the Chapter 3. In plants, N is present in protein form, and digestion of the sample with H_2SO_4 containing digestion mixture (10 parts potassium sulphate and 1 part copper sulphate) is required for estimation. Sample size may be 0.5 - 1.0 g depending on the type of crop and the plant part. The procedure for sample digestion, distillation and estimation of N is the same as for total N estimation in soil.

Phosphorus Estimation

The estimation of total P can be carried out by any of the following methods:

- Gravimetric quinolinium phosphomolybdate
- Gravimetric ammonium phosphomolybdate
- Volumetric quinolinium phosphomolybdate
- Volumetric ammonium phosphomolybdate and
- Spectrophotometric vanadium phosphomolybdate.

The selection of a method depends on a number of factors, the important ones are:

- Speed
- Accuracy
- Reproducibility of results
- Cost of chemicals and
- Applicability in the presence of most commonly occurring/ interfering cations and anions.

Some of these factors are affected by the quantity and the form of the element to be estimated. Generally, gravimetric methods (which are quite accurate) can be used when the quantity of the element in the sample is quite large.

Therefore, the gravimetric quinolinium phosphomolybdate method is widely used for P estimation in fertilizer samples. The spectrophotometric vanadiumphosphomolybdate method is used for P estimation in plant samples where the content is small. Similarly, volumetric methods are also considered suitable for P estimation in plant samples.

Spectrophotometric Vanadium Phosphomolybdate Method

The P content of the plant sample is converted to orthophosphates by digestion with an acid mixture (di-acid or tri-acid). The digested sample is used for P estimation. When orthophosphates are made to react with molybdate and vanadate, a yellow-coloured vanadomolybdo phosphoric heteropoly complex is formed.

The intensity of the yellow colour is directly proportional to the concentration of P present in the sample, which can be read on the spectrophotometer.

Apparatus required

- A digestion block
- A spectrophotometer &
- Some beakers/flasks.

Reagents required

- Ammonium molybdate
- *Ammonium vanadate in HNO_3* (vanadomolybdate): Dissolve 22.5 g of $(NH_4)_6MO_7O_2.4H_2O$ in 400 ml of distilled water. Dissolve1.25 g of ammonium vanadate in 300 ml of boiling distilled water. Add the vanadate solution to the molybdate solution and cool to room temperature. Add 250 ml of concentrated HNO_3 and dilute to 1 litre.
- *Standard phosphate solution*: Dissolve 0.2195 g of analytical-grade $KH_2PO_4$and dilute to 1 litre. This solution contains 50 µg P/ ml.

Procedure

- *Preparation of the standard curve*: Put 0, 1, 2, 3, 4, 5 and 10 ml of standard solution (50 µg P/ml) in 50ml volumetric flasks. Add 10 ml of vanadomolybdate reagent to each flask and make up the volume. The P contents in these flasks are 0, 1, 2, 3, 4, 5 and 10 µg P/ml, respectively. The standard curve is prepared by measuring these concentrations on aspectrophotometer (420nm) and recording the corresponding absorbance.
- Take 1 g of plant sample and digest as per the wet digestion method, and make the volume up to 100 ml.
- Put 5 ml of digest in a 50-ml volumetric flask, and add 10 ml of vanadomolybdate reagent.
- Make up the volume with distilled water, and shake thoroughly. Keep for 30 minutes.

- A yellow colour develops which is stable for days and is read at 420 nm on spectrophotometer.
- For the observed absorbance, determine the P content from the standard curve.

Calculation

P content (μg) in 1 g of sample = C x df

P content (g) in 100 g sample (% P) = (C x df x 100 x C)/1000000

P content (g) in 100 g sample (% P) = (C x 1000 x 100)/1000000

= C/10

Where,

- C = concentration of P (μg /ml) as read from the standard curve;
- df = dilution factor, which is 100 x 10 = 1000, as calculated below:
  - 1 g of sample made to 100 ml (100 times)
  - 5 ml of sample solution made to 50 ml (10 times)
  - 1000000 = factor for converting μg to g.

Potassium Estimation by AAS

Potassium estimation can be done on a flame photometer (see Section 3.6.11), an AAS or by the volumetric sodium tetraphenyl boron method. In a soil/plant analysis laboratory, the use of an AAS is very common and a large number of elements are estimated using this equipment. The acid-digested or dry-ashed plant sample is used for determining K.

Apparatus

- An AAS
- Some volumetric flasks.

Reagents

- Di-acid/tri-acid digestion mixture.
- *KCl (AR-grade) standard solution*: Dissolve 1.908 g of pure KCl in 1 litre of distilled water. This solution contains 1 mg K/ml.

Take 100 ml of this solution and dilute to 1 litre. This will give 100 µg K/ml as stock solution.

- *KCl working standard solution*: Put 5, 10, 15 and 20 ml of stock solution in100.ml volumetric flasks. Make up the volume. This will give 5, 10, 15 and 20 µg K/ml, respectively.

Procedure

- Set up the AAS and standardize. The relevant parameters for K estimation on an AAS are:
  - Lamp current = 6mA^0
  - Wavelength = 766.5 nm
  - Linear range = 0.4-1.5 µg /ml
  - Slit width = 0.5 nm
  - Integration time = 2 seconds
  - Flame = air acetylene.
- Preparation of the standard curve: Prepare the standard curve using 0, 5, 10, 15 and 20 µgK/ml. The curve will show a linear relationship between the concentration of K and absorbance on a specific wavelength as read from the AAS.
- Acid-digest 1 g of plant sample and make up to 100 ml. Keep the sample for estimation in the range 5-10 mgK/kg (5-10 µgK/ml) by further diluting as appropriate.
- Prepare a blank in the same way without adding plant digested material.
- Take an aliquot of 5 ml for estimation and make up to 100 ml. Atomize on the calibrated AAS, on which the standard curve has also been prepared.
- Record the absorbance against each sample.
- From the standard curve, note the concentration of K for the particular absorbance observed for the sample.

Calculation

K content (µg) in 1 g of sample = C x df

K content (g) in 100 g sample (% K) = (C x df x 100)/1000000

= (C x 2000 x 100)/1000000

= C/5

where,

- C = concentration of K (μg/ml) as read from the standard curve
- df = dilution factor, which is 100 x 20 = 2000, as calculated below:
  - 1 g of sample made to 100 ml (100 times)
  - 5 ml of sample solution made to 100 ml (20 times)
  - 1000000 = factor for converting μg to g.

Sulphur Estimation

As dry ashing leads to volatilization loss of S present in the organic combination, and the wet oxidation based on tri-acid mixture includes H_2SO_4, these two methods cannot be used for S determination in plant samples. Therefore, di-acid (HNO_3-$HClO_4$) digestion is used. The turbidimetric method as described for soil. The method for S analysis is given in the Chapter 3 recommended for S analysis of plant samples too. In soils, it is the available S, while in plants; it is the total S, which is brought into solution by di-acid mixture digestion.

Apparatus

- A spectrophotometer
- A mechanical shaker
- Some volumetric flasks.

Reagents

The reagents required are the same as given for S estimation in soil (Chapter 3), except monocalcium phosphate extracting solution.

Procedure

- *Preparation of the standard curve*: Same as for S estimation in soil.
- Digest 1 g of plant sample in di-acid and make the volume up to 100 ml.
- Transfer 10 ml of the aliquot to a 100 ml volumetric flask.
- Add 1 g of sieved $BaCl_2$ and shake for 1 minute.

- Add 1 ml of gum acacia acetic acid solution, make the volume up to the mark and shake for 1 minute.
- Run a blank in an identical manner.
- Measure the turbidity 25-30 minutes after the precipitation at 440nm.
- Read the S content in the sample from the standard curve against the similar absorbance as noted for the sample.

Calculation

S content (µg) in 1 g of sample = C x df

S content (g) in 100 g sample (%S) = (C x df x 100)/1000 000

= (C x 1000 x 100)/ 1000 000

= C /10

where,

- C = concentration of S (µg/ml) as read from the standard curve
- df = dilution factor, which is 100 x 10 = 1000, as calculated below:
  - 1g of sample made to 100 ml (100 times)
  - 10 ml of sample solution made to 100 ml (10 times).
  - 1000000 = factor for converting µg to g.

Calcium Estimation

Estimation by AAS is described here. However, Ca estimation in the acid digest can also be done by the EDTA titration method (Chapter 3).

Apparatus

- An AAS
- Some volumetric flasks
- A fumehood
- A hotplate
- A muffle furnace (when dry ashing has to be done).

Reagents

Standard Ca solution: Take 0.2247 g of primary standard $CaCO_3$ and add 5 ml of deionized water. Add about 10 ml of HCl to ensure complete dissolution of $CaCO_3$. Dilute to 1 litre with deionized water. This will give Ca solution of 100 µg Ca/ml. Dilute 10 ml of this solution to 100 ml to obtain 10 µg Ca/ml.

Procedure

- Take 1 g of prepared plant sample. Digest in di-acid, and make the volume up to 100 ml
- Dilute the sample solution to 10.20 times depending on expected content of Ca, which can be estimated from the standard curve prepared for the purpose
- Set up and calibrate the AAS using the relevant parameters:
  - Lamp current = 10 mA^0
  - Wavelength = 422.7nm
  - Linear range = 1- 4µg /ml
  - Slit width = 0.5nm;
  - Integration time = 2 seconds
  - Flame = nitrous oxide acetylene.
- After setting the AAS, atomize the standard solutions of different concentrations of Ca and record the absorbance for the respective concentrations of Ca. Plot the concentration of Ca on the x-axis and the corresponding absorbance on the y-axis in order to prepare the standard curve.
- Put 5ml of the sample solution in a 100 ml volumetric flask and make up the volume, atomize, and observe the absorbance. Note the corresponding concentration for the absorbance recorded that represents the content of Cain the sample solution.

Calculation

Ca content (µg) in 1 g of sample = C x df

Ca content (g) in 100 g sample (% Ca) = (C x df x 100)/1000 000

= (C x 2000 x 100)/ 1000 000

= C/5

where

- C = concentration of Ca (μg /ml) as read from the standard curve;
- df = dilution factor, which is 100 x 20 = 2000, as calculated below:
  - 1 g of sample made to 100 ml (100 times)
  - 5 ml of sample solution made to 100 ml (20 times).
  - 1 000 000 = factor for converting μg to g.

Magnesium Estimation by AAS

Though Mg is estimated by AAS, the acid digest can be done by the EDTA titration method.

Apparatus

- An AAS and some volumetric flasks.

Reagents

- *Standard Mg solution*: Dissolve 10.141 g of $MgSO_4.7H_2O$ in 250 ml of deionized water, and make the volume up to 1 litre. This will give 1 000 μg Mg/ml solution.
- Under this procedure, the preparation of the standard curve, the estimation and the calculation procedure are the same as described for Ca estimation (above). The relevant parameters for estimation by AAS are:
  - Lamp current = 3 mA^0
  - Wavelength = 285.2nm
  - Linear range = 0 - 0.5μg /ml
  - Slit width = 0.5nm
  - Integration time = 2seconds
  - Flame = air acetylene.

Procedure

The procedure for Mg estimation is given the Chapter 3 (methods for soil analysis).

Micronutrients Estimation by AAS

The estimation of Zn, Mn, Cu, Fe, B and Mo can be done in the same manner as the estimations of K, Ca and Mg (above) using an AAS. However, for B and Mo, chemical methods are preferred, which have been described in Chapter 3. The preparation of the standard curve for each of these metal elements is different and full descriptions are given in Chapter 3. In brief, they are:

- **Zn**: 1 g of pure zinc dissolved in 20 ml of HCl (1:1) and diluted to 1 000 ml gives 1 mg/ml/Zn stock solution. Working solutions can be obtained by diluting the stock solution from 100 to 1000 times to obtain 10µg to1 µg /ml.
- **Fe**: 1 g of pure iron wire is dissolved in 30 ml of HCl (1:1) and diluted to1000 ml to obtain 1 mg/ml of standard Fe. By diluting further, a working solution of a different concentration is obtained.
- **Mn** and **Cu**: Standard Mn and Cu solutions are prepared by dissolving 1 g each of pure Mn and Cu metal in 30 ml of HCl (1:1) and making the volume up to 1 000 ml. It will give 1 mg/ml Mn and Cu solutions. Further dilutions can be done to obtain working solutions.
- **B**: Dissolve 8.819 g of $Na_2B_4O_7.10H_2O$ in warm water. Dilute to 1 litre to obtain 1 mg/ml B stock solution. Dilute further for working solutions and preparation of standard curve.
- **Mo**: Dissolve 0.15 g of MoO_3 in 100 ml of 0.1M NaOH. Dilute to 1 litre to obtain 1000 µg /ml or 1 mg/ml of Mo stock solution. Dilute further for working solutions and preparation of standard curve.

The list of parameters of different hollow cathode lamps and the fuel to be used for estimation of micronutrients is given below in the Table 4.4.

Table 4.4 : Parameters for micronutrient estimation by AAS

Element	Wave length (nm)	Flame	Approximate working range of standard (μg /ml)
Zn	213.8	Air acetylene	0.4–1.5
Fe	248.3	Air acetylene	2.0–9.0
Mn	279.5	Air acetylene	1.0–3.6
Cu	324.7	Air acetylene	1.0–5.0
B	249.7	Nitrous oxide acetylene	1–4
Mo	313.3	Nitrous oxide acetylene	1–4

The estimation on an AAS is carried out first by making the standard curve for each element and then estimating the plant sample digested in acid. The quantity of the element in the sample is calculated by multiplying the concentration observed from the standard curve by the dilution factor. This quantity is present in 1 g of sample taken for estimation. By further multiplying this value by 100, the percentage content is determined.

Calculation

Micronutrient content (μg) in 1 g of sample = C x df

$$\text{Micronutrient content (g) in 100 g sample (\%)} = \frac{(C \times df \times 100)}{1000000}$$

$$= (C \times 1000 \times 100) \div 1000000$$

$$= C/10$$

where,

- C = concentration of micronutrient (μg / ml) as read from the standard curve
- df = dilution factor, which is 100 x 10 = 1000, as calculated below:
  - 1 g of sample made to 100 ml (100 times);
  - 10 ml of sample solution made to 100 ml (10 times).
  - 10,00,000 = factor for converting μg to g.

5

Methods for Water Analysis

Introduction

Irrigation water always contains some soluble salts irrespective of its source. The suitability of waters for a specific purpose depends on the types and amounts of dissolved salts. Some of the dissolved salts or other constituents may be useful for crops. However, the quality or suitability of waters for irrigation purposes is assessed in terms of the presence of undesirable constituents, and only in limited situations is irrigation water assessed as a source of plant nutrients. Some of the dissolved ions, such as NO_3, are useful for crops.

Sometimes, effluents and domestic sewage water is utilized for irrigating field crops. For using these water safely in the farming system, assessment of undesirable pollutants and organic and microbial constituents with regard to their suitability is fore-most important. Determination of organic constituents is generally carried out under two categories viz., (i) organic substances that quantify an aggregate amount of organic C and (ii) individual or specific organic substances, such as benzene, DDT, methane, phenol and endosulphan. Important determinations are the chemical oxygen demand (COD), which gives the total organic substances, and the biochemical oxygen demand (BOD), which gives the amount of total biodegradable organic substances in the water sample.

Sampling

Materials for water samples collection

Common sampling tools and accessories are:

- Clean plastic /glass bottles (500ml)
- Cotton/nylon thread
- Water table recorder
- Glass markers and
- Labels and tags.

Method of sample collection

Water sample is collected in the bottle after rinsing it with the same water 3 - 4 times. Sample from tube well should be collected directly from the outlet point. When sampling from open wells and piezometers, the sample bottle may be tied to a good quality thread and then lowered into the well till it is filled with water. Care should be taken to collect the sample only after continuous discharge of the source for 10 - 20 minutes. From shallow ponds, lakes, canals and rivers, water sample should be collected from centre of the width after avoiding the floating debris on the top. About half a litre of the sample is sufficient. After proper marking and labelling, immediately the sample must be sent to the laboratory for analysis in order to avoid any change/deterioration in its quality due to chemical/microbial activity. While collecting sample, the following points keep in mind:

- Water sample should not be collected in dirty, used and contaminated bottles
- Time interval between collection and analysis should be short in order to get reliable results
- If a delay is inevitable, water sample must be protected against bacterial growth either by adding 2-3 drops of pure toluene or by keeping it under refrigeration (4°C) for the time required.

The parameters generally used to assess quality of water are given in the Table 5.1.

Table 5.1 : Parameters generally used to assess quality of water are given below:

Physical	Chemical	Biological
Temperature	BOD, COD, DO	Bacteria
Colour	pH, hardness, total salt, Cations,	Coliforms
Odour	Anions	Algae
Turbidity	Toxic elements	Virus
Foam and froth, suspended solids	Heavy metals Detergents Pesticides	

Nitrate content of water is of interest not only because plants can absorb nitrate to meet their nutrient demands but also from environment and health point of view because excess of nitrate in drinking water can be toxic to animals and humans. However, the water samples are mainly analysed for total salt, relative proportion of cations, anions, and toxic substances such as boron and fluorine, whereas in case of sewage and effluent water, estimation of bio-chemical oxygen demand (BOD) and chemical oxygen demand (COD) is desirable.

Parameters of Water Quality

Electrical conductivity

The concentration of total salt content in irrigation waters, estimated in terms of EC, is the most important parameter for assessing the suitability of irrigation waters. Generally, all irrigation waters with an EC of less than 2.25 mS/cm are considered suitable except in some unusual situations, e.g. very sensitive crops and highly clayey soils of poor permeability. The ideal value is less than 0.75 mS/cm (Richards, 1954).

Sodium adsorption ratio

The SAR is calculated in order to determine the sodicity or alkalinity hazard of irrigation waters:

$SAR = [Na^{+} \div (Ca^{2+} + Mg^{2+} \div 2)^{1/2}]$, where, the concentration of cations is in me/litre.

Based on the SAR value, waters can be rated into different categories of sodicity (Richards, 1954).

Table 5.2 : Category of water based on SAR

Sl No.	SAR value	Category
1	<10	Safe
2	10 -18	Moderately safe
3	19 – 26	Moderately unsafe
4	>26	Unsafe

Residual sodium carbonate

The RSC index is important for carbonate - and bicarbonate-rich irrigation waters. It indicates their tendency to precipitate Ca as CaCO3. The RSC is calculated by:

RSC (me/litre) = $(CO_3^{2-} + HCO^-_3) - (Ca^{2+} Mg^{2+})$

Concentrations of both cations and anions are in me/litre. The sodicity hazard in terms of RSC is categorized (Richards, 1954).

Table 5.3 : Category of water based on RSC

Sl. No.	RSC (me/litre)	Category
1	1.25	Safe
2	1.25-2.5	Moderate
3	> 2.5	Unsafe
4		

The limits can vary depending on the type of soil, rainfall and climate conditions. Higher RSC values can be considered safe for sandy soils in a high rainfall area (> 600 mm/year).

Ratio of magnesium to calcium

It is widely reported that Ca and Mg do not behave identically in soil systems, and the Mg deteriorates soil structure particularly where waters are sodium-dominated and highly saline. A high level of Mg usually promotes a higher development of exchangeable Na in irrigated soils. Based on the ratio of Mg to Ca, waters are categorized (Table 5.4).

Table 5.4 : Category of water based on Mg/Ca ratio

Mg/Ca Ratio	Category
< 1.5	Safe
1.5 - 3.0	Moderate
> 3.0	Unsafe

Boron content

Crops require B in very small quantities. It becomes toxic where present beyond a certain level. In relation to B toxicity, water quality ratings are:

- Low hazard: < 1μgB/ml
- Medium hazard: 1μgB/ml;
- High hazard: 2 4 μgB/ml and
- Very high hazard: > 4 gB/ml.

Each of the above parameters has a bearing on the quality of irrigation water. However, each water source will have its specific suitability or hazardous nature depending on the presence (and the degree) or absence of each of the constituents. Different chemical constituents interact with one another and cause a complex effect on soil properties and plant growth.

Waters with a low SAR and low EC are widely suitable. However, when a value of any one of these parameters (or both) increases in its content, the waters become less suitable for irrigation purposes. The selection of crops for such situations becomes critical. Salt-tolerant crops can be grown in such areas. Soil type is also an important consideration under such situations.

Table 5.5 indicates the upper permissible limits of EC, SAR, RSC and B for soils with different amounts of clay and for growing tolerant and semi-tolerant crops. These limits are based on extensive trials conducted by Paliwal and Yadav (1976).

Table 5.5 : Suitability of irrigation water for semi-tolerant and tolerant crops in different soil types

Soil Texture	Upper permissible limit							
	EC (dS/m)		SAR (me/L)		RSC		B (μg /ml)	
	ST	T	ST	T	ST	T	ST	T
> 30% clay	1.5	2.0	10	15	2	3	2	3
20-30% clay	4.0	6.0	15	20	3	4	2	3
10-20% clay	6.0	8.0	20	25	4	5	2	3
< 10% clay	8.0	10.0	25	30	5	6	3	4

(*Note:* ST = semi-tolerant crop; T = tolerant crop)

Trace elements

The presence of trace elements or heavy metals reduces crop growth where their concentration increases beyond a certain level in irrigation waters and where such waters are used continuously. However, such elements are not normally a problem in common irrigation waters. They can be of concern where industrial effluent water is used for irrigation.

Analytical Methods

Estimation of pH

The pH is determined by putting about 50 ml of the water sample in a clean 100 ml beaker and using a pH meter as described in Chapter 3.

Estimation of EC

A conductivity meter cell is filled with the water sample, and the EC is determined as described in Chapter 3.

Estimation of Calcium and Magnesium

The usual method for determination of Ca and Mg is by versenate (EDTA) titration (Cheng and Bray, 1951). The estimation of Ca and Mg can also be done using an AAS, as described in Chapter 4. Estimation of Ca and Mg in water by the EDTA method is described below.

Apparatus required

- A porcelain dish
- Some volumetric flasks
- A burette.

Reagents required

- *Standard versenate solution (EDTA):* Prepare an approximately 0.01N solution of EDTA disodium salt (versenate) by dissolving 2.0 g in distilled water, add0.05 g of magnesium chloride ($MgCl_2.6H_2O$) and dilute to 1 litre. Standardize against 0.01N calcium chloride solution prepared by weighing 0.5 g ARgrade$CaCO_3$ (oven-dried) and dissolving in minimum excess of dilute HCl (AR), followed by making the volume up to 1 litre with distilled water.

- *Ammonium chloride-ammonium hydroxide buffer (pH 10)*: 67.5 g of pure ammonium chloride dissolved in 570 ml of concentrated ammonium hydroxide and made up to 1 litre; pH adjusted to 10.
- *EBT indicator*: 0.5 g of EBT and 4.5 g of hydroxylamine hydrochloride (AR) dissolved in 100 ml of 95 percent ethyl alcohol.

Procedure

- Put 5 ml of the water sample in a porcelain dish (8 cm in diameter).
- Dilute to about 25 ml with distilled water.
- Add 1 ml of ammonium chloride-hydroxide buffer and 3–4 drops of EBT indicator.
- Titrate with the standard versenate solution. The colour change is from winered to bright blue or bluish green. At the end point, no tinge of the red colour should remain.

Calculation

From the volume of 0.01N EDTA (standardized against 0.01N $CaCl_2$) solution required for titration, the concentration of Ca and Mg is obtained directly as follows:

$$\text{Ca + Mg (me/litre)} = \text{(ml versenate-EDTA) used} \times \text{normality of EDTA} \times 1000) \div \text{Aliquot (ml)}$$

$$\text{Ca + Mg (g/litre)} = (\text{Ca+Mg in me/litre} \times \text{equivalent wt.}) \div 1000$$
$$= (\text{Ca+Mg in me/litre} \times 32.196) \div 1000$$

Estimation of Sodium

A small amount of Na is generally present even in the best-quality irrigation water. The concentration of Na may be quite high in saline water with an EC higher than 1 mS/cm and containing relatively less Ca and Mg. Its estimation is of interest when the water sample tests saline (i.e. an EC higher than 1.0 mS/cm at 25°C). The determination of Na is carried out directly with the help of a flamephotometer using appropriate filters and standard curves prepared by taking a known concentration of Na.

Apparatus required

- A Flamephotometer
- Some volumetric flasks
- Some beakers.

Reagent

NaCl (AR-grade)

Procedure

- *Preparation of the standard curve*:
- Take 2.5413 g of NaCl (AR), dissolve in water to make to the volume up to 1 litre; this gives a solution of 1000 µg Na/ml. From this solution, take 100 ml and dilute to 1 litre to obtain 100 µg Na/ml as stock solution.
- To prepare working standards, take 5, 10, 15 and 20 ml of stock solution in 100.ml volumetric flasks and make up the volume. This gives 5, 10, 15 and 20 µg Na/ml.
- Feed the standards on the flamephotometer one by one in order to obtain a standard curve, with absorbance on the y-axis and the respective concentrations of Na on the x-axis.
- Feed the water samples on the flamephotometer, and record the absorbance for each sample.
- Observe the concentration of Na against each absorbance (in µg Na/ml).

Calculation

Na in mg/litre of water = (A x 1000) ÷ 1000 = A

Where,

A = absorbance reading (µg/ml) from the standard curve.

Note

- If a water sample is diluted for estimation, the quantity of Na as observed on the standard curve is multiplied by the dilution factor.

- If the water sample is concentrated before estimation, the quantity noted from the standard curve is divided by the concentration factor.
- Normally, no dilution or concentrated is required.

Estimation of Carbonates and Bicarbonates

The estimation is based on simple acidimetric titration (Richards, 1954) using different indicators that work in the alkaline (higher than 8.2) or acidic pH range (lower than 6.0).

Apparatus required

- A porcelain dish and
- A burette.

Reagents required

- *Phenolphthalein indicator*: 0.25 percent solution in 60 percent ethyl alcohol.
- *Methyl orange indicator*: 0.5 percent solution in 95 percent alcohol.
- Standard sulphuric acid (0.01M).

Procedure

- Put 5 ml of the water sample (containing not more than one milli-equivalent of carbonate plus bicarbonate) in a porcelain dish.
- Dilute with distilled water to about 25 ml.
- A pink colour produced with 2-3 drops of phenolphthalein indicates the presence of carbonate, and it is titrated with 0.01M sulphuric acid until the colour just disappears (phenolphthalein end point) because of alkali carbonate having been converted to bicarbonate. This is called the half-neutralization stage. This burette reading (volume used) is designated Y.
- To the colourless solution from this titration (or to the original sample of water if there was no colour with phenolphthalein), add 1-2 drops of methyl orange indicator, and continue titration with brisk stirring to the methyl orange end point (yellow); the final reading (volume used) is designated Z.

Calculation

Carbonates (me/litre) = 2(volume of H_2SO_4) x molarity of H_2SO_4 x (1000 ÷ ml of aliquot)

= 2Y x 0.01 x (1000 ÷ 5)

= 2Y x 2 = 4Y

Carbonates (g/litre) = 2(Volume of H_2SO_4) x molarity of H_2SO_4 x Eq.wt.of CO_3 (30)] ÷ (sample-ml x 1000)

= (2Y x 0.01 x 30) ÷ 5 = 0.12Y

The volume of acid used for half-neutralization of carbonate is Y. Hence, for full neutralization it has been assumed as 2Y:

Bicarbonates (me/litre) = (Z -2Y) x molarity of H_2SO_4 x (1000 ÷ ml of aliquot)

= [(Z -2Y) x 0.01 x 1000)] ÷ 5

= Z – 2Y) x 2 (*Note:* where carbonate is absent: Z x 2).

Estimation of Residual Sodium Carbonate

This is an important characteristic for assessing the suitability of irrigation water in consideration of a probable sodium hazard. It is calculated from the analysis data for carbonates, bicarbonates and Ca plus Mg as follows (all expressed in me/litre):

$$RSC\ (me/litre) = (CO_3^{2-} + HCO^{3-}) - (Ca^{2+} + Mg^{2+})$$

Estimation of Boron

The method for B estimation is same as described in Chapter 3 (methods for soil analysis). The determination is carried out using the azomethine-H colorimetric method. It can also be estimated on an AAS. Suitable quantities of the sample should be taken depending on the B content in the waters.

Estimation of Fluorine

In arid and semi-arid regions, saline ground waters are usually rich in fluorine content. Its content beyond one ppm in drinking water and 10ppm in irrigation water is harmful. It is not directly toxic to the plants but to animals feeding on plants which have been irrigated with high fluoride waters. Fluorine in irrigation waters can be determined either volumetrically or colorimetrically. However, volumetric determination involving titration of test sample against thorium nitrate after adding suitable organic indicator is more precise and accurate (Hesse 1971).

Principle

Fluorine in water sample reacts with thorium and forms thorium tetrafluoride, when titrated against thorium nitrate. At the end point, excess thorium ions produce a coloured lake in the presence of suitable organic indicator such as chrome azural-S and alizarin red-S.

Reagents

- *Standard fluorine solution*: Dissolve 2.211 gm NaF (oven dried at 100°C) per litre. It contains 1000 ppm F. Store it in a polythene bottle.
- *Sodium hydroxide solution, 0.1 M :* Weigh 4.0 gm of pure salt in distilled water and make the volume to one litre.
- Perchoric acid, 1N : Dilute 83.5 ml of 70% acid to one litre.
- *Thorium nitrate (0.025M):* Weigh and dissolve 13.8 gm of thorium nitrate $Th(NO_3)_4.4H_2O$ per litre. Dilute it by 10 and 50 times to have 0.0025 M and 0.0005 M solutions, respectively.
- *Chrome Azural-S indicator*: Weigh and dissolve 0.016 gm of indicator in 100 ml of double distilled water.

Procedure

- Add 1.0 M perchloric acid dropwise to a suitable aliquot of water until the yellow color of the P-nitrophenol solution present is discharged
- Adjust pH of the solution to 3.3 by 0.1 M perchloric acid or 0.1 M NaOH
- Prepare a colour blank by taking 50 ml of distilled water in to Nessler comparison tube and adding 1 ml of indicator and 0.1 ml of thorium nitrate (0.0005 M) until the colour matches with colour blank.
- If more than 2 ml of $Th(NO_3)_4$ are used, titrate against stronger solution of 0.0025 M and multiply the reading by five. Make a fresh colour blank every 15 minutes.
- Pipette 2 ml of standard fluorine solution in Nessler tube and dilute to 50 ml. This contains 20 ppm F.

- Add 1 ml of indicator and titrate with thorium nitrate to match colour blank. Similarly prepare a reagent blank.

Calculation

Test solution reading - reagent blank = A

Standard fluorine reading: 0.1 ml x 20 = B

Fluorine (µg)/50 ml = A x B

Practical Suggestions

- Colour blank should be prepared afresh every 15 minutes.
- Before F determination, water sample may be distilled to separate fluorine from other non-volatile constituents especially in case of sewage and industrial effluents.
- High concentrations of Chlorine usually interfere in F determination. Add silver sulphate to distilling mixture for complexing chloride with silver and minimizing its volatilization.

Estimation of Chloride

Mohr's titration method is the one most commonly used for chloride estimation. It depends on the formation of a sparingly soluble brick-red silver chromate ($AgCrO_4$) precipitate at the end point when the sample is titrated against standard silver nitrate ($AgNO_3$) solution in the presence of potassium chromate (K_2CrO_4) as indicator. Initially, the Cl ions are precipitated as AgCl and the dark brick-red precipitate of Ag_2CrO_4 starts just after the precipitation of AgCl has finished.

Apparatus required

- Some beakers
- A porcelain dish
- A burette.

Reagents required

- *Potassium chromate (K_2CrO_4) indicator (5%) solution*: Dissolve 5 g of K_2CrO_4 in about 75 ml of distilled water, and add saturated solution of $AgNO_3$ drop by drop until a slight permanent red precipitate is formed. Filter and dilute to

100 ml. With high-purity AR, the indicator solution can be prepared directly.

- *Standard silver nitrate solution (0.05M):* Dissolve 8:494 g of silver nitrate ($AgNO_3$) in distilled water, and make the volume up to one litre. Standardize it against standard NaCl solution, and keep it in an amber-coloured bottle away from the light.

Procedure

- Put 5 ml of the sample in a 100.ml beaker or a porcelain dish, and dilute to about 25 ml with distilled water.
- Add 5-6 drops of K_2CrO_4 indicator (making it dark yellow), and titrate against the standard AgNO3 solution with continuous stirring until the first brick-red tinge appears.
- Run a blank to avoid error caused by any impurity in the chemicals.

Calculation

Cl^- mg/litre of water = X x 1.775 x (1000/ml of sample)

where,

- ml of water sample taken = 5
- X = ml of 0.05M $AgNO_3$ consumed in titration
- 1.775 = factor representing mg of Cl in aliquot/sample as calculated below:
  - 1 ml of 1M $AgNO_3$ = 1 me of Cl
  - 1 ml of 0.05M $AgNO_3$ = 0.05 me of Cl
    = 35.5 x 0.05
    = 1.775 mg of Cl (in aliquot).

Estimation of Sulphate

While traces of sulphate occur universally in all types of waters, its content may be appreciably high in several saline water showing an EC higher than 1dS/m at 25^0C. Sulphate can be determined gravimetrically, colorimetrically, turbidimetrically or titrimetrically. Here, the turbidimetric method is described.

Sulphate content is determined by the extent of turbidity created by precipitated colloidal barium sulphate suspension. Barium chloride solid crystals are added to ensure fine and stable suspension of $BaSO_4$ at a pH of about 4.8. This also eliminates interference from phosphate and silicate. This fine suspension of $BaSO_4$ is stabilized by gum acacia, and the degree of turbidity is measured with a turbidity meter or estimated spectrophotometrically at 440nm.

Apparatus required

- A spectrophotometer
- Some beakers
- Some volumetric flasks.

Reagents required

- *Sodium acetate - acetic acid buffer*: Dissolve 100 g of pure sodium acetate in 200 ml of distilled water. Add 31 ml of glacial acetic acid, and make the volume up to 1 litre. Adjust the pH to 4.8.
- *Gum acacia*: Dissolve 2.5 g of gum acacia in 1 litre of distilled water. Keep overnight and filter.
- *Barium chloride*: Grind pure $BaCl_2$ crystals to pass through a 0.5 mm sieve but be retained on a 0.25 mm sieve.
- *Potassium sulphate solution*: To make a stock solution of 10 me S/litre, weigh 1.74 g of pure K_2SO_4 salt and dissolve in 1 litre water.

Procedure

- Put 5 ml of the water sample (< 1 me S/litre) in a 25.ml volumetric flask. If the EC of water is > 1dS/m, dilute it with distilled water to bring the EC to lower than 1dS/m.
- Add 10 ml of sodium acetate-acetic acid buffer to maintain the pH at about 4.8.
- Add 1 ml of gum acacia and 1 g of $BaCl_2$ crystals, and shake well.
- Make the volume up to 25 ml with distilled water.
- Invert the flask several times, and measure the turbidity with aspectrophotometer at 440 nm using a blue filter.
- *Preparation of the standard curve*: For 0, 1, 2, 3, 4 and 5 meS/litre, pipette 2.5, 5, 7.5, 10 and 12.5 ml from stock solution containing

10 meS/litre into 25 ml volumetric flasks. Then develop the turbidity and measure its intensity as in the case of samples. Draw a curve showing S concentration on the x-axis and absorbance on the y-axis.

- The S content of the samples is calculated using the standard curve, taking into account the dilution factor of five (5 ml made to 25 ml) and expressed as meS/litre of water.

Estimation of Nitrate Nitrogen

This method depends on the reduction of nitrate to ammonia by adding Devarda's alloy and alkali. The nitrites (NO^{2-}) (if present) in the sample are also reduced and determined along with NO^{3-}-N.

Apparatus

- A Kjeldahl distillation assembly
- An electric muffle furnace and
- A desiccator.

Reagents

- *Magnesium oxide (MgO):* Heat the MgO at 65°C for 2 hours in an electric muffle furnace to remove any traces of $MgCO_3$ that may be present. Cool in a desiccator over solid KCl, and store in a tightly stoppered bottle.
- *Boric acid with mixed indicator*: Weigh 20 g of boric acid, and add about 900 ml of hot distilled water. Cool and add 20 ml of mixed indicator, and make the volume up to 1 litre.
- *Mixed indicator*: Dissolve 0.066 g of methyl red and 0.099 g of bromocresol green in 100 ml of alcohol.
- Standard sulphuric acid (0.02M).
- *Devarda's alloy*: Mix Cu, Al and Zn in the ratio of 50:45:5 and grind to pass through a 0.15.mm sieve.

Procedure

- Put 50 ml of the water sample in the distillation flask.
- Add 0.5 g of MgO and 0.2 g of Devarda's alloy.

- Put the heaters on and collect the NH4 (NO_3 converted into NH_4 by reducing agent - Devarda's alloy) in boric acid (20 ml) having mixed indicator into a conical flask, which is connected with the distillation apparatus.
- Continue distillation to collect about 35 - 40 ml.
- Remove the distillate first and then switch off the heating system.
- Titrate the distillate against 0.02M H_2SO_4 until the pink colour appears.
- Carry out a blank simultaneously.

Calculation

NO_3^-- N (mg/litre) ={[(X –Y) x 0.56] ÷ (50ml of sample)} x 1000

Where,

X = volume (ml) of 0.02M H_2SO_4 consumed in sample titration

Y = volume (ml) of 0.02M H_2SO_4 consumed in blank titration

(***Note:*** 0.56 = factor; 1 litre 1M H_2SO_4 = 28 g N, therefore 1 ml 0.02M H_2SO_4= (28 x 0.02 x 1000) ÷ 1000 mg N = 0.56 mg N).

Estimation of Phosphorus

Phosphorus (P) occurs in natural wastes and in waste waters mainly as phosphates. Orthophosphates are more important from crop growth point of view as compared to other forms of P. Main sources of phosphate in irrigation waters are through contribution from fertilizers and manures in most cases. In sewage waters, phosphates are contributed by detergents and food residues. Phosphorus analysis of water has two steps viz.

(i). conversion of organic and other condensed forms (sewage and waste water) into soluble orthophosphates and

(ii). determination of orthophosphates colorimetrically (APHA, 1989).

The important colorimetric methods are:

- Vanadomolybdo-phosphoric acid method (for range of 1- 20 mg P/L)
- Stannous chloride (for range of 0.01 – 6 mg P/L) and
- Ascornic acid method (for range of 0.01 – 6 mg P/L).

For irrigation water and waste water, the ascorbic acid method is commonly used because of its precision, stability of blue colour and simplicity (Murphy and Riley, 1962).

Principle

Ammonium molybdate and potassium antimony tartrate react in acid medium with orthophosphates to form a heteropoly acid - phosphomolybdic acid, which is reduced to intensely coloured molybdenum blue by ascorbic acid.

Reagents

- *Solutions A:* weigh 1 g of ammonium molybdate and 0.02g of potassium antimony tartrate in 1000 ml measuring flask. Add 16 ml of conc. H_2SO_4 slowly by touching outlet point of measuring cylinder to the inner neck of the flask. Add distilled water slowly, dissolve the contents by shaking and make upto the mark.
- *Solution B:*_weigh 0.88 g of ascorbic acid and dissolve in one litre of solution A. It should be prepared fresh.
- *Standard phosphate solution:* dissolve 0.2195 g anhydrous KH_2PO_4 in distilled water and dilute to one litre. This is a 50ppm P solution or 1 ml = 50 µg P. Prepare a series of standard solutions containing 0, 2, 4, 6, 8 and 10 µg P/ml by pipetting same volume of stock solution into 50 ml conical flask and making up to its mark with by distilled water.

Procedure

- Pipette 10ml of water sample and standard P solutions in 50 ml conical flasks (total P not to exceed 500 µg approximately).
- Add 10 ml of reagent B. Make the volume to 50 ml with distilled water and let the blue colour develop for 30 minutes.
- Measure absorbance/transmittance of the colour at 600 nm wave length.
- Prepare a blank with distilled water and adjust 100% transmittance before reading the samples.
- Draw graph of the standards P solutions (µg P ml v/s absorbance) and plot the straight line relationship. Read P concentration of unknown water samples from this graph in µg P / ml.

Calculation

P (mg/L) = [mg P (in 50ml)/ ml Sample] x 1000

Practical suggestions

- For getting better color development use very clean glassware which has been washed with dilute HCL at one stage of cleaning.
- Prepare solution B fresh since it decolorizes on stage.
- For colored samples, either removed the color by activated charcoal treatment or deduct blank absorbance from the sample absorbance after adding all reagents except ascorbic acid and potassium antimony tartrate.
- In sewage and other industrial effluents, the organic and condensed forms of phosphates are converted into orthophosphates by acid digestion. Add 1 ml conc. H_2SO_4 and 5 ml conc. HNO_3 to water sample into a Kjeldahl flask and digest till it is colourless. Cool and add 20 ml distilled water to dissolve the contents. Transfer into volumetric flask and make the volume as original after filtration, if necessary.
- If necessary, remove nitrite and sulphide interference by adding excess bromine water or saturated $KMnO_4$ solution.

Alternate Methods for P Estimation in Water

- Vanadomolybdo- phosphoric acid method (minimum detectable concentration is 20 µg P/L)
- Colorimetric methods using stannous chloride (minimum detectable concentration is 7 µg) P/L).

Determination of Potassium in Water

Potassium (K) generally constitutes a small fraction of water cations. Being a plant nutrient, its presence in saline water counteracts the adverse effect of Na on crop growth. Hence, its determination is essential in saline waters along with that of Na. Flame photometry is the most rapid and realisable method of K determination.

Procedure

- *Preparation of standard curve*: Weigh 191 mg of KCl (AR) salt and dissolve in distilled water. Make the volume upto 1 litre mark. This is 100 ppm or mg/L K solution. For preparing working standard solutions of 0, 2, 4, 6, 8 and 10 ppm, pipette same volume in each case into 100 ml measuring flasks and mark up to 100 ml.
- Start Flame-Photometer and first atomize distilled water and adjust galvanometer reading to zero.
- Now feed 10me/L standard and adjust galvanometer reading to 100 or any highest value displayed on the dial T.
- Then feed 2, 4, 6, 8 and 10 ppm /L standards and record galvanometer readings.
- Draw curve by plotting flamephotometer reading on y-axis and K on x-axis. This should be straight line. If it not straight, reduce the range of working standards and draw the above relationship.
- Now atomize the unknown samples into the flame and record the readings.

Practical suggestions

- Water sample must be very clear, free from turbidity and suspended particles. It can be filtered through a good quality filter paper.
- Range of K concentration in standard solutions must be kept as per the sensitivity of the flamephotometer used.
- After 10 -15 samples, it is better to feed the highest standards solution and adjust its reading if it varied slightly.
- During operation, air pressure and gas supply must be kept constant. A small variation can affect the readings.

6

Methods for Fertilizers and Manures Analysis

Introduction

The main objective in analysing fertilizers is to assess their quality. The analysis examines both their physical and chemical composition. The quality of fertilizers is stated by the manufacturers and, in most countries, it is statutorily notified. Hence, analysis is carried out to determine whether the stated quality meets the statutorily notified standards or not. Together with the statutory notified composition of the fertilizers, the testing methods are specified. In situations where the testing methods are not notified, the prevalent standard methods are followed. Generally, the term fertilizer refers to mineral fertilizers, which are manufactured chemical products of standard composition, while the term manures refers to organic manures, compost, agro-industrial wastes, etc. The compositions of organic fertilizers, unlike mineral fertilizers, are quite variable and, thus, difficult to regulate precisely.

Fertilizer quality is notified in terms of physical and chemical characteristics. The physical parameters include moisture content and particle size. The chemical parameters refer to the amount and form of nutrients, and to various impurities that may be toxic to plants above a critical limit, e.g. biuret in urea. The efficiency of a fertilizer depends on its form of nutrient content. A phosphatic fertilizer may have water-soluble, citrate-soluble, water-insoluble or citrate-insoluble forms of phosphate. A nitrogenous fertilizer may contain ammoniacal, nitrate and amide forms of N in various proportions.

The accompanying ions also reflect the quality of a fertilizer, such as SO_4 ions in ammonium sulphate, potassium sulphate, superphosphates and many micronutrient fertilizers. They supply S in addition to the main nutrient. Many fertilizers are fortified with micronutrients such as boronated single superphosphate (SSP) and zincated urea.

Therefore, in fertilizer analysis, in addition to estimating total nutrient content, it is necessary to estimate the forms of nutrients and other associated compounds in order to assess their quality properly. For organic fertilizers, the C content and the total content of nutrients are considered relevant and not their forms as they are low-analysis materials.

The analytical methods for fertilizers as described are applicable to most common fertilizers and the forms of nutrient content in them. The procedures as applicable to a particular nutrient could be applicable to any fertilizer with the Guide to laboratory establishment for plant nutrient analysis nutrient in that particular form. To conform to the scope of this guide, this chapter considers only commonly used solid fertilizers and their major constituents, including impurities.

Sampling

Collection and Preparation of Fertilizer Sample

The collection of a representative sample of a fertilizer is an important step in fertilizer analysis and quality control. The method of sample collection depends on the type and source of fertilizer. Fertilizers are manufactured commodities. They are stored in silos at the manufacturing site for different periods. They are transported using various means (e.g. ship, rail and road) and stored again at various locations including port godowns, warehouses and dealers shops. Fertilizers are stored/moved both in bulk and as bagged. Therefore, the sample collection methods can be classified broadly as concerning:

- Collection from bulk stock in godowns
- Collection from ship hatches or while the ship is being loaded/ unloaded
- Collection from bagged stock in godowns of various types
- Sample collection from damaged stock.

Scale of Sampling

The number of samples to be collected from a given stock depends on the quantity available in the stock. In a ship, each hold/hatch is treated separately from the others, and samples are collected accordingly. In practice, one representative sample is taken from 100 tonnes of material. A similar scale of sampling is followed for factory silos where bulk fertilizers are stored.

In the case of bagged material, stored in smaller quantities (e.g. at dealers godowns), generally, 1 sample (minimum) is drawn from 10 bags; 2 samples from100 bags, 6-7 samples from 1000 bags; and 10 samples from 2000 bags. There is no fixed number of samples that can be defined to represent a given quantity. However, it is necessary to ensure that the sample is truly representative of the lot it designates.

In the case of bulk material being loaded into or unloaded from ships, samples are taken from the conveyor belt at certain intervals of time. The material so collected is stored in a container, and from such quantity collected, three representative samples each weighing about 400-500g is taken. Samples from the bulk material are collected with the help of sampling cups made of corrosion-free metal. Bagged fertilizers are sampled with the help of a sampling probe/tube. This is often a slotted double tube with a solid cone tip made of stainless steel or brass, about 60-65 cm long, about 1.5 cm in diameter, and with a slot width of about 1.2 - 1.3 cm. The sampling probe should be inserted diagonally from one corner to another, keeping the slit down and rotated while withdrawing. The samples collected from the bags or bulk representing one lot is composited and, through the quartering method of leaving aside the portions of two opposite quarters successively, three identical samples of about 450 - 500 g each are retained for analysis. These samples are labelled with details showing:

- Name of the fertilizer
- Source
- Date when collected and
- Signature, name and details of authority of the person who collected the sample.

Unlike soil, plant and water samples, fertilizer samples are generally collected in triplicate. Of the three samples, one goes to the designated laboratory for analysis; another goes to the owner of the fertilizer (e.g. ships captain, godown manager, or dealer), and the third sample is kept for further reference by the sample collector.

Such a procedure is necessary because in the event of deficiencies in the quality parameters, there has to be provision to analyse the reference sample before holding the party concerned responsible for the poor quality of the fertilizer manufactured/Imported/ sold to the farmers.

Sample Preparation for Analysis

The sample received for analysis is recorded in the laboratory with adequate details, and a laboratory code number is assigned in order to identify the sample and to keep its identity confidential.

About half of the sample is ground, sieved through a 1 mm sieve, and stored in a sample bottle for analysis. The remaining half is kept ungrounded for particle size estimation. The samples are stored in an air tight glass bottle or taken for analysis in a moisture-free room (fitted with a dehumidifier) as most fertilizers are hygroscopic in nature.

Analytical Methods for Fertilizer Analysis

There are a number of estimation methods available for each of the constituents. Fertilizer analysis is carried out primarily for quality control and statutory purposes. Each country has adopted certain methods in its fertilizer statute, and only these methods are relevant for that country. Fertilizer is a widely traded commodity, and it is necessary that the methodology adopted in checking quality be acceptable to all concerned. While there are no internationally accepted or common methods, the methods adopted, verified and notified by the AOAC are widely used (Motsara, 1984). The AOAC adopts a method after its verification and validation by a large number of analytical laboratories in various countries. In view of this, this book describes the AOAC based methods of fertilizer analysis in most cases, with simplification of the procedures for ease of comprehension.

Estimation of Moisture Content

Two important forms of water present in fertilizers are: (i) absorbed/adsorbed water; and (ii) free water. They are interchangeable depending on the degree of moisture saturation and temperature. Some fertilizers also contain water as an establishment for plant nutrient analysis integral part of their composition, which is referred to as water of crystallization, as in the case of $ZnSO_4.7H_2O$ and $CuSO_4.5H_2O$. As fertilizers are generally hygroscopic in nature, they tend to absorb moisture from the atmosphere (depending on the relative humidity and their packing and storage conditions). Excessive moisture may damage the granular structure of fertilizers, affect their quality and influence their nutrient content by increasing the weight of fertilizers in a given container.

Therefore, moisture estimation is critical to determining the quality of a fertilizer. The method used depends on the type of fertilizer and the nature of moisture held by it. Some common methods are:

- Gravimetric method
- Vacuum desiccator method and
- Karl Fischer titration method.

With the gravimetric or oven-drying method, the loss of water on heating fertilizer samples at a certain temperature is estimated. This method is suitable for fertilizers such as ammonium sulphate, sodium nitrate, superphosphates, muriate of potash (MOP) and sulphate of potash (SOP). It is not suitable for fertilizers that yield volatile substances (such as NH_4) other than moisture on drying at a specified temperature, e.g. calcium ammonium nitrate and di-ammoniumphosphate (DAP).With the vacuum desiccator method, the free moisture present in the fertilizer is absorbed by the desiccant (sulphuric acid), and the loss in weight is reported as moisture. This method is suitable for fertilizers such as calcium ammoniumnitrate, DAP, and NPK complexes. The Karl Fischer titration method is suitable for fertilizers such asnitrophosphates, urea, and urea-based fertilizers, which do not withstand high temperatures.

Gravimetric Method

Moisture is estimated by the gravimetric method where the loss in weight at a constant temperature of 100° ± 1°C for 5 hours is measured, e.g. zinc sulphate, and copper sulphate. In the case of sodium nitrate, superphosphates, ammoniumsulphate, SOP and MOP, the heating is at 130 ^{0}C ± 1 ^{0}C. For urea and urea-based fertilizers, the heating is at 70 ^{0}C. However, heating at 70 ^{0}C does not reflect full moisture content. Therefore, the Karl Fischer method is preferred.

Apparatus

- A glass weighing bottle;
- An electronic balance;
- A temperature-controlled oven.

Procedure

- Weigh 2.0 g of fertilizer sample in a pre-weighed glass weighing bottle.
- Heat in a temperature-controlled oven for about 5 hours at the specified temperature, as given above for different types of fertilizers.
- Cool in a desiccator, and weigh.

Calculation

Moisture (%) by weight = [(B - C) x 100] ÷ B - A

Where,

A = weight in grams of the empty sample bottle

B = weight in grams of the bottle plus material before drying

C = weight in grams of the bottle plus material after drying.

Vacuum Desiccator Method

In this method, the sample is kept in a vacuum desiccator over sulphuric acid. Free moisture present in fertilizers is absorbed by the acid, and the loss in weight of the sample is recorded as the moisture content in the sample.

Apparatus

- A vacuum desiccator
- A porcelain dish and
- A balance.

Procedure

- Weigh (accurately) 5 g of sample in a porcelain dish, and keep it in a desiccators for 24 hours.
- Take the weight again after 24 hours. The loss in weight is equal to moisture content in the sample.

Calculation

Moisture (%) by weight = [(B – C ÷ B - A)] x 100

Where,

A = weight in grams of the porcelain dish;

B = weight in grams of the porcelain dish plus the fertilizer sample;

C = weight in grams of the porcelain dish plus the fertilizer sample after desiccation for 24 hours.

Karl Fischer Method

Apparatus

- A Karl Fischer titrator
- A balance
- A beaker or flask;
- A graduated cylinder.

Reagents

- Karl Fischer reagent (pyridine-free).
- Disodium tartrate dihydrate ($Na_2C_4O_6 2H_2O$) - AR grade.
- Methanol - Karl Fischer grade / spectroscopy grade containing less than 0.05 percent water.

Procedure

- *Standardization of Karl Fischer reagent*
  - Set up the instrument.
  - Add about 25 ml of methanol to the titration vessel until the electrodes are dipped, and titrate with Karl Fischer reagent to a pre-set end point that persists for 30 seconds.
  - Add 100 mg of the disodium tartrate dihydrate to the titration vessel carefully, and titrate with Karl Fischer reagent to a pre-set end point (the end point should persist for 30 seconds). Note the volume (ml) of Karl Fischer reagent used as V1.
- Weigh accurately about 1 g of the prepared sample, transfer it carefully to the titration vessel, and stir until dispersed.
- Titrate with Karl Fischer reagent to the same pre-set end point as above, and note the volume (ml) of Karl Fischer reagent used as V2.

Calculation

Moisture % in sample = [(F x V2)/Wt. of sample (g)] x [100 (for %)/1000 (for mg to g)]

Where,

F (factor) in mg H_2O/ml of Karl Fischer reagent =

(0.1566 x mg of sodium tartarate dihydrate added) ÷ V1.

(*Note:* Disodium tartrate dihydrate contains 0.1566 percent moisture).

Estimation of Particle Size

Fertilizers are manufactured with varying degrees of particle size. This property of fertilizer has a bearing on its efficiency when used in various types of soil for crop production. The size and strength of the particle determine its dissolution time when applied in soil. Most fertilizers are highly water soluble; hence, they dissolve quickly when they come into contact with soil moisture. Fertilizers can be crystalline or granular. With a view to reducing losses caused by rapid dissolution, fertilizers with large granules are also being manufactured, e.g. granular urea and super granular urea.

Granular fertilizers are considered superior for machine application, for preparing bulk blends with greater homogeneity and uniformity, and they are also less vulnerable to adulteration. Therefore, particle size estimation is an important aspect in determining the fertilizer quality. Most granular fertilizers range between 1 and 4 mm, with a specific particle size for a specific fertilizer. The apparatus required for particle size estimation consists of sieves of various sizes.

The procedure consists of sieving through a given sieve size. The material is passed through a sieve with a mesh equal to the maximum particle size prescribed for a given fertilizer. The material so sieved is retained on a sieve with a mesh equal to the minimum particle size prescribed for that fertilizer. For example, a fertilizer is sieved through a 4 mm sieve and is retained on a 1 mm sieve, kept below the 4 mm sieve. The material retained on the 4 mm sieve is larger than 4 mm in size and that passed through the 1 mm sieve is less than 1.0 mm in size. The material retained on the 1 mm sieve is that with a particle size of between 1 and 4 mm. Generally, 250 g of the fertilizer is taken and sieved as per the requirement. Sieving can be done mechanically or manually.

Estimation of Nitrogen

Estimation of Total Nitrogen

Nitrogen in fertilizers may be present in various forms such as NH_4-N, NO_3-N, urea-N (amide) and organic N. The estimations are carried out for total N and its forms. For urea, the total N estimation method is followed. The principle of N estimation is based on the Kjeldahl method. For including or excluding a particular form of N in total N estimation, specific chemicals/catalysts are used. For example, in nitrate-containing fertilizers, 2 g of salicylic acid and 5 g of sodium thiosulphate are added in the digestion mixture. This helps to bind the NO_3-N in the form of nitrosalicylic acid, and it is converted eventually into NH_4-N in the presence of H_2SO_4 and is estimated along with other forms of N present in the sample. Devarda's alloy (2/3 g per sample) can also be used instead of salicylic acid and thiosulphate.

Total Nitrogen by the Kjeldahl Method

The method and procedure are the same as described for total N estimation in soil (Chapter 3). Specific care is required for sample size. It may vary between 0.2 and 0.5 g depending on the N content of the sample. A smaller amount of sample may be taken for high-analysis fertilizers (e.g. urea) and a larger amount for low analysis fertilizer (e.g. ammonium sulphate).

Ammoniacal Nitrogen by the Distillation Method

Apparatus

- A Kjeldahl distillation unit;
- Some flasks, beakers and pipettes;
- A burette.

Reagents

- Freshly ignited carbonate-free MgO.
- Standard acid (0.1M HCl).
- Standard alkali (0.1M NaOH).
- NaOH (40 percent) for distillation.
- Methyl red indicator.

Procedure

- Put 0.5 g of the sample in a 600 ml distillation flask with about 250 ml of water.
- Add 2 g of freshly ignited carbonate-free MgO or 5 ml of NaOH solution
- (40 percent) by tilting the flask and through the side of the flask so that the contents do not mix at once.
- Connect the flask to a condenser by a Kjeldahl connecting bulb and connecting tube.
- Start heating, and distil about 100 ml of liquid into a measured quantity of standard acid (0.1M HCl).
- Titrate the distillate with standard NaOH (0.1M) to determine the remaining amount of unused acid, using methyl red indicator. The acid used to neutralize ammonia is equivalent to the N content in the sample.
- Carry out a blank.

Calculation

Percent NH_4 N = {[(A - C) - B] x (0.0014 x 100)} ÷ W

Where

- A = ml of standard acid (0.1M HCl) taken to receive ammonia
- B = ml of standard alkali (0.1M NaOH) used in titration
- W = weight of the sample taken
- C = ml of standard alkali used in the blank
- 1 ml 0.1M HCl = 0.0014 g N

Ammoniacal plus Nitrate-Nitrogen by the Distillation Method

Devarda's alloy (50 percent Cu, 45 percent Al, and 5 percent Zn) reduces NO_3 to NH_4 in an alkaline condition. The method is same as for NH_4-N estimation (above), except that 2-3 g of Devarda's alloy is added before distillation in order to take into account the NO_3 by reducing it to ammonia form.

Nitrate-Nitrogen

In fertilizers containing both NH_4 and NO_3-N, first ammoniacal nitrogen is estimated followed by NH_4 plus NO_3 estimation. From the combined value of $NH_4$and NO_3, the value of ammoniacal N is subtracted to obtain the nitrate-N content.

Urea Nitrogen

The urea form of N can be estimated together with total N by digestion with sulphuric acid. For example, total N is estimated for urea fertilizer. However, for some NPK complexes, urea N has to be estimated separately. In such cases, it is done by the urease method.

Apparatus

- Some beakers;
- Some flasks;
- A Gooch crucible;
- Some filter paper.

Reagents

- *Neutral urease solution:* Shake 1 g of jack bean meal with 100 ml of water for 5 minutes. Transfer 10 ml of the solution to a 250 ml Erlenmeyer flask, dilute with 50 ml water, and add 4 drops of methyl purple indicator. Titrate with 0.1M HCl to reddish purple, then back titrate to green colour with 0.1MNaOH. From the difference in volume used, calculate the amount of 0.1M HCl required to neutralize 10 ml of solution. Based on the calculated acid required, add 0.1M HCl to the remaining 90 ml of solution (about 2.5 ml of acid is required per 100 ml of solution), and shake well.
- *HCl (0.1M):* Dilute 100 ml of concentrated HCl to 1 litre, and titrate with the standard alkali to establish the exact strength of the acid.
- *NaOH (0.1M):* Dissolve 4 g of NaOH in 900 ml of water in a 1-litre volumetric flask, make the volume up, and standardize with the standard acid.
- Sodium carbonate (10 percent).
- Barium hydroxide (saturated).

Procedure

- Weigh 10 ± 0.01 g of the sample and transfer it to 15 cm No. 12 fluted filter paper.
- Leach with about 300 ml of water into a 500 ml volumetric flask.
- Add 75-100 ml of saturated barium hydroxide solution to precipitate phosphates.
- Let it settle, and test for complete precipitation with a few drops of saturated barium hydroxide solution.
- Add 20 ml of 10 percent sodium carbonate solution to precipitate excess barium and any soluble Ca salts.
- Let it settle, and test for complete precipitation (when the addition of a few more drops of sodium carbonate does not show further precipitation).
- Dilute to volume, mix, and filter through 15 cm No. 12 fluted paper.
- Transfer 50 ml of aliquot (equivalent to 1 g of sample) to a 200 or 250 ml Erlenmeyer flask, and add 1-2 drops of methyl purple indicator.
- Acidify solution with 0.1M HCl, and add 2-3 drops in excess (after colour change is noticed).
- Neutralize (titrate) solution with 0.1M NaOH to the first change in colour of the indicator.
- Add 20 ml of neutral urease solution, close flask with rubber stopper, and let it stand for 1 hour at 20-25°C.
- Cool the flask in ice water slurry, and titrate at once with 0.1M HCl to full purple colour, then add about 5 ml in excess.
- Record total volume added, back titrate excess HCl with 0.1M NaOH to neutral end point.

Calculation

%Urea N = [(ml 0.1M HCl ml 0.1M NaOH) x 0.0014 x 100] ÷ Wt. of sample (1 g contained in 50 ml aliquot)

Estimation of Biuret Content

Biuret ($C_2O_2N_3H_5$) is a chemical compound formed by the combination of two molecules of urea with a release of a molecule of ammonia when the temperature during the urea manufacturing process exceeds the controlled level. Fertilizer grade urea contains biuret, which usually varies between 0.3 and 1.5 percent. Biuret is toxic to plants particularly when applied through foliar spray.

Apparatus

- A water-bath shaker;
- A spectrophotometer;
- Some beakers and flasks;
- A burette.

Reagents

- Alkaline tartrate solution: Dissolve 40 g NaOH in 50 ml of cold water and50 g of $NaKCl_4H_4O_6.4H_2O$, and dilute to 1 litre. Let it stand for 1 day before use.
- Copper sulphate solution: Dissolve 15 g of $CuSO_4.5H_2O$ in CO_2-free water, and dilute to 1 litre.
- Biuret standard solution (1 mg/ml): Dissolve 100 mg of reagent-grade biuret in CO_2-free water, and dilute to 100 ml.
- Standard H_2SO_4.

Procedure

- *Preparation of the standard curve*
  - Transfer a series of aliquots, 2-50 ml of standard biuret solution, to a 100ml volumetric flask.
  - Adjust the volume to about 50 ml with CO_2-free water. Add one drop of methyl red, and neutralize with 0.1M H_2SO_4 to a pink colour.
  - Add, with swirling, 20 ml of alkaline tartrate solution and then 20 ml of $CuSO_4$ solution.
  - Dilute to volume. Shake for 10 seconds, and place in a water-bath for 15minutes at 30°C ± 5°C.

- Also prepare a reagent blank.
- Determine absorbance of each solution against the blank at 555 nm on the spectrophotometer with a 2.4 cm cell, and plot the standard curve.

- Stir continuously 5 g of the sample in 100 ml of water for 30 minutes.
- Filter and wash in 250 ml volumetric flask and dilute to volume.
- Transfer 25 ml of aliquot to 100 ml volumetric flask and proceed as given under preparation of standard curve.

Calculation

Biuret % = [(C x 100)/ W] x df

Where,

C = concentration in mg/ml of biuret as read from the standard curve;

W = weight of sample;

df = 200 (5 g of fertilizer extracted to 250 ml, and 25 ml taken for further dilution to 100 ml).

Determination of Free Acid in Ammonium Sulphate as (H_2SO_4)

The presence of free acid is needs to be regulated in fertilizers such as ammonium sulphate. It is generally kept below 0.025 percent. Its estimation is necessary in order to check the quality of fertilizers.

Apparatus

- Some beakers and flasks and
- A burette.

Reagents

- Standard sodium hydroxide solution (0.02M).
- Methyl red indicator: Dissolve 0.15 g of water-soluble methyl red in 500 ml of water.
- *Methyl red-methylene blue mixed indicator solution*: Mix equal volumes of 0.2 percent solution of methyl red and 0.1 percent solution of methylene blue in rectified spirit.

Procedure

- Dissolve about 20 g of the prepared fertilizer sample, accurately weighed, in about 50 ml of cold water.
- Filter and make the volume up to about 200 ml.
- Titrate with standard sodium hydroxide solution, using 1-2 drops of methyl red as indicator.
- If a satisfactory end point (change from red to yellow-orange) with methyl red is not obtained, methyl red - methylene blue mixed indicator may be used.

It is important to use a micro-burette for this titration. The filtering medium should be neutral and should not contain any alkaline material (which would neutralize free acid).

Calculation

Free acid as H_2SO_4 % by weight = (4.9 x A x M)/ W

Where,

A = volume in millilitres of standard NaOH solution

M = Molarity of standard NaOH solution

W = weight in grams of prepared sample taken for the test

4.9 = factor (1 M 1 000 ml NaOH = 49 g H_2SO_4; thus, 1 M 100 ml NaOH = 4.9 g H_2SO_4).

Determination of Phosphorus

Phosphate (P_2O_5) in fertilizers may be present in different forms: (i) water soluble; (ii) neutral ammonium citrate soluble or insoluble; (iii) citric acid soluble or insoluble; and (iv) acid soluble. Phosphate is generally present as bound with Ca as monocalcium phosphate, dicalcium phosphate and tricalcium phosphate. It may present with other metal elements, e.g. aluminium phosphate and iron phosphate. In phosphate rock, it is present as apatite of chlorine and fluorine. Being in water soluble form, monocalcium phosphate is considered available, while dicalciumphosphate becomes available in slightly acidic situations. Tricalcium phosphate is in an unavailable form and can be available only in acidic situations. Similarly, the aluminium and iron phosphates are also in plant unavailable forms.

Neutral ammonium citrate soluble form is also considered as available, which includes both monocalcium phosphate and dicalcium phosphate. In view of the variability in availability to plants, the estimation of different forms of phosphate is critical. For the so-called "available" forms of P, appropriate extractants have been designed to extract P from fertilizers under a set of well-defined sampling conditions: extractant ratio, temperature, time of extraction, shaking period, etc. The form of P as a fraction of the total P is extracted by a particular method. Estimation of the extracted P utilizes various testing methods: (i) gravimetric; (ii) volumetric; and (iii) colorimetric. The following methods are used for P estimation in fertilizers:

- Gravimetric ammonium phosphomolybdate
- Gravimetric quinolinium phosphomolybdate
- Volumetric ammonium phosphomolybdate
- Volumetric quinolinium phosphomolybdate and
- Spectrophotometric vanadium phosphomolybdate.

All the methods are used in various laboratories. For total phosphate estimation, the gravimetric quinolinium phosphomolybdate method is generally preferred because of the minimal interference of other ions and its accuracy and simplicity. Another common method providing acceptable accuracy and simplicity is volumetric ammonium phosphomolybdate.

Gravimetric Quinolinium Phosphomolybdate Method

Various forms of P present in fertilizers are first converted into orthophosphate through chemical treatments. On reaction with quimociac reagent, theorthophosphate precipitates as quinolinium phosphomolybdate $[(C_9H_7N)_3H_3PO_4.12\,MoO_3]$ in a boiling medium. The precipitate is weighed gravimetrically, which gives the P content of the sample.

In the gravimetric method, Ca, Fe, Mg, alkali metals and citrates do not affect the analysis. The citrate in the reagent complexes the ammonium ions, thus preventing interference from precipitation of ammonium phosphomolybdate by the ammonium salts usually present in mixed fertilizers. The citrates also reduce interference from soluble silica.

Apparatus

- A volumetric flask
- Some beakers

- A Gooch crucible
- Some filter paper and
- An analytical balance.

Reagents

- Concentrated nitric acid.
- Concentrated hydrochloric acid.
- Magnesium nitrate solution (9%): Dissolve 90 g of P-free $Mg(NO_3)_2$ in water, and dilute to 1 litre.
- Acetone.
- Citric acid.
- Sodium molybdate dihydrate.
- Quinoline.
- *Quimociac reagent*: Dissolve 60 g of citric acid in a mixture of 85 ml of HNO_3 and 150 ml of water, and cool. Dissolve 70 g of sodium molybdatedihydrate in 150 ml of water. Gradually add the sodium molybdate solution to the citric acid - nitric acid mixture, with stirring. Dissolve 5 ml of synthetic quinoline in a mixture of 35 ml of HNO_3 and 100 ml of water. Gradually add this solution to the molybdate citric-nitric acid solution, mix, let it stand for 24 hours, and filter. Add 280 ml of acetone, dilute to 1 litre with water, admix well. Store in a polyethylene bottle.

According to the nature of the fertilizer, the sample solution should be prepared using one of the following methods:

- *For materials and fertilizer mixtures with a high OM content*: Put 1 g of the sample in an evaporation dish. Add 5 ml of $Mg(NO^{3-})_2$ solution, and evaporate to dryness. Ignite to destroy the OM, and dissolve in 10 ml of HCl.
- *For materials with a low OM content*: Put 1 g of the sample in a 50 ml beaker. Add 30 ml of HNO_3 and 5 ml of HCl, and boil gently until the OM is destroyed and red-brown fumes cease to appear.
- *For basic slag and fertilizers containing iron or aluminium phosphate*: Treat 1g of the sample with 30 ml of HCl and 10 ml of HNO_3, and boil gently until red-brown fumes disappear.

- Cool the solution, prepared by any of the above three methods, dilute to 250 ml, mix, and filter through a dry filter, if required (may contain some insoluble material).

Procedure

- Pipette 5-25 ml of aliquot (sample solution) depending on the P content (containing not more than 25 mg P_2O_5 in the aliquot) into a 250 ml beaker, and dilute to 100 ml with distilled water.
- Add 50 ml of quimociac reagent, cover with a watch glass, place on a hotplate, and boil for 1 minute.
- Cool the material to room temperature, swirl carefully 3-4 times during cooling.
- Filter the precipitate with fibreglass filter paper (or Gooch crucible G4) previously dried at 250°C and weighed. Wash 4-5 times with 25 ml portions of water. Dry the crucible/filter paper and contents for 30 minutes at 25°C. Cool in a desiccator to a constant weight.
- Run a reagent blank with each batch. Subtract the weight of the blank from the weight of the sample precipitate.

Calculation

Total phosphate (as P_2O_5) % = [3.207(S - B)/100] x df x (100 ÷ W)
= [3.207 (S – B) ÷ W] x df

Where,

S = weight of sample precipitate in grams;

B = weight of blank precipitate in grams;

df = dilution factor for aliquot taken:

- Suppose volume of the aliquot (solution) taken for estimation = 5 ml, and total volume of fertilizer solution prepared = 250 ml;
- df = (Total volume of fertilizer solution)/ aliquot taken = 250/5 = 50
- For percentage = 100/Wt. of fertilizer

W = weight of sample taken in grams;

Factor 3.207 = the quinolinium phosphomolybdate precipitate

contains 3.207 percent P_2O_5 on weight basis.

In cases where $MoO_3.Na_2MoO_4.2H_2O$ (quinoline) is not of standard quality, the exact volume of quimociac reagent to be added for precipitation should be calculated by running a series of known standards and observing the phosphate recovery in them.

Volumetric Ammonium Phosphomolybdate Method

Phosphorus is precipitated from the acidic solution as ammonium phosphomolybdate $[(NH_4)_3PO_4.12MoO_3]$ by adding ammonium molybdate solution. The precipitate is dissolved in a measured excess of the standard alkali after filtration and washing until free of the acid.

Apparatus

- Some volumetric flasks / beakers
- A burette
- A shaker
- A water-bath and
- Some No. 44 filter paper.

Reagents

- *Magnesium nitrate solution (9%):* Dissolve 90 g of P-free $Mg(NO_3)_2$ in water, and dilute to 1 litre.
- Concentrated nitric acid.
- Concentrated hydrochloric acid.
- *Ammonium molybdate solution (3%)*: Dissolve 30 g of ammonium-molybdate in hot distilled water, and make the volume up to 1 litre.
- *Standard NaOH solution (0.1M):* Dissolve 4 g of NaOH in 1 litre of water, and standardize against standard acid.
- *Standard H_2SO_4 solution (0.1M):* Take 5.6 ml of concentrated H_2SO_4 and make the volume up to 1 litre. Standardize against a primary standard alkali such as Na_2CO_3 (procedure as detailed in Chapter 3).
- *Sodium nitrate (2%):* Dissolve 20 g of AR-grade sodium nitrate in 1litre of distilled water.
- Phenolphthalein indicator (1%): Dissolve 1 g of phenolph-

thalein in 100 ml of 95.5% ethanol.

- Ammonium nitrate (AR-grade).
- Sodium carbonate (AR-grade).

The sample solution should be prepared using one of the methods indicated fort the gravimetric quinolinium phosphomolybdate method (above).

Procedure

- Pipette 5-25 ml of aliquot (sample solution) depending on the P content (containing not more than 25 mg P_2O_5 in the aliquot) in a 250 ml beaker, and dilute to 100 ml with distilled water.
- Add about 5-10 ml of concentrated HNO_3 and about 10 g of ammoniumnitrate.
- Heat this mixture on a water-bath at 55- 60°C for 10 minutes.
- Add 3 percent ammonium molybdate solution in the beaker drop by drop with the help of a burette. Continue stirring with a glass rod until about 50 ml of molybdate solution is added. Stir for another few minutes until the yellow precipitate appears to become granular.
- Cover the beaker with glass and allow it to settle for some time. Decant the clear solution through No. 44 filter paper, and wash the precipitate with 2 percent sodium nitrate solution, agitate thoroughly, and allow the precipitate to settle. Transfer the precipitate to the filter paper, and wash with $NaNO_3$ solution until free from acid (by test with a litmus paper).
- Transfer the precipitate and filter paper to a beaker, and add 10 ml of 0.1M NaOH at a time by pipette until the precipitate becomes soluble.
- Add 1-2 drops of 1 percent phenolphthalein, and titrate the excess of alkali against 0.1M sulphuric acid.
- Run a reagent blank with each batch.

Calculation

$$\text{Total phosphate (as } P_2O_5\%) = F \times (V_1M_1 - V_2M_2) \times df$$
$$= 0.0031 \times (40 \times 0.1 - 10 \times 0.1) \times (250/5) \times 100$$
$$= 46.5$$

Where,

F = factor for P_2O_5 corresponding to 1 ml of 1M alkali (NaOH).

The calculation is as follows:

23 g equivalent of NaOH = 31 g P = 71 g P_2O_5 (P x 2.29 = P_2O_5)

1equivalent of NaOH or 1000 ml of 1M NaOH = (71/23) g P_2O_5

1ml of 1M NaOH = (71/23) x (1/1000) g P_2O_5 = 0.0031 g P_2O_5

V1 = volume of 0.1M NaOH required to dissolve the precipitate (e.g. 40ml);

V2 = volume of 0.1M H_2SO_4 used for titration to neutralize excess alkali (e.g.10 ml);

M1 = molarity of the standard alkali (NaOH)

M2 = molarity of the standard acid (H_2SO_4)

df = dilution factor for aliquot taken:

Suppose, volume of the aliquot (solution) taken for estimation = 5 ml

Total volume of fertilizer solution prepared = 250 ml.

df = (Total volume of fertilizer solution/ Aliquot taken) = 250/5 = 50

For percentage = 100 ÷ Wt. of fertilizer

Water-soluble Phosphate (P_2O_5)

The water-soluble phosphate is obtained from the sample by dissolving it in distilled water or by washing the sample successively with distilled water. As a procedure, put 1 g of the sample on a filter paper fitted on a 12 cm funnel. Wash with small portions of water at a time to collect about 250 ml of filtrate and makeup the exact volume. Pour water into the funnel only when the earlier portion has drained fully. Otherwise, filtration and complete washing may be prolonged (which should be completed in 1 hour). The filtrate so obtained is used for estimation of phosphate by the gravimetric quinolinium phosphomolybdate method or volumetricammonium phosphomoly-bdate method as described above. The residue remaining on the filter paper contains the water-insoluble portion of P in the sample.

Available Phosphate (Neutral Ammonium Citrate-Soluble P_2O_5)

For estimating available phosphate, an indirect method is followed whereby total, water-soluble and ammonium citrate-insoluble fractions are estimated. By subtracting citrate-insoluble P from total P, estimates are made for the available P.

Apparatus

- A volumetric flask / beaker;
- A burette;
- A water-bath-cum-shaker;
- A Buchner funnel.

Reagents

- Concentrated HNO_3
- Concentrated HCl
- Concentrated H_2SO_4
- Ammonium hydroxide
- Ammonium nitrate (5%)
- Quimociac reagent (same as described in total P_2O_5 estimation)
- Filter paper
- *Neutral ammonium citrate solution*: Dissolve 370 g of pure citric acid in 1500 ml of distilled water. Add about 345 ml of 28-29% ammoniumhydroxide so that the acid is neutralized. After neutralization, the solution must attain a pH of 7.0, if it does not, adjust the pH by adding NH_4OH or citric acid solution.

Procedure

- Follow the procedure as described above for the preparation of a sample solution for estimation of water-soluble phosphate. Within 1 hour, transfer the filter paper and residue to a 250 ml conical flask containing 100 ml of ammonium citrate solution previously heated to 65°C.
- Close the flask tightly with a smooth rubber stopper, shake vigorously until the filter paper is transformed to pulp, and release pressure by removing stopper occasionally.
- Agitate continuously the contents of the stoppered flask in a controlled temperature (65 ± 0.5°C) water-bath-cum-shaker for 1 hour.
- Exactly 1 hour after adding the filter paper and residue, remove the flask from the shaker, and filter immediately by

suction as rapidly as possible through No. 5 filter paper or equivalent, using a Buchner or ordinary funnel.

- Wash with distilled water at 65^0C until the volume of filtrate is about350 ml, allowing time for thorough draining before adding more water. If the material is such that it will yield a cloudy filtrate, wash with 5 percent NH_4NO_3 solution.
- Determine the P_2O_5 in the citrate-insoluble residue (remainder on filter paper) after digestion by one of the following methods:
  - Transfer the dry filter paper and contents to a crucible; ignite until all OM is destroyed. Digest with 10-15 ml of HCl until phosphates are dissolved.
  - Transfer the filter paper and residue to a 250 ml Kjeldahl flask, boil for 30 - 45 minutes with 30 ml of HNO_3 and 10 ml of HCl. Boil very gently until it is colourless and white dense fumes appear in the flask.
  - Dilute the solution to 250 ml, mix well, and filter through dry filter paper if required. Pipette out 25 ml of aliquot containing not more than 25 mg of P_2O_5 into a 500 ml Erlenmeyer flask, and proceed as described for estimation of total P_2O_5 using quimociac reagent (above).

Calculation

Citrate insoluble (as P_2O_5%) = [3.207 (S-B) ÷100] x df x (100 ÷W)

Where,

S = weight of sample precipitate in grams

B = weight of blank precipitate in grams

W = weight of sample in grams

df = Dilution factor = (Volume of fertilizer solution/ Aliquot taken)

For percentage = 100 ÷ W

Percent available (citrate-soluble) P_2O_5 = (% total P_2O_5 - % citrate-insolubleP_2O_5). The procedure for total P_2O_5 estimation is described above.

Method for Estimation of Free Phosphoric Acid (as P_2O_5)

In the specifications of superphosphates, a certain content of free acid (a maximum of 4 percent as phosphoric acid) is allowed in order to check the conversion of water-soluble P into non-water-soluble P during long storage. Therefore, its estimation is essential in determining the quality of superphosphates.

Apparatus

- A shaker;
- Some flasks and beakers;
- A burette.

Reagents

- Acetone
- Standard sodium hydroxide solution (0.1M)
- Bromocresol green indicator solution: Dissolve 0.1 g of bromocresol green in 100 ml of rectified spirit.

Procedure

- Weigh accurately about 2.5 g of the prepared sample in a 250 ml Erlenmeyer flask.
- Add 100 ml of neutral acetone. Fix to a wrist-action shaker. Shake for 1 hour.
- Filter rapidly through No. 1 filter paper into a 250 ml Erlenmeyer flask, wash with acetone 2-3 times, adding 10 ml of acetone each time.
- Evaporate the acetone as much as possible.
- Add about 50 ml of water and drops of bromocresol green indicator.
- Titrate with standard NaOH solution until the colour changes from yellow to blue.

Calculation

Free phosphoric acid (as P_2O_5) percent by weight = $(7.1\ M \times V) \div W$

where,

M = molarity of standard NaOH solution

V = volume of standard NaOH solution

W = weight in grams of sample taken for the test

7.1 = factor (1ml 1M NaOH = 0.098 g H_3PO_4; thus, 100 ml 1M NaOH = 9.8 g H_3PO_4. The relationship between H_3PO_4 and P_2O_5 is 196:142 = 0.72. Hence, the factor is 9.8 x 0.72 = 7.1.

Determination of Potassium

In all potassic fertilizers, K is generally present in water-soluble form. Therefore, it is estimated directly in fertilizer solution either gravimetrically, volumetrically or flame photometrically. In manures and organic fertilizers, wet digestion with acid is required prior to determination of K in order to bring the element into solution form, as described for plant digestion in the Chapter 4. The methods used for K determination in fertilizers and manures are:

- Gravimetric perchloric acid method
- Gravimetric chloroplatinate method
- Gravimetric and volumetric cobaltinitrite method and
- Gravimetric and volumetric sodium tetraphenyl boron (STPB) method.

The AOAC-based STPB volumetric method is commonly used in laboratories because of its accuracy and simplicity.

STPB Method

Potassium from the fertilizer sample is first extracted with water or ammonium-oxalate. The K in extracted solution is precipitated with an excess of STPB as potassium tetraphenyl boron. The excess of STPB is back titrated with benzalkonium chloride (BAC) or quaternary ammonium chloride using Clayton yellow as indicator: $Na[B(C_6H_5)_4] + K \rightarrow K [B(C_6H_5)_4] + Na^+$. Interference of NH^{4+} takes place during K precipitation. It is avoided by complexing NH^{4+} with formaldehyde under slightly alkaline conditions before precipitation of K. The chlorides and sulphates do not interfere in the titration.

Apparatus

- Some volumetric flasks and beakers;
- A burette / semi-microburette;
- Some filter paper.

Reagents

- *Sodium hydroxide solution (20%)*: Dissolve 20 g of NaOH in 100 ml of distilled water.
- Formaldehyde (HCHO) solution (37%).
- *STPB solution (about 1.2%)*: Dissolve 12 g of STPB in about 800 ml of water. Add 20 -25 g of $Al(OH)_3$, stir for 5 minutes, and filter through No.42 filter paper (or equivalent) into a 1 litre volumetric flask. Rinse the beaker sparingly with water and add to the filtrate. Collect the entire filtrate, add 2 ml of 20 percent NaOH solution, dilute to volume (1 litre) with water, and mix. Let it stand for 48 hours, and then standardize (as described below). Adjust (by using K salt of known composition for prior standardization by trial and error) so that 1 ml of STPB = 1 percent K2O. Store at room temperature.
- *BAC or quaternary ammonium chloride solution (about 0.625%)*: Dilute 50 ml of 12.8% BAC to 1 litre with water, mix and standardize (as described below). If a different concentration is used, adjust the volume accordingly (BAC of 0.625%strength is required so the dilution can be done according to the concentration available).
- *Clayton yellow (0.04 %) indicator*: Dissolve 40 mg of Clayton yellow powder in 100 ml of water.
- *Ammonium oxalate solution* $[(NH_4)_2\ C_2O_4]$ (4%): Dissolve 40 g of ammonium oxalate in 1 litre of distilled water.

Standardization of the solutions

- *BAC solution*: Put 1 ml of STPB solution in a 250 ml Erlenmeyer flask; add 20-25 ml of water, 1 ml of 20% NaOH, 2.2 ml of HCHO, 1.5 ml of 4% ammonium oxalate, and 6-8 drops of Clayton yellow indicator. Titrate to pink end point with BAC solution, using a 10 ml semimicroburette.
- Adjust by increasing or decreasing the strength of the BAC solution so that 2 ml = 1 ml of STPB solution (keeping 1 ml STPB = 1% K_2O).
- *STPB solution*: Dissolve 2.5 g of KH_2PO_4 in about 150 ml of water in a 250 ml volumetric flask, add 50 ml of 4% ammonium oxalate solution, dilute to volume with water, and mix. Transfer 15 ml of aliquot (51.92 mg of K_2O or 43.10 mg of K) to a 100 ml volumetric flask, add 2 ml of 20 percent NaOH, 5 ml of HCHO

and 43 ml of STPB solution. Dilute to volume (100ml) with water, and mix thoroughly. Let it stand for 5-10 minutes, and then pass through dry No. 42 filter paper. Transfer 50 ml of aliquot of filtrate to a 250 ml Erlenmeyer flask, add 6-8 drops of Clayton yellow indicator, and titrate excess STPB with BAC solution to pink end point.

Calculate factor (f) by:

f = % K_2O ÷ ml of STPB solution 43 ml of BAC used for standardization

= 34.61÷ 43-ml of BAC used for standardization

Where, 34.61 = % K_2O present in standard KH_2PO_4.

Procedure

- *K extraction/preparation of sample solution*: Dissolve a known weight (2.5 g) of straight K fertilizer (MOP, SOP, potassium magnesium sulphate) in 200 ml of distilled water, and make the volume up to 250 ml for estimation. For NPK complex fertilizers or NPK fertilizer mixtures, dissolve the sample in 125 ml of water, add 50 ml of 4% ammonium oxalate solution, and boil for 30 minutes; after cooling, filter through dry No. 12 filter paper, and make the volume up to 250 ml for further estimation.
- Transfer 15 ml of aliquot of sample solution to a 100 ml volumetric flask and add 2 ml of 20 percent NaOH and 5 ml of HCHO.
- Add 1 ml of standard STPB solution for each 1% of K_2O expected in the sample plus an additional 8 ml in excess in order to ensure complete precipitation.
- Dilute to volume (100 ml) with water, mix thoroughly, let it stand for 5-10 minutes, and pass it through No. 12 filter paper (or equivalent).
- Transfer 50 ml of filtrate to a 250 ml Erlenmeyer flask, add 6-8 drops of Clayton yellow indicator, and titrate excess STPB with standard BAC solution to pink end point.

Calculation

% K_2O = (ml STPB used - ml BAC used) x f

Where,

f = % K_2O/ml of STPB solution. This factor applies to all fertilizers where 2.5 g of sample is diluted to 250 ml, and 15 ml of aliquot is taken for analysis. To express the results as K rather than K_2O, substitute 28.73 for 34.61 in calculating the value of f.

Determination of Micronutrients

The methods for estimating micronutrients in soils using an AAS are described in the Chapter 3. In the case of soils, the available micronutrient content is first extracted with the help of appropriate extractants such as DTPA. After standardization of the AAS, the micronutrient content in the extract is estimated.

For mineral fertilizers, that are in 100% water-soluble form, the estimation of micronutrients is carried out using water-dissolved samples. The NPK complex/ compound fertilizers and fertilizer mixtures with water-insoluble ingredients need to be acid digested (similar to organic fertilizers) before analysis is carried out.

Standard curves are prepared for the relevant micronutrients in the same manner as described in Chapter 3. The water-soluble or acid-digested fertilizer samples are used in appropriate quantities so that the content is within the range of concentration used in the standard curve. The nutrient content is calculated taking into account the weight of the sample, the volume made and the aliquot used for estimation.

Analytical Methods for Manures Analysis

Unlike soil analysis where available nutrients and fertilizers where (both mineral and organic) the total contents of nutrients are estimated. In the case of organic fertilizers, the C content and the total content of nutrients are considered relevant and not their forms as they are low-analysis materials. Therefore, organic fertilizers are first acid digested as per the di-acid digestion method described in Chapter 4 (wet digestion method) in order to bring them into solution. From this solution, nutrient estimations are carried out using standards methods. The method for C content estimation is the same as described in Chapter 3. The methods for estimation of total N, P and K in organic fertilizers are the same as described above for mineral fertilizers. From wet digested solution of manures, micronutrient estimations are carried out using an AAS as described in Chapter 3. The sample size should be 1.0 g (to be weighed exactly).

7

Modern Techniques in Analysis of Soil, Plant, Water and Fertilizer/ Manures

Introduction

In view of the accepted importance of analysis, the workload on soil, plant and water testing laboratories has increased considerably in recent years. Therefore, analytical methods have needed to be accelerated through the automation of instruments. Almost all instruments either contain inbuilt computers or can interface directly with microprocessors, thereby simplifying instrument operation and providing versatility for the analyst. Most operations can be performed through keyboard commands. This type of instrument automation enables:

- Higher working speeds
- Lower labour requirements
- Added consistency and accuracy
- Flexible and extensive data processing
- Various modes of display and
- Potential for unattended measurements.

Commonly used automated advance equipments are:

- Atomic Absorption Spectrometry (AAS)
- Inductively Coupled Plasma (ICP) emission spectrometry
- Mass spectrometry (MS)
- Near Infrared Reflectance spectrometry (NIR)
- Ion Chromatography (IC) and
- Electrochemical methods (to a lesser extent).

In combination with the above techniques, continuous flow analysis (CFA) and flow injection analysis (FIA) are often used. An ICP emission spectrophotometer cannot be operated without the use of microprocessors. The microprocessor (with the help of software) enables the automatic sampling, setting of instrument operating parameters, calibration, result evaluation, data storage and retrieval, data transfer, etc. required for the operation of the instrument for the analysis of a particular element.

The entire laboratory operation from sample preparation to calculating and reporting of concentration of analyte can be automated with the help of robotic systems, which are available and undergoing continuous development. The type of robot that may work best in a soil testing laboratory is one that travels on a track, the length of which can be essentially unlimited (Munter, 1990).

Through the use of a laboratory information management system (LIMS), the automatic control of the functioning of the system, computations and data management can be carried out efficiently. Skotnikov (1998) developed an automated workstation for soil analysis. The methods and uses of some modern multi-element analysing are discussed below (adapted from Singh, Chhonkar and Pandey, 1999). Each item of equipments has an operational manual supplied by the manufacturers.

Modern Equipments

Autoanalysers

Autoanalysers are versatile modularized instruments used for automatic chemical analysis of soil, plant, water and fertilizer samples. These systems are mainly of two types, i.e. CFA and FIA. They are designed to offer automatic simulation of operations used in manual procedures for the estimation of an element on a conveyer-belt principle.

Usually, autoanalysers use the same reagents as those used in manual assays.

Principle

In autoanalysers based on the CFA mechanism, the samples are loaded into cups or test-tubes on the sampler. The samples and a number of streams of reagents are made to flow from one module to the next through plastic or glass tubings by the action of multiple-channel peristaltic pumps operating continuously. Each module automatically performs a different function in the analysis. Air bubbles are added to the flowing analytical stream to segment the streams of samples and reagents (Ferreira, Rangel and Lima, 1998). The samples and reagents are brought together under controlled conditions in the mixing coils that are part of the manifold, causing a chemical reaction that produces colour. The FIA system is similar to the CFA system in its modules. However, there is no air segmentation and the sample is injected rapidly into the carrier stream via an injection valve or syringe as a "plug".

Operating procedure

The operating procedure is:

- Prepare working standards of required concentrations, reagents and carrier solutions.
- Switch on the sampler, analyser and spectrophotometer and allow at least 30 minutes to warm up.
- Set the wavelength, gain factor, pump times, injection valve cycle, plotting parameter, etc. through keyboard commands of the modules as per the requirement of the analysis. Where the instrument interfaces with a microprocessor, the above parameters may be set automatically by the default choice.
- Place the blank, working standards and samples in cups or test-tubes on circular tray of sampler in proper sequence.
- Place the carrier and reagent solution bottle in the holder.
- Loosen the tube holders of the pumps and insert the pump tubes. Connect the aspiration ends of all the pump tubes except one to a bottle containing degassed water. Then press the ends of all the pump tubes except one, which is connected to the manifold (chemifold). Connect the aspiration end of the remaining pump tube to the injection valve outlet and its pressed end to the waste tube.

- Attach the pump tube holders, and release the tension by turning the tension screws counter-clockwise.
- Lubricate the pump tubes and the rollers with a small amount of silicon oil.
- Assemble the manifold (chemifold) as per the requirement of the procedure and flow diagram. The reaction coils and tubes used for various connections should be checked carefully according to the prescribed colour code.
- Connect the inlet stream of the flow cell to the manifold, and the out stream to the waste bottle.
- Check the flow pattern of the carrier stream by running the pumps. Apply sufficient pressure on the pump tube holders by turning the tension screws clockwise until liquid starts flowing through the pump tubes. In the event of any leakage, stop the pump and correct it.
- After checking the flow pattern, remove the aspiration end of the pump tube from degassed water bottle and connect it to the carrier and reagent solution bottles according to the requirement of the method (see application note). Now the instrument is ready for the actual run.
- Start the pumps and set the baseline zero from the keyboard on the spectrophotometer by injecting the blank. Then, run the instrument for calibration and sample analysis.
- Generate a calibration curve by recording absorbance from the display of the recorder of a series of standard solutions of increasing concentrations. From the absorbance of the test solution, determine the concentration using the calibration curve. With microprocessor-interfaced instruments, the sample peaks are compared automatically with the calibration curve after being corrected for baseline and sensitivity drift, and the results are displayed on the monitor screen.
- If the instrument shows signs of "over" or "error", then dilute the samples considering the observed absorbance of the sample, and feed the sample again.
- The procedure for closing down the instrument is:
  - Before closing down, operate the instrument using degassed distilled water from all the channels until the detector reading returns to zero.

- Loosen the pump tube holders immediately after the analysis.
- Switch off the instrument in the following order: spectrophotometer, analyser, sampler and computer.

Precautions

It is important to observe the following precautions at all times:

- Never use any component of the instrument if it is in need of adjustment and/or repair.
- Always keep the equipment clean. It is important to clean the sampler and manifold immediately after the analysis is over.
- Clean the rollers and the pump tube holders every month. Lubricate the rollers and the pump tube holders with silicon oil regularly.
- Replace flattened and dirty pump tubes. While using new pump tubes, care should be taken for the change in the flow rate.
- Use all the tubings of prescribed diameter or colour code for a particular method as given in the operating manual.
- Check all the tubings before use for clogging of the passage.
- Develop different manifold (chemifold) units for different analytical methods in order to avoid sample contamination.
- Use solvent-resistant manifold for organic solvents. Never use organic solvent on perspex manifold, not even for cleaning stains.
- Check the manifold bores regularly for plugging. Use a nylon wire or steel to remove solid particles.
- Keep the external walls of the flow cell absolutely clean. Fingerprints, grease, etc. can be removed using tissue paper soaked in acetone or absolute ethanol.
- Care should be taken in handling cadmium during column preparation as itis toxic.

Atomic Absorption Spectrophotometer

Principle

In an analysis employing an atomic absorption spectrophotometer (AAS), the sample in the form of a homogeneous liquid is aspirated into a flame where "free" atoms of the element to be analysed are created. A light source (hollow cathode lamp) is used to excite the free atoms formed in the flame by the absorption of the electromagnetic radiation. The decrease in energy (absorption) is then measured. It follows the Lambert–Beer law, i.e. the absorbance is proportional to the number of free atoms in the ground state (Baker and Suhr, 1982).

Preparation of Standards and Sample Solutions

- Prepare stock standards in concentrations of 1000 mg/litre from pure metal wire, granules, foil, metal oxides or other suitable primary standard compounds of the elements.
- Prepare a blank sample using the same reagents as used for standard samples but without the elements intended to be estimated.
- Free the sample solution from interfering elements and suspended solids, which may cause clogging of the nebulizer.
- Adjust both standards and unknowns to a concentration range that is compatible with the analytical range of the instrument. It should preferably be at least 5–10 times the detection limit of the instrument.

Operation procedure

- Check the instrument for the proper fitting of all the tubings, required type of burner (air acetylene or nitrous oxide acetylene) and hollow cathode lamps.
- Fill the liquid trap with the solvent to be used for the analysis.
- Align the hollow cathode lamp of the element to be analysed with the optical path of the instrument by rotating the lamp turret.
- Switch on the instrument and allow at least 30 minutes for warming up.
- Switch on the deuterium lamp for background correction, which is generally required when the wavelength of the resonance line of the element is less than 250 nm.
- Use the lamp current recommended by the lamp manufacturer.
- Select the desirable wavelength and the band pass width or slit width.

- Optimize the burner position by using the vertical, horizontal and rotational adjustment knobs until the burner slot is aligned with the beam and is just below the position from where it starts to block the light path.
- Switch on the compressor in order to generate air supply in the case of an air acetylene flame. If an N_2O acetylene flame is used, turn on the N_2O supply cylinder. Select air with the support selector knob. Adjust the support flow (air) reading to between 6 and 9 flow units.
- If a nitrous oxide acetylene flame is used, then first ignite an air acetylene flame and then change over to a nitrous oxide acetylene flame.
- Turn on the gas supply from cylinder, use the fuel-control knob of the instrument and light the flame.
- Adjust the fuel control (acetylene) and support control (air or nitrous oxide) knobs to produce the required kind of flame of air acetylene or nitrous oxide acetylene flame.
- Set the instrument to zero by means of the "zero" control against a reagent "blank" solution.
- Aspirate a standard (or sample) and optimize fuel, oxidant and sample flow rates by adjusting the fuel knob, fuel support knob and nebulizer so that a maximum signal (absorbance) is achieved.
- Prepare a calibration curve by recording the absorbance of a series of working standards. The calibration must be done for each set of analysis.
- If the instrument shows signs of "over" or "error", then dilute the samples depending on the absorbance of the sample, and feed the sample again.
- If the instrument has been used in a higher concentration range, then operate the instrument using distilled water until the reading returns to zero, before closing down.
- Procedure for closing down the instrument is:
  - Turn off the gas from the cylinder.
  - Wait for extinction of the flame, and then turn off the fuel-control knob.
  - Turn off the air compressor and fuel-support knob.

- The shutdown sequence for a nitrous oxide acetylene flame involves first changing over to an air acetylene flame and then extinguishing it.
- Switch off the instrument.

Precautions

- Acetylene cylinders should always be used in a vertical position in order to prevent liquid acetone entering the gas line.
- Acetylene cylinders should not be run at a pressure lower than 500 kPa. Never operate acetylene lines at more than 100 kPa. At higher pressures, acetylene can decompose or explode spontaneously.
- Never run the nitrous oxide acetylene flame without the "red feather" visible, or with less than five flow units of acetylene.
- Do not leave uncovered containers of the volatile organic solvents near the uncovered flame.
- Do not look at flame without the aid of safety glasses or the flame shield.
- Do not leave the flame completely unattended.
- Do not ignite the flame if the air flow is below six flow units.
- Do not adjust the air (or N_2O) and gas supply to alter the sensitivity of the instrument after calibration of the instrument.

Inductively Coupled Plasma - Atomic Emission Spectroscopy

A new analytical technique called inductively coupled plasma - atomic emission spectroscopy (ICP-AES) is used for simultaneous multi-element analysis of biological materials and soils. This technique offers advantages over an AAS and other multielement methods because matrix problems are eliminated or minimized through the use of the high-temperature argon plasma. Apart from multielement capability at all concentration levels, plasmas are noted for their relative freedom from the chemical and ionization interferences that are common with an AAS.

The detection limits are equal to or better than an AAS (depending on the element analysed). Elements such as aluminium, phosphorus, sulphur and boron, which are either poorly measured at low concentrations or not possible with an AAS, arereadily determined with higher sensitivity by ICP-AES.

Principle

The ICP–AES method is based on the observation of atomic emission spectra when samples in the form of an aerosol, thermally generated vapour or powder are injected into an ICP atomization and excitation source. By definition, plasma refers to a hot gas in which a significant fraction of the atoms or molecules is ionized. Plasmas are electrically conducted and have been referred to as electrical flames, as no combustion takes place. This is because instruments using a plasma source generally use inert argon gas.

The ICP is produced by passing initially ionized argon gas through a quartz torch located within an induction coil (copper coil) that is connected to a radiofrequency (RF) generator. The RF generator produces 1.5–3 kW of power at a frequency of 27.1 MHz. An oscillating magnetic field is formed within the quartz torch in response to the RF energy passing through the coil. Electrons and ions passing through the oscillating electromagnetic field flow at high acceleration rates within the quartz torch space. As argon gas enters the magnetic field associated with the induction coil, its atoms collide with the accelerated ions and electrons, resulting in the ionization of the argon gas. These collisions give rise to ohmic heating, which produces plasma with temperatures ranging from 4 000 to 6 000 °C.

The resultant plasma is contained within the torch by means of argon flow. The method of presenting the sample to the plasma is similar to that used in flame atomic absorption. The liquid sample is aspirated into the plasma through a nebulizer system, using argon carrier gas at a rate of about 1 litre of argon per minute. The prevailing high temperature in the plasma leads to complete vaporization, atomization and excitation of the element to be analysed. The exited neutral atoms or ions of the sample emit radiation of characteristic wavelengths. The intensity of the emitted radiation is measured by the spectrophotometer component of the ICP–AES instrument.

Preparation of Soil and Plant Samples

The digestion of soil and plant samples for total elemental analysis by ICP–AES is similar to that used for other emission instruments. Universal/multielement soil extractants are used for the extraction of soil samples. Recently, acidified ABDTPA and Mehlich No. 1 extracts have been analysed by ICP–AES (Soltanpour *et al.*, 1998).

Preparation of Standard Solution

The procedure for the preparation of stock standard solution containing 1 000 mg/litre of an element from pure metal wire or suitable compounds of the element is similar to that described for AAS. However, multielement working standard solutions (secondary standards) should be made in such a way that these contain the maximum number of the elements compatible with stability considerations and match with the sample solutions in kind and strength of acids. In soil and plant analysis, one set of secondary standards is required for each multielement extracting solution, and one for each soil and plant digest. Mc Quaker, Kluckner and Chang (1979) devised a calibration scheme for 30 elements that satisfies the needs of analysts engaged in soil, water, tissue, and particulate matter analysis.

Operation procedure

The general principles that allow the determination of the optimal analytical conditions for the operation of ICP–AES are similar to those for AAS. Microprocessors are used for the automatic control of instrument components, setup and optimization of required operational parameters, instrument calibration, and manipulation and storage of data through key commands. As the actual operation of different ICP spectrometers varies with the type, make and computer software of the instrument, the operation manual provided by the manufacturers should be consulted. Usually, when an ICP spectrophotometer is purchased, the manufacturer/dealer provides training to the analysts on operating procedures.

Precautions

It is important to observe the following precautions at all times:

- Filter soil extracts and soil and plant tissue digests with No. 42 filter paper to prevent clogging of the nebulizer.
- To prevent clogging of the nebulizer tip, use either a high salt nebulizer (Babington-type) or standards and samples with a very low salt content.
- Avoid mixing chemicals that cause precipitation during the preparation of multielement working standard solutions.

References and Further Reading

Baker, D.E. and Suhr, N.H. 1982. *Atomic absorption and flame emission spectrometry. Methods of soil analysis, Part 2*. 2nd edition. Agronomy Monogram. Madison, USA, ASA and SSSA.

Bear, F.E. 1964. *Chemistry of the soil.* American Chemical Society.

Black, C.A. 1965. Methods of Soil Analysis, *Soc. Agron. In., Madison, USA.*

Chopra, S.L. and Kanwar, J.S. 1991. *Analytical agricultural chemistry.* New Delhi, Kalyani Publishers.

Day, P.R. 1965. Particle fractionation and particle-size analysis p. 545-56. *In* C.A. Black et al (ed.) Methods of soil analysis, Part 1. Agronomy 9:545-567. Gee, G. W., and J. W. Bauder. 1979. Particle size analysis by hydrometer: a simplified method for routine textural analysis and a sensitivity test ofmeasured parameters. *Soil Sci Soc. Am. J.* 43:1004-1007.

FAI 1985. *Fertilizer (Control) Order.* India.

FAO 1998. *Guidelines for quality management in soil and plant laboratories,* by L.P. van Reeuwijk and V.J.G. Houba. *FAO Soils Bulletin No. 74.*

FAO. 2004. *Integrated nutrient management – A glossary of terms,* by H.L.S. Tandon and R.N. Roy. Rome.

Gee, G. W., and J. W. Bauder. 1986. Particle-size Analysis. P. 383 - 411. *In* A.L. Page (ed.). Methods of soil analysis, Part1, Physical and mineralogical methods. Second Edition, Agronomy Monograph 9, American Society of Agronomy, Madison, WI. U.S. Salinity Lab. Staff. 1954. Methods for soil characterization. p. 83-147. Diagnosis and improvement of saline and alkali soils. Agr. Handbook 60, USDA, Washington, D.C.

Gupta, P.K. 2000. *Soil, plant, water and fertilizer analysis.* Jodhpur, India, Agrobios.

Hanway, J.J. and Heidel, H. 1952. Soil analysis methods as used in Iowa State College Soil Testing Laboratory. *Iowa Agric.*, 57: 1–31.

Hesse, P.R. 1994. *A text book of soil chemical analysis.* Delhi, CBS Publishers and Distributors.

Indian Agricultural Research Institute. *Soil, plant and water testing methods – A laboratory manual,* India.

Jackson, M.L. 1962. *Soil chemical analysis.* New Delhi, Prentice Hall of India Pvt. Ltd.

Jackson, ML. 1958. *Soil Chemical Analysis*. Prentice-Hall Inc., New Jersey.

Jones, J.B. Jr., Wolf, B. and Mills, H.A. 1991. *Plant analysis handbook: a practical sampling, preparation, analysis, and interpretation guide.* Athens, USA, Micromacro Publishing Inc.

Keen, B. and H.J. Rackzonski (1921). Relationship between clay content and certain physical properties of the spoil, *J Agric Sci*, **11:** 441-449.

Lindsay, W.L. and Norvell, W.A. 1978. Development of a DTPA soil test for zinc, iron, manganese, and copper. *Soil Sci. Soc. Am. J.*, 42: 421–448.

Motsara, M.R. and Tripathi, N. 1983. *A laboratory handbook for fertilizer analysis.* Faridabad, India, CFQCTI.

Muhr, G.R., Datta, N.P., Shankarsubramoncy, H., Leley, V.K. and Donahue, R.L. 1965. *Soil testing in India*. USDA.

Norris, D.O. and Date, R.A. 1976. Legume bacteriology in tropical pasture research principles and methods. *CAB International (Comm. W. Bur. Past. Field Crops Hurl. Berks. Bull.)*, 51: 134–174.

Page, A.L., Miller, R.H. and Keeney. D.R. eds. 1982. *Methods of soil analysis.* Part 2. No. 9, Agronomy series. Madison, USA, ASA-SSSA.

Palaskar, M.S., Babrekar, P.G. and Ghosh, A.B. 1981. A rapid analytical technique to estimate sulphur in soil and plant extracts. *J. Ind. Soc. Soil. Sci.*, 29: 249–256.

Paliwal, K.V. and Yadav, B.R. 1976. *Irrigation water quality and crop production in Delhi territory.* Tech. Bull. No. 9. New Delhi, IARI. pp.166.

Perur, N.G., Subramanian, C.K., Muhr, G.R. and Ray, H.E. 1973. *Soil fertility evaluation to serve Indian farmers.* USDA.

Piper, C.S. 1966. *Soil and plant analysis*. Bombay, India, Hans Publishers.

Prasad, R. 1998. *A Practical manual for soil fertility.* New Delhi, Division of Agronomy, IARI.

Reuter, D.J. and Robinson, J.B. 1986. *Plant analysis – an interpretation manual.* Melbourne and Sydney, Australia, Inkata Press.

Richards, L.A. 1954. *Diagnosis and improvement of saline and alkali soils.* Handbook No. 60. USDA.

Schoonover, W.R. 1952. *Examination of soils for alkali*. Berkeley, USA, University of California Extension Services.

Shoemaker, H.E., McLean, E.O. and Pratt, P.F. 1961. Buffer methods for determining lime requirement of soils with appreciable amounts of extractable aluminium. *Proc. Soil Sci. Soc. Am.*, 25: 274–277.

Singh, D., Chhonkar, P.K. and Pandey, R.N. 1999. *Soil plant water analysis – a methods manual.* New Delhi, IARI.

Skotnikov, A. 1998. Automated unit for soil sample preparation and processing. *Soil Sci. Plant Anal.*, 29(11–14): 2015–2033.

Soltanpour, P.N., Johnson, G.W., Workman, S.M., Jones, J.B. Jr. and Miller, R.O. 1998. Advances in ICP emission and ICP mass spectrometry. *Adv. Agron.*, 64: 27–113.

Subbiah, B.V. and Asija, G.L. 1956. A rapid procedure for the determination of available nitrogen in soils. *Curr. Sci.*, 25: 259–260.

Tandon, H.L.S. ed. 1993. *Methods of analysis of soils, plants, waters and fertilizers.* New Delhi, FDCO.

Tandon, HLS. 2001. *Methods of Analysis of soils, plants, waters & Fertilizers*. Fertilizer Development & Consultation Organization, New Delhi.

Tisdale, S.L., Nelson, W.L. and Beaton, J.D. 1985. *Soil fertility and fertilizers*. New York, USA, Macmillan Publishing Company.

Veihmeyer, F.J. and Hendrickson, A.H. 1931. The moisture equivalent as a measure of the field capacity of soils. *Soil Sci.*, 32: 181–194.

Walsh, L.M. and Beaton, J.D., eds. 1973. *Soil testing and plant analysis*. Madison, USA, SSSA, Inc.

Wilde, S.A., R.B. Corey, J.G. Iyer and G.K. Voigt. 1979. *Soil and Plant Analysis for Tree Culture*. Oxford IBH, Bombay and New Delhi. Reprinted 1985.

Willard, H.H., Merrit, L.L. Jr. and Dean, J.A. 1965. *Instrumental methods of analysis*. New Delhi, Affiliated East-West Press Pvt. Ltd.

Yoder, R.A. 1936. A direct method of aggregate analysis of soils and a study of the physical nature of erosion losses. *J. Am. Soc. Agron.*, 28: 337–351.

Annexures

1. Annual Requirements for the Soil, Plant and Water analysis laboratory (Capacity: 10000 Soil Samples, 1000 Plant Samples and 500 Water Samples Per Year)

Sl. No	Name/specification/description	Quantity
A.	**Equipment Requirement**	
1.	Analytical / semi-micro balance Capacity = 300 g Resolution = 0.1 mg Pan size = 100 mm	2 (1 of each type)
2.	Two-pan balance Capacity = 500 g Resolution = 0.2%	1
3.	**pH meter:** range 0-14 pH with accuracy of ±0.05 pH, complete with combination electrode, mains operated; to work on 220 V, 50 cycles	2
4.	**Conductivity bridge:** single range 0-15 mS/cm directly calibrated with temperature compensation and cell constant adjuster, complete with pipette-type conductivity cell having platinum electrodes duly coated with platinum black and having a cell constant of 1.00±0.01%; mains operated with electronic "eye" null indicator; to work on 220 V, 50 cycles	1

Contd.

5.	**Photoelectric colorimeter:** with dual-barrier-type matched photocells with sensitive galvanometer for null adjustment and logarithmically calibrated potentiometer to read directly optical density on dial, complete with optical glass filters for maximum transmission at 420, 540 and 660 nm wavelengths; mains operated; to work on 220 V, 50 cycles Or spectrophotometer	1
6.	(i). **Shaking machine:** reciprocating type, variable speed of 70-300 strokes per minute, with box-type platform carrier (size: 79 cm long × 43 cm wide × 8 cm high) fitted with heavy-duty electric motor for continuous operation and built-in 0-60 minutes times witch; to work on 220 V, 50 cycles	1
7.	(ii). Water-bath shaker with 50 cm × 38 cm water-bath size mounted on the shaking machine as 6(i)	1
8.	**Centrifuge:** clinical type with head to take 12 tubes of 15 ml capacity, complete with metal shields, rubber cushions and 15 ml centrifuge polyethylene tubes; to work on 220 V, 50 cycles	1
9.	**Voltage stabilizers (constant voltage transformers):** input 170-250 V, AC output 220 V Capacity: 1, 2 & 5 kW	1 each
10.	**Voltage stabilizers** (constant voltage transformers): Input 170-250 V, AC output 220 + 5 V	2
11.	**Pressure vacuum pump:** to deliver 0.04 m3 of air per minute at a maximum pressure of 1.1 kg/cm^2 and create vacuum of 28° mercury column, complete with pressure gauge and ballast; to work on 220 V, 50 cycles (SI unit)	2
12.	**Automatic pipetting machine:** Brewer-type, adjustable volume and frequency of cycling, to deliver up to 50 ml solution; syringe, plunger cylinder, valves and intake and delivery tubes made of neutral hard glass or resistant plastic material; to work on 220 V, 50 cycles	2
13.	**Demineralizer plant:** For obtaining deionized water, regenerating type, separate or mixed-bed resin columns treated water to have pH 6.8-7.0, portable model, capacity - 75 litres of deionized silica free water per hour	1
14.	**Oven:** laboratory model, made of stainless steel inside and outside, maximum temperature 180 °C, thermostatically controlled, ±1.0 °C accuracy, inside chamber - 30 cm × 30 cm × 30 cm	1
15.	**Trolleys** (push carts) made of tubular frame mounted on rubber casters, with mild steel top; size 60 cm × 75 cm and with a height of 90 cm	4
16.	**Flask stand:** To hold eleven 100 ml conical flasks, with adjustable base and collar - total length of stand 75 cm,	10

Contd.

	width 8 cm, overall height 12 cm, distance between flasks 6.5 cm to fit multiple dispensing equipment (wood)	
17.	**Funnel stand:** To hold eleven 5-7 cm diameter glass funnels, to correspond to flask stand	10
18.	(i). **Beaker stand:** To hold eleven 50 ml beakers - to fit multiple dispensing equipment (wood)	10
	(ii). Burette stand with clamps	4
19.	**Test-tube stand:** To hold 11 test-tubes of 25 mm × 150 mm, distance between test tubes 6.5 cm, overall height 16 cm (wood)	10
20.	**Multiple dispensing equipment:** with 11 units each 50 ml, to fit 75 cm tray, distance between flasks from centre to centre 6.5 cm, width of tray 8 cm, distance from centre of outer flasks and end of tray 4.5 cm, overall height of tray 12 cm	2
21.	**Multiple dispensing equipment:** with 11 units each 25 ml, to fit 75 cm tray, distance between flasks from centre to centre 6.5 cm, width of tray 8 cm, distance from centre of outer flasks and end of tray 4.5 cm, overall height of tray 12 cm	2
22.	**Multiple dispensing equipment:** With 11 units each 20 ml, to fit 75 cm tray, distance between flasks from centre to centre 6.5 cm, width of tray 8 cm, distance from centre of outer flasks and end of tray 4.5 cm overall, height of tray 12 cm	2
23.	**Washing assembly:** for washing glassware used with multiple dispensing equipment, pipe and jet made of PVC, combined unit for both tap-water washing and distilled water rinsing, complete with brackets for mounting in sink	1
24.	**Scoops:** for soil sampling, made of brass with wooden handle. A set of 5 scoops to measure 1 , 2.5 , 5.0 , 10 and 12.5 g of soil	2
25.	**Mortar and pestle:** heavy cast-iron mortar or porcelain mortar, glazed outside only, size 160 mm diameter with wooden rubber-tipped pestle	2
26.	(i). **Sieves:** 20 cm in diameter, 5 cm high with 2 mm round holes, preferably made of stainless steel, complete with cover lid and receiver pan	3
	(ii). 1 mm sieve with similar specifications	1
27.	**Trays:** for drying soil samples, made of aluminium sheet, 22 cm × 22 cm × 8 cm 100 27.	100
28.	**Hotplate:** rectangular 45 cm × 60 cm with three positions: low, medium and high, heavy-duty rotary switch, 1 kW to work on 220 V, 50 cycles	2

Contd.

29.	Kjeldahl assembly, both as digestion and distillation set, having a capacity to hold 6 round-bottomed flask of 300 ml capacity each complete with condenser and connecting tubes Heating capacity of 500 W of each heater	1
30.	Fumehood - digestion chamber to hold Kjeldahl assembly of 6 sets 1	1
31.	**Atomic absorption spectrophotometer:** double-beam with spare hollow cathode lamps for zinc, copper, manganese, iron, boron and molybdenum	1
32.	Muffle furnace with temperature 1 000 °C ± 5 °C, size of furnace 10 cm × 15 cm 1	1
B.	**Annual Chemicals Requirement**	
1.	Acetic acid (glacial)	10 litre
2.	Activated charcoal - P-free	10kg
3.	Ammonium ferrous sulphate (CP)	10kg
4.	Ammonia solution (CP)	10 litre
5.	Ammonium acetate (CP)	40kg
6.	Ammonium bicarbamate (AR)	1kg
7.	Ammonium metavanadate (AR)	1kg
8.	Ammonium molybdate (AR)	3kg
9.	Ammonium vanadate (AR)	500g
10.	Ascorbic acid	100g
11.	Barium chloride (CP and AR)	1kg each
12.	Boric acid (CP)	10kg
13.	Bromocresol green	500g
14.	Buffer solutions (pH 4.0, 7.0 & 9.2)	2bottles each
15.	Calcium acetate (CP)	500g
16.	Calcium carbonate (CP)	500g
17.	Calcium sulphate (CP)	500g
18.	Copper sulphate (AR)	500g
19.	Copper sulphate (CP)	500g
20.	Calcium sulphate (CP)	1kg
21.	Copper sulphate (AR)	500 g
22.	Copper sulphate (CP)	1kg
23.	Diethylene triamine pentaacetic acid	2kg
24.	Digestion mixture containing potassium sulphate and copper sulphate	10kg
25.	Diphenyl amine indicator	100g

Contd.

26.	EDTA - disodium salt	1kg
27.	Eriochrome black - T	50g
28.	Ethyl alcohol	5 litres
29.	Ferrous sulphate (AR)	500 g
30.	Ferrous sulphate (CP)	500 g
31.	Filter paper, No. 1 (460 mm × 570 mm)	2500 sheets
32.	Filter paper, 110 mm, No. 40	5 packets
33.	Filter paper, 110 mm, No. 42	5 packets
34.	Gum acacia	0.5 kg
35.	Hydrochloric acid (CP)	100 litres
36.	Hydrogen peroxide	5 litres
37.	Hydroxylamine hydrochloride	1 kg
38.	Magnesium chloride (AR)	500 g
39.	Manganese sulphate (AR)	500 g
40.	Manganese chloride (CP)	1 kg
41.	Methyl orange	25 g
42.	Methyl red	25 g
43.	Methylene blue	50 g
44.	Monocalcium phosphate (AR)	500 g
45.	Mureoxide indicator	100 g
46.	Nitric acid (CP)	10 litres
47.	Nitric acid (AR)	10 litres
48.	Nitrophenol (CP)	500 g
49.	Paranitrophenol (CP)	1 kg
50.	Perchloric acid (CP)	10 litres
51.	pH indicator papers (full pH range)	10 books
52.	Phenolphthalein indicator	100 g
53.	Phosphoric acid (LR)	5 litres
54.	Potassium dihydrogen phosphate (KH2PO4) (AR)	500 g
55.	Potassium chloride (AR)	2 kg
56.	Potassium chromate (CP)	500 g
57.	Potassium dichromate (AR)	2 kg
58.	Potassium dihydrogen orthophosphate	500 g
59.	Potassium hydrogen phthalate (AR)	500 g
60.	Potassium permanganate (CP)	2 kg
61.	Potassium sulphate (AR)	1 kg
62.	Salicylic acid (CP)	1 kg

Contd.

63.	Silver sulphate	1 kg
64.	Sodium bicarbonate (LR)	30 kg
65.	Sodium carbonate (AR)	500 g
66.	Sodium carbonate (CP)	1 kg
67.	Sodium cyanide	100 g
68.	Sodium diethyl dithiocarbamate	500 g
69.	Sodium fluoride (CP)	500 g
70.	Sodium hydroxide (CP)	50 kg
71.	Sodium thiosulphate (CP)	500 g
72.	Stannous chloride (AR)	500 g
73.	Sucrose (AR)	500 g
74.	Sucrose (CP)	1 kg
75.	Sulphuric acid (conc./CP)	50 litres
76.	Toluene	500 ml
77.	Tri-ethanol amine granule (CP)	500 g
78.	Tri-ethanol amine	500 ml
79.	Universal indicator	100 ml
80.	Zinc sulphate (AR)	500 g

C. Annual Glassware requirement

1.	Bottle (polyethylene) 20 litres	5
2.	Bottle (polyethylene) 10 litres	5
3.	Bottle (glass) for reagents with glass stoppers Glass-stoppered	
4.	125 ml	10
5.	250 ml	10
6.	500 ml	20
7.	1 000 ml	5
8.	2 000 ml	5
9.	Bottle (glass), amber 250 ml	5
10.	Bottle (glass), amber 500 ml	5
11.	Bottle (polyethylene) - wash bottle 250 ml	6
12.	Bottle (polyethylene) 500 ml	6
13.	(i) Burettes fitted with screw-thread stopcocks Graduation interval (ml) & size	2each
	0.05 & 10 ml	
	0.05 & 25 ml	
	0.1 & 10 ml	
	0.1 & 25 ml	

Contd.

14.	(ii) Burette (automatic) (mounted on reservoir) Graduation interval (ml) & size 0.1 & 25 ml, 0.1 & 50 ml	2 each
15.	Cylinder (glass) graduated with an interval & size of: 0.5 ml & 10 ml 1 ml & 25 ml 2 ml & 50 ml 2 ml & 100 ml 5 ml & 500 ml	2 each
16.	Crucible (silica) 30 ml	10
17.	Desiccator with approx. I.D. of ground flange as 200 mm	2
18.	Dishes, evaporating flat-bottom with pour out, having outer diameter as 150mm and height as 80 mm	20
19.	Water distilling unit, mounted with borosilicate condenser, with a capacity (output) to distil 2.5 litre/hour	2
20.	Flask distilling/Kjeldahl, round-bottom, long-neck Capacity & O.D. × height (mm) 100 ml & 64 x 210 250 ml & 85 x 226	12 each
21.	Flask (conical)	
	100 ml cap., 64 × 105 mm (O.D. × height) with approx. neck O.D as 25 mm	50
	250 ml cap., 85 × 140 mm (O.D. × height) with app. neck O.D as 34 mm	50
	500 ml cap., 104 × 180 mm (O.D. × height) with app. neck O.D. as 34 mm	10
	1 000 ml cap., 131 × 225 mm (O.D. × height) with app. neck O.D. as 34 mm	10
22.	Flask (volumetric): Capacity (ml) & Tolerance (± ml)	
	25 & 0.04	50
	50 & 0.06	50
	100 & 0.10	100
	250 & 0.15	25
	500 & 0.25	25
	1000 & 0.40	10
23.	Funnel, plain, 60-degree angle	
	Diameter: 50 mm, 65 mm, 75 mm, 100 mm	20 each

24.	Pipette (measuring)			
	Capacity (ml)	**Graduation interval(ml)**	**Tolerance (± ml)**	
	1.0	0.1	0.006	2
	2.0	0.1	0.01	2
	5.0	0.1	0.05	2
	10.0	0.1	0.05	5
	25.0	0.2	0.1	5
	50.0	0.5	0.1	2
25.	Porcelain dish - 100 and 150 ml			6 each
26.	Test-tube: O.D. × height (mm): 12 × 10, 15 × 125 & 18 × 150			60 each
27.	Watch glass: App. diameter (mm): 100 & 200			60 each
28.	Rubber stopper 15, 18, 20, 25 & 30 mm diameter			12 each
29.	Spatula (stainless) with wooden handle, blade length 100 mm			12
30.	Wire gauge with asbestos centre 150 × 150 mm			20

Notes : Twenty percent of glassware may need annual replacement because of breakage or changed requirement. O.D. = outer diameter; I.D. = internal diameter. When estimating boron, boron-free glassware must be used. Commonly required glassware includes beakers, flasks, pipettes, funnels and water distilling sets. Generally, marketed glassware is made of borosilicates, which contains traces of boron, hence, not suitable for boron estimation.

2. Common Methods for Nutrient Estimation

Nutrient	**Type of sample**		
	Soil	**Plant**	**Fertilizers/Manures**
Total N	Kjeldahl method	Kjeldahl method	Kjeldahl method
Mineralizable N	Alkaline $KMnO_4$ method	-	
NO_3-N	Phenoldisulphonic acid method	-	Estimation of (below) - NH_4-N (below)
NH_4-N	Indophenol blue method	-	Distillation with MgO/ alkali
NH_4+NO_3-N	-	-	NH_4+NO_3-N - Devarda's treatment followed by distillation with MgO/alkali
P	Available P: Bray's method No. 1 for	Total P: Spectrophotometric	Total P: Gravimetric

Contd.

	acid soils Olsen's method for alkali soils	vanadium phosphomolybdate method	quinolinium phosphomolybdate method Volumetric ammonium phosphomolybdate method
K	Available K: Flame photometric method (neutral ammonium acetate extraction)	Total K: Estimation by AAS	Total K: Sodium tetraphenyl boron (STPB) method
S	Available S: Spectrophotometric barium sulphate precipitation method	Total S: Spectrophotometric barium sulphate precipitation method	-
Ca/Mg	EDTA titration method	Estimation by AAS EDTA titration method	-
Zn, Cu, Fe & Mn	DTPA extraction and estimation by AAS	Estimation by AAS	Estimation by AAS
B	Hot water extraction and estimation by AAS Hot water extraction and determination by azomethine- H colorimetric method	Estimation by AAS Colorimetric method as in soils	Estimation by AAS
Mo	Ammonium acetate extraction and estimation by AAS Ammonium oxalate extraction and estimation by colorimetric method	Estimation by AAS Colorimetric method as in soils	Estimation by AAS

3. Equivalent and Molecular Weights of Chemicals

Chemical compounds	Formula	Molecular weight (g)	Equivalent weight (g)
Ammonium acetate	CH_3COONH_4	77.08	77.08
Ammonium chloride	NH_4Cl	53.49	53.49
Ammonium fluoride	NH_4F	37.04	37.04
Ammonium nitrate	NH_4NO_3	80.04	80.04
Barium chloride	$BaCl_2.2H_2O$	244.28	122.14
Boric acid	H_3BO_3	61.83	20.61
Calcium acetate	$(CH_3COO)2Ca$	158.00	79.00
Calcium carbonate	$CaCO_3$	100.09	50.05
Calcium chloride (dihydrate)	$CaCl_2.2H_2O$	147.02	73.51
Calcium hydroxide	$Ca(OH)_2$	74.00	37.00
Calcium nitrate	$Ca(NO_3)_2$	164.00	82.00
Calcium sulphate	$CaSO_4.2H_2O$	172.17	86.08
Ferrous ammonium sulphate	$FeSO_4.(NH_4)$ $2SO_4.H_2O$	392.13	392.13
Ferrous sulphate	$FeSO_4.7H_2O$	278.01	139.00
Magnesium chloride	$MgCl_2.6H_2O$	203.30	101.65
Magnesium nitrate	$Mg(NO_3)2.6H_2O$	256.41	128.20
Potassium chloride	KCl	74.55	74.55
Potassium dichromate	$K_2Cr_2O_7$	294.19	49.04
Potassium hydroxide	KOH	56.10	56.10
Potassium permanganate	$KMnO_4$	158.03	31.60
Potassium nitrate	KNO_3	101.10	101.10
Potassium sulphate	K_2SO_4	174.27	87.13
Potassium hydrogen phthalate	$COOH\ C_6H_4\ COOK$	204.22	204.22
Oxalic acid	$C_2H_2O_4.2H_2O$	126.00	63.00
Silver nitrate	$AgNO_3$	169.87	169.87
Sodium acetate (anhydrous)	CH_3COONa	82.04	82.04
Sodium bicarbonate	$NaHCO_3$	84.01	84.01
Sodium carbonate	Na_2CO_3	106.00	53.00
Sodium chloride	$NaCl$	58.45	58.45
Sodium hydroxide	$NaOH$	40.00	40.00
Sodium nitrate	$NaNO_3$	84.99	84.99
Sodium oxalate	$Na_2C_2O_4$	134.00	67.00
Sodium sulphate	Na_2SO_4	142.04	71.02
Sodium thiosulphate	$Na_2S_2O_3.5H_2O$	248.18	248.18

4. Information Sheet for Sample

1. Sample No. ____________________
2. Name of sample collector ____________________________________
3. Address ______________________________ Date ____________________
4. Area ____________________ Location (Late & Long)________________
5. Name of farmer ______________________ Farm size _______________
6. Vegetative cover ____
7. Source of water _______________ Water quality __________________
8. Sample depth _______________ Previous crop ____________________
9. Purpose of analysis

   Land capability assessment

   Fertility evaluation and fertilizer recommendation

   Salinity appraisal and causes of the source of salinity, if known

   Soil classification
10. Slope

    1-2 percent

    2-5 percent

    5-10 percent

    10-25 percent

    > 25 percent
11. Irrigation

<u>Method</u>	<u>Years of irrigation</u>
Flood	Never irrigated
Furrow	1-5
Sprinkler	5-15
Drip	-
Rainfed	-

12. Years of cultivation

    Never cultivated

    1-5

    5-15

    >15

13. Drainage:
    Good
    Moderate
    Poor
14. Manure used in the previous crop and dose ____________
15. Fertilizers used in the previous crop and dose ____________

5. Units and Conversion Factors

To convert unit in Column 1 to unit in Column 2 multiply by	Column 1: SI unit	Column 2: non-SI unit	To convert unit in Column 2 to unit in Column 1 multiply by
Area			
2.47	hectare, ha	Acre	0.405
2.47	square kilometre, km2 $(10^3\ m)^2$	acre	4.05×10^{-3}
0.386	square kilometre, km^2 $(10^3\ m)^2$	square mile, mi^2	2.590
2.47×10^{-4}	square metre, m^2	acre	4.05×10^3
10.76	square metre, m^2	square foot, ft^2	9.29×10^{-2}
1.55×10^{-3}	square millimetre, mm2 $(10^{-3}\ m)^2$	square inch, in^2	645
Volume			
9.73×10^{-3}	cubic metre, m^3	acre-inch	102.8
35.3	cubic metre, m^3	cubic foot, ft^3	2.83×10^{-2}
6.10×10^4	cubic metre, m^3	cubic inch, in^3	1.64×10^{-5}
1.057	litre, L $(10^{-3}\ m^3)$	quart (liquid), qt	0.946
3.53×10^{-2}	litre, L $(10^{-3}\ m^3)$	cubic foot, ft^3	28.3
0.265	litre, L $(10^{-3}\ m^3)$	gallon	3.78
33.78	litre, L $(10^{-3}\ m^3)$	pint (fluid), pt	0.473
Mass			
2.20×10^{-3}	gram, g $(10^{-3}$ kg)	pound, lb	454
3.52×10^{-2}	gram, g $(10^{-3}$ kg)	ounce (avdp), oz	28.4
2.205	kilogram, kg	pound, lb	0.454
0.01	kilogram, kg	quintal (metric), q	100
1.10×10^{-3}	kilogram, kg	ton (2000 lb), ton	907

Contd.

1.102	megagram, Mg tonne)	ton (U.S.), ton	0.907
1.102	tonne, t	ton (U.S.), ton	0.907
Length			
0.621	kilometre, km (10^3 m)	mile	1.609
1.094	metre, m	yard, yd	0.914
3.28	metre, m	foot, ft	0.304
3.94×10^{-2}	millimetre, mm (10^{-3} m)	inch, in	25.4
10	nanometre, nm (19^{-9} m)	angstrom, å	0.1
Yield and rate			
0.893	kilogram per hectare, kg ha^{-1}	pound per acre, lb $acre^{-1}$	1.12
7.77×10^{-2}	kilogram per cubic metre, kg m^{-3}	pound per bushel, lb bu^{-1}	12.87
1.49×10^{-2}	kilogram per hectare, kg ha^{-1}	bushel per acre, 60 lb	67.19
1.59×10^{-2}	kilogram per hectare, kg ha^{-1}	bushel per acre, 56 lb	62.71
1.86×10^{-2}	kilogram per hectare, kg ha^{-1}	bushel per acre, 48 lb	53.75
0.107	litre per hectare, L ha^{-1}	gallon per acre	9.35
893	tonne per hectare, t ha^{-1}	pound per acre, lb $acre^{-1}$	1.12×10^{-3}
893	megagram per hectare, Mg ha^{-1}	pound per acre, lb $acre^{-1}$	1.12×10^{-3}
0.446	megagram per hectare, Mg ha^{-1}	ton (2000 lb) per acre, ton $acre^{-1}$	2.24
2.24	metre per second, m s^{-1}	mile per hour	0.447
Pressure			
9.90	megaPascal, MPa (106 Pa)	atmosphere	0.101
10	megaPascal, MPa (106 Pa)	bar	0.1
1.00	megagram per cubic metre, Mg m^{-3}	gram per cubic centimetre, g cm^{-3}	1.00

Contd.

2.09×10^{-2}	Pascal, Pa	pound per square foot, lb ft^{-2}	47.9
1.45×10^{-4}	Pascal, Pa	pound per square inch, lb in^{-2}	6.90×10^{3}
Temperature			
1.00 (K - 273)	Kelvin, K	Celsius, °C	1.00 (°C + 273)
(9/5 °C) + 32	Celsius, °C	Fahrenheit, °F	5/9 (°F - 32)
Water measurement			
9.73×10^{-3}	cubic metre, m^3	acre-inch, acre-in	102.8
9.81×10^{-3}	cubic metre per hour, $m^3 h^{-1}$	cubic foot per second, ft3 s^{-1}	101.9
4.40	cubic metre per hour, $m^3 h^{-1}$	U.S. gallons per minute, gal min^{-1}	0.227
8.11	hectare-metre, ha-m	acre-foot, acre-ft	0.123
97.28	hectare-metre, ha-m	acre-inch, acre-in	1.03×10^{-2}
8.1×10^{-2}	hectare-centimetre, ha-cm	acre-foot, acre-ft	12.33
Concentration			
1	centimole per kilogram, cmol kg^{-1} (ion exchange capacity)	milli-equivalents per 100 grams, me 100 g^{-1}	1
0.1	gram per kilogram, g kg^{-1}	percent, %	10
1	milligram per kilogram, mg kg^{-1}	parts per million, ppm	1
Plant nutrient conversion			
	Element	**Oxide**	
2.29	P	P_2O_5	0.437
1.20	K	K_2O	0.830
1.39	Ca	CaO	0.715
1.66	Mg	MgO	0.602
1.216	N	NH_3	0.777
4.426	N	NO_3	0.226
6.25	N	Protein	0.160
3.00	S	SO_4	0.330
2.5	S	SO_3	0.440
1.724	Organic C	Organic matter	0.580

6. Some Important Concepts and Contributors

Sl No	Particulars	Name of the contributor
1.	Law of limiting factor	Blakman
2.	a). Electro-chemical theory of nutrient up take	
	b). Theory of Relativity	Lundegardh
3.	Electro-ultrofiltration Theory	Nymith (Q/I)
4.	Target Yield Theory	Ramamoorthy et al
5.	a). Equilibrium Phosphate Potential	Ramamoorthy - Subramanium
	b). Phosphate Equilibrium Potential	Beckett -White
6.	"E" Value	Russell
7.	Soil is an in-exhaustible source of nutrients	Cameroon
8.	a) Per cent Yield Concept	Baule
	b) Nutrient sufficiency concept	
9.	a) Nutrient Mobility Concept	Bray
	b) Per cent Sufficiency Concept	
10.	Law of Minimum/ Law of Limiting Nutrient of Law of Restitution	Liebig
11.	Critical Soil Test Level Concept	Cate & Nelson
12.	Benchmark soils of India	Murthy et al
13.	Ultra-micronutrient concept	Nicholas
14.	a). CEC is next to Photosynthesis	Marshall
	b). pH is physical phenomenon	
15.	Carrier Theory	Epstein
16.	Biogas	S V Desai & S C Biswas
17.	Auto-radiography	La cassageue
18.	Lignin theory	Waksman
19.	Water - essential for plant	Van Helment
20.	Water - transpiration	Woodward
21.	Ionic strength	Lewis & Randol
22.	Isotopic Dilution	Hevesy & Hoffer
23.	Auto Radioactivities	Reinganum
24.	CEC	Thompson & Way
25.	Root Exchange (contact)	Jenny & Over steet
26.	Root CEC	Devaux
27.	pH Concept	Sorenson

Contd.

28.	pE Concept	Silen
29.	a). Prescription Approach b). Father of soil Testing	Troug
30.	Integrated Soil Test Approach	Colwell
31.	DRIS concept	Beaufils
32.	Radio Carbon Dating	Libbby et al
33.	Lime potential	Aslyng & Schofield (later)
34.	Q/I	Beckett
35.	Salt Index	Puri
36.	Soil Catena	Milne
37.	Polyphenol theory of organic matter	Stevenson
38.	Fertility / Nutrient Index	Parker
39.	DTDP - Extractable micronutrients	Lindsay and Norvell
40.	Isotopic Dillution Techniques for phosphorus	Research Scientists of US & Europe
41.	"A" value	Fried and Dean
42.	"Y" or "L" value	Larsen
43.	Mathematical equation indicating relationship between plant growth response & growth factor	Mitscherlich
44.	Phenomenon of radioactivity	Bacquerel
45.	Liquid scintillation counting	Kallman and Reynold

7. Important Journals of Soil Science in India and Abroad

Name of the Journal	Periodicity of Publication	Published by
In India		
Journal of the Indian Society of soil science	Quarterly	Soil Science & Agrl. Chemistry Division, IARI, New Delhi
The Indian Journal of Agricultural sciences	Monthly	IARI, New Delhi
The Indian Journal of Agricultural Chemistry	Quarterly	Indian Society of Agricultural chemists, University of Allahabad, Allahabad.
Oryza	Quarterly	Central Rice Research Institute, Cuttack
Indian Agriculturist	Quarterly	The Agricultural Society of India, Kolkata
Madras Agricultural Journal	Monthly	TNAU, Coimbatore

Contd.

Journal of Maharashtra Agricultural Universities crop research	Thrice in a year	College of Agriculture, Pune
Crop Research	Thrice in a year	Agricultural Research Information Centre, Hissar
Annals of Agricultural Research	Quarterly	Indian Society of Agricultural Science, Agronomy Division, IARI, New Delhi
Fertilizer News	Monthly	Fertilizer Association of India, New Delhi
Journal of Nuclear Agriculture and Biology	Quarterly	Nuclear Research Lab, IARI, New Delhi
Clay Research	Twice in a year	The Clay Minerals Society of India, IARI, New Delhi
In Abroad		
Soil Science Society of America Journal	Once in 2-months	USA
European Journal of Soil Science	Monthly	USA
Agrochimica	Once in 2-months	Italy
Plant and soil	Quarterly	The Netherlands
Geoderma	Once in 3-months	The Netherlands
Fertilizer Research	Quarterly	The Netherlands
Soil and Tillage Research	Quarterly	The Netherlands
Advances in Soil Science	Twice in a year	USA
Advances in Agronomy	Twice in a year	USA
Journal of Soil Science	Twice in 3-months	UK
Soil Biology and Biochemistry	Twice in 2-months	UK
Biology and fertility of soils	Quarterly	Germany
The journal of Agricultural Science	Twice in 2-months	UK
Soil Science and Plant Nutrition	Bi-monthly	Japan
Australian Journal of Soil Research		Australia
Water, Air and Soil Pollution		The Netherlands

❑❑❑

FSC
www.fsc.org
MIX
Papier | Fördert
gute Waldnutzung
FSC® C083411

Kolibri 360 GmbH
Ferdinand-Jühlke-Straße 7
99095 Erfurt, Deutschland
produktsicherheit@kolibri360.de